BEFORE CHICANO

AMERICA AND THE LONG 19TH CENTURY

General Editors: David Kazanjian, Elizabeth McHenry, and Priscilla Wald

Before Chicano

*Citizenship and the Making of Mexican American
Manhood, 1848–1959*

Alberto Varon

NEW YORK UNIVERSITY PRESS
New York

NEW YORK UNIVERSITY PRESS
New York
www.nyupress.org

References to Internet websites (URLs) were accurate at the time of writing. Neither the author nor New York University Press is responsible for URLs that may have expired or changed since the manuscript was prepared.

Library of Congress Cataloging-in-Publication Data
Names: Varon, Alberto, author.
Title: Before Chicano : citizenship and the making of Mexican American manhood, 1848–1959 / Alberto Varon.
Description: New York : NEW YORK UNIVERSITY PRESS, 2018. | Series: America and the long 19th century | Includes bibliographical references and index.
Identifiers: LCCN 2017044868 | ISBN 9781479863969 (cl : alk. paper) | ISBN 9781479831197 (pb : alk. paper)
Subjects: LCSH: Mexican Americans—History—19th century. | Mexican Americans—History—20th century. | Mexican Americans—Ethnic identity—History—20th century. | Mexican Americans—Ethnic identity—History—20th century. | Citizenship—United States—History—19th century. | Citizenship—United States—History—20th century.
Classification: LCC E184.M5 V3435 2018 | DDC 973/.046872—dc23
LC record available at https://lccn.loc.gov/2017044868

New York University Press books are printed on acid-free paper, and their binding materials are chosen for strength and durability. We strive to use environmentally responsible suppliers and materials to the greatest extent possible in publishing our books.

Manufactured in the United States of America

10 9 8 7 6 5 4 3 2 1

Also available as an ebook

Para ma y pa

CONTENTS

LIST OF FIGURES

Introduction

Against Xenophobic Citizenship

This is not a book about immigration. Or, perhaps put more directly, this is a book about not immigrating. It is a cultural history of Mexican American manhood from the mid-nineteenth to the mid-twentieth centuries that underscores Mexican Americans' long-standing place in American political and cultural life. Decades before the Border Patrol, César Chávez, Dolores Huerta, the Delano grape strike, the Chicano Moratorium, or the 2006 immigration protests, Mexican Americans, living in cities and homes they had occupied for generations, found ways to imagine themselves as U.S. citizens. These Mexican American men and women worked to build safe, happy, and productive lives within the United States and as U.S. citizens, but to do so, found themselves time and again excluded from the country they called home and worked diligently to support.

In turning to an earlier historical period, this book challenges prevailing, facile, and often flawed associations between Mexican Americans and immigration that typecast Mexican Americans as immigrants. To access the long history of Mexican American culture, this book examines manhood and asks how the experience of being a man—and how that experience was represented—shaped the lives of Mexican American men and women. By focusing on manhood, we can see how Mexican Americans understood themselves as racial, gendered citizens and how that experience impacted the way they organized socially, how they functioned politically, and how they connected to broader, mainstream, and usually white American society. In examining Mexican American manhood during this period, this book reevaluates the Anglocentric focus of existing studies of U.S. manhood and illuminates the myriad ways that Mexican Americans produced competing notions of U.S. citizenship.

In 1848, U.S. expansionist ambitions resulted in the acquisition of what is now the American West and Southwest, known as the Mexican Cession and a familiar fact among historians of the U.S. and Mexico. Following the cessation of hostilities with the Treaty of Guadalupe Hidalgo, vast swaths of territory in what is now the U.S. Southwest traded national hands, and along with it, the nationality of those we know as Mexican American.[1] The agreement granted citizenship to those Mexicans now living in the U.S., under certain stipulations.[2] In short, since at least the mid-nineteenth century, Mexican Americans have found themselves in the paradoxical position of U.S. citizen and perceived foreigner.

The outcomes of this conflict are captured by Maria Amparo Ruiz de Burton in her 1872 Civil War novel *Who Would Have Thought It?*—the first novel written in English by a Mexican American woman living in the United States. One of the main characters, Mrs. Norval, finds herself in a bind. Her husband, recently returned from extended travels in the American Southwest, brought back with him a young orphaned girl, Lola, daughter of a Mexican woman held captive by an unnamed group of Native Americans.[3] Lola enters the narrative with her skin dyed dark but possessing fabulous wealth, and Mrs. Norval is caught between her racial prejudices against Lola and a consuming desire to control her wealth. Responding to a comment on the diversity and complexity of the U.S. population, Mrs. Norval exclaims, "How I do hate foreigners!"[4] She struggles to makes sense of the racial status of Mexican Americans while acting on and rationalizing her desire to acquire that which the U.S. Southwest offers. She is not alone in this conundrum, and the encounter between these disparate ideas fuels much of the narrative. Later in the novel, Julian, the Norvals' son, demands an audience with President Lincoln as "an American who will not cast a fellow citizen down into a mire of disgrace, and as a man who will not let a fellow man perish in despair."[5] Julian, desperately fighting false accusations of treason and working to clear his family's name, places his faith in two interlocked ideas: citizenship and manhood. These are pitted in part against the discourse of "foreignness" but also as the terrain on which the very ideals underpinning American democracy are at stake, exposing the tension between nativist impulses and democratic idealism.[6]

Her novel presents a complicated portrait of Californio racial identity, but as a woman facing her own legal challenges that sought to classify her as non-white, Ruiz de Burton was keenly aware of Mexican Americans' precarious position and how that position was further complicated by gender. Ruiz de Burton cleverly delivers a critique of U.S. racialization through her white characters that, by invoking and challenging the terms under which Mexican Americans were portrayed, opens up a complex history of Mexican American gendered political participation.[7] While her novel offers a powerful example, she is only one of numerous writers, both male and female, who used manhood to frame Mexican American citizenship and group identity for a U.S. national audience—in part, simply by writing in English.

Just as contemporary political discourse regularly neglects or forgets Mexican American citizenship, Ruiz de Burton's novel fell out of cultural and critical memory. It was recently recovered by scholars, and with it the imbricated histories of Mexican Americans and U.S. national culture.[8] For Mexican Americans, and for Latinos more generally, debates about national identity and racial difference are often subsumed under the category of immigration. The current nativist position popular among conservatives has its earlier counterpart, when some began to bemoan the demographic changes that accompanied territorial expansion and "manifest destiny."[9] Yet since at least 1848, and arguably since the nation's founding, Mexican Americans have been active participants in the formation of U.S. national culture and manhood, though their participation is routinely left out of the historical record and popular memory.[10] *Before Chicano* offers a historical alternative to the xenophobic accounts that frequently populate contemporary media and overlook Mexican Americans by examining Mexican American manhood and citizenship within U.S. American culture on several fronts. First, it argues against the characterization of Mexican Americans primarily as immigrants by exploring their longstanding investment in the U.S. national project. Second, it offers an analysis of some of the major figures or types of Mexican American manhood, how these evolved historically, and how that development illuminates the emergence of a national category now identifiable as Latino. In doing so, it asks us to reconsider the cultural history of U.S. American manhood and Mexican Americans' role within it. Third, it demonstrates Mexican American participation in U.S. public life and how Mexican Americans developed more expansive and inclusive no-

tions of citizenship that distinguished between local, regional, and national political participation.

Portraying Mexican Americans as recent arrivals to the United States
is nothing new. Polemical political discourse from the 1840s onward de-
risively referred to Mexican Americans as immigrants in an effort to
diminish their social and political power, a patent nativist response. In
its most basic form, nativism opposes a minority group because of a
perceived difference or foreignness (political, social, or cultural) in order
to prevent, exclude, or excise that group's participation.[11] In a seminal
work on immigration and nativism, John Higham defines nativism "as
intense opposition to an internal minority on the ground of its foreign
(i.e., 'un-American') connections" and points to how nativist responses
are always inextricable from nationalism, as whatever the "ideological
core of nativism in every form [. . . the nativist] stood for a certain kind
of nationalism."[12]

Nowhere is this entanglement between nativism and nationalism
more visible and more complex than in the case of Mexican Americans. Just before the U.S.-Mexican War and riding on waves of anti-
Catholic sentiment directed toward immigrants (first European but
later Mexicans), a group of Protestant men organized the short-lived
Know-Nothing Party under a platform of restricting immigration and
naturalization.[13] Responding to the Know-Nothing Party's attempts to
limit Mexican American social intergration, the Los Angeles weekly
newspaper *El Clamor Público* (which evolved out of the English-language
Los Angeles Star to serve the area's Spanish-speaking population) notes
how the Know-Nothings opposed a government working "en favor de
derechos iguales y libertad religioisas [. . .] y que ha firmado leyes que
protejen los intereses de los nativos del pais" [in support of equal rights
and religious liberty and who has passed laws to protect the interests of
the country's native residents].[14] (In retort to "aquellos hombres cuyos
proyectos de leyes que no hacian mucho honor" [those men whose proposed laws have no honor], the newspaper centers the Spanish-speaking
population as "native," inverting the Know-Nothings' strategy of ostracization.) Half a century later, calling for Congress to extend the 1922-
era three-percent quota on immigration, an editorialist of a separate
newspaper charged, "The immigration peril from which this country
has been spared is not fictional," and elaborated on the "real threat" im-

migrants posed to U.S. society.[15] Just a few years later, demand grew for a police force to regulate the national borders in response to changes in the demographic makeup of the country. Like so often seen in contemporary political rhetoric, the *Kansas City Star* shifted the blame to Mexico and condemned the movement of people across the U.S.-Mexico border, stating "the entry laws and regulations of the United States are a laughing stock to that very nation whose shortcomings in law enforcement we are frequently protesting—the Mexicans!"—a call which would feed into the creation of the Border Patrol in 1924.[16] Across the country, in the nation's metropolitan heart, the *New York Times* reported on Congressional debates about immigration reform and stated that the argument "in favor of unlimited Mexican immigration was that American workers were rising out of the ranks of manual laborers so fast, through education and in other ways, that unskilled workers were needed to replace them. It was added that Mexican labor would not likely develop a racial problem for the United States, due to the Mexican's roving temperament, and that the majority of them, once their temporary work was done, would return to their homeland."[17]

Although these examples reveal slippage between Mexican and Mexican American, since the U.S.-Mexican War these groups have been linked to immigration, and nativist calls continually displace Mexican Americans from the national imaginary.[18] While immigrants from Europe in the nineteenth and early twentieth centuries were also seen as disruptive to the national character, most groups ultimately found a pathway to social incorporation.[19] In contrast, immigrants from Mexico were typically described as temporary, transitory, and readily deportable. As Mae M. Ngai has shown for both Asian and Mexican Americans, "The legal racialization of these ethnic groups' national origin cast them as permanently foreign and unassimilable to the nation [. . . possessing] formal U.S. citizenship but who remained alien in the eyes of the nation."[20] Conceiving of Mexican Americans as expendable, the Bracero Program (1942–1964) invited several million Mexicans to cross the border into the United States as temporary agricultural workers, though the legal structures through which these workers entered offered neither the expectation nor the path to permanent residency or citizenship.[21] The specifics shift dramatically over time, yet there remains a persistent historical representation of Mexican Americans and Latinos as an immigrant presence. (In fact, many opportunistic politicians and pundits frequently elide the difference between Mexican Americans and other Latina/o national groups, and "Mexican" becomes reductive or derogatory shorthand to stereotype Latina/os generally.) In critiquing the immigration label I am not recommending assimilation as the ultimate or even desired marker of social integration. Such binaries between exclusion and assimilation are too simplistic to adequately represent the complexity of cultural development. Rather, I point to the long-standing understanding of Mexican Americans, and more broadly Latinos, as immigrant (and, alongside it, the metonymic tendency to collapse one group with the other).

Indeed, in many ways the terms "Latino" and "immigration" have become ontologically linked, each fundamentally dependent on the other in the context of the U.S. nation-state. To be clear, immigration has historically been, will continue to be, and should be central to the category "Latino," in the U.S. and elsewhere. It is a crucial aspect of national and international policy, especially in a global climate in which migration is increasingly at the center of debates about international conflict. Latino studies, which as a field has historically been concerned with the movement of people across and within national borders, is poised at the forefront of this debate and hence has much to offer the global conversation about the impact of immigration. However, conceiving of Latinos solely through frameworks of immigration or immigration rights in relation to public policy diminishes the ability of Latinos to participate in U.S. cultural and national life by perpetually deferring their place as agents of a U.S. national project in the making. My aim here is to engage a historical record that reveals Mexican Americans as producers of and longtime participants in U.S. national culture.

The coupling of Latinos and immigration has its domestic equivalent in understandings of citizenship and the political body: specifically, the concept of the "sleeping giant."[22] Corky Gonzales deployed this image in one of the foundational documents of the Chicano movement, the poem "I Am Joaquin" (1967), where he describes an emergent Chicano consciousness as "the music of the people stirs the revolution / Like a sleeping giant it slowly / rears its head."[23] The sleeping giant represents the statistical call for Latinos as a demographic group ready to be mobilized in the exercise of suffrage as a remedy to centuries-old political alienation, rendered in the poem as a bubbling resistance to the nation-state. It represents the future-oriented potentiality of Mexican Americans—as revolution or as new voters—but its antithesis is the negative portrayal of "the Latino threat," the perceived destabilizing effect and illegality often associated with Latino immigrants, as Leo Chavez has described.[24] More so than any other ethnic group, Latinos are now associated with not only the issue of immigration but also with "illegality." One of the questions this book thus asks is, what would it mean to recast the immigration debate with Latinos at the center of a U.S. national culture?

Manhood and Citizenship

My readings of manhood and citizenship operate somewhat counterintuitively, asking us to reconsider both the nation and Mexican American cultural history within it. One of the implications of thinking beyond resistance is to move past a notion of early Latino literature as recuperation or primarily a recovery project and into a more integrated intellectual history and U.S. *national* narrative. This requires us to decouple the idea of the Latino subject from immigration. This book counters the hegemonic view of Latinos as perennial immigrants by turning to Mexican Americans' long historical investment in ideas of national manhood.

Whereas during the Chicano movement and its subsequent affiliated projects manhood was positioned as resistance to the U.S. nation-state (and the state's concomitant policies of exclusion and oppression), *Before Chicano* demonstrates how Mexican American manhood shaped U.S. national culture in tension and conversation with prevailing discourses about Mexican Americans. The book's analyses of gender bring together disparate actors working across vastly divergent geographic terrains, temporal distances, political spectrum, and nationality, but who come to see themselves as participating in a unified U.S. national culture, connecting a network of writers from California, to Texas, to New York. As such, manhood allows for asynchronous development that better reflects the multiple, diverse, and transnational registers in which contemporary Latina/os operate, as well as the complexity of the Latina/o experience. *Before Chicano* also shows how U.S. citizenship developed in a dialogue with external democratic projects, exploding the nativist fabrication of the U.S. as isolated or insulated from external influence. Manhood—a gendered cultural practice through which men understood themselves and were understood as men and as political agents—functioned domestically between racial and ethnic groups, and transnationally as people moved across and within nations. For example, Mexican American bandit manhood discussed in chapter one was one of the primary cultural forms through which the nation reconciled itself with the vast former Mexican territories, as well as provided a justification for imperial expansion. To understand how Mexican Americans responded to and engaged with banditry is to recognize how the discourses of Mexican American manhood were part of the development of the U.S. nation as a continental power.

Mexican Americans developed a variety of views on manhood—some that emerged in part as a response to nativist movements—that reflected the community's disparate values about the individual, the family, and the potential for intracultural integration. Manhood, to borrow from Darieck Scott's description of blackness and sexuality, "makes tangible to us, visible, the operation of sociogenesis by which all of our human world comes into being."[25] The convergence of these categories through representation, left as a cultural archive and through literary documents, stabilizes, if briefly, the multitude of ideas surrounding gendered cultural identity—in the body, as a social relation, through national affiliation, or in the simultaneous distancing and tethering of all of these. In these ways, Mexican American manhood traded on an ambiguity between legal and racial conditions of citizenship and belonging: legally white though socially excluded; not quite white, black, nor native, yet enmeshed within the national social fabric.

Dana Nelson is among the best-known critics to analyze manhood and citizenship in the United States, and among the first to link those concepts to racial difference. Focusing on early U.S. history through the mid-nineteenth century, her study shows how "national manhood" privileged the goals of the white, northern European founders of the nation, giving priority to English-speaking Protestant men with access to East Coast centers of power.[26] Centering "white *manhood* [as] the legal criteria of civic entitlement, attaching the 'manly confidence' idealized by defenders of the Constitution to the abstractly unifying category of 'whiteness,'" Nelson contends that the fraternity of white national manhood promised civic equality and that white "manhood's identification with national unity has worked historically to restrict others from achieving full entitlement in the United States."[27] In other words, white manhood provided an umbrella of inclusion that relied on the exclusion of others. What might it mean, then, to formulate national manhood from the position of that exclusion? Where white manhood was often defined in opposition to or in exclusion of people of color, Mexican American manhood defined itself from a position of exclusion. Mexican Americans, legally white but actively racialized, sought to disrupt the social boundaries imposed on their racial identity. Mexican Americans developed ideas of manhood that allowed them to draw on and define themselves in relation to racialization that was exclusionary and de jure, but not always legal or legislated. And while Mexican Americans turned to manhood to find common ground with their Anglo neighbors, to borrow from Eve Sedgwick, "when something is about masculinity, it is not always 'about men.'"[28] Mexican American women actively constructed manhood in order to express an array of social positions and to intervene in developing forms of citizenship, and both Mexican American men *and* women publicly represented their individual and communal concerns through manhood, even as those representations often excluded others.

The dialectic between inclusion and exclusion operated at several levels, internally within Mexican American cultural circles and externally between Mexican American and other ethnic groups. Mexican American men and women sought to overcome the exclusion of fraternal white manhood by, at times, appealing to whiteness; at others, they sought to redefine democratic ideals, appealing to and even beyond the U.S. nation. In some instances, Mexican American men and women differentiated between degrees of "authenticity" among Mexican American manhood in order to assert national inclusion; in others, they used manhood to reinterpret long-standing Anglo American political traditions within Mexican American culture. For instance, early twentieth-century Mexican Americans debated the degree to which certain groups, such as Mexican political exiles, could make claims to geographic attachment—the "how long have you lived here?" discourse is still prevalent in contemporary immigration debates—while both the late nineteenth-century revolutionary Juan Nepomuceno Cortina and mid-twentieth-century novelist José Antonio Villarreal triangulated Mexican American manhood against other ethnic groups, including white, Mexican, Italian, and Japanese.

The archival record reflects values associated with recognizable white or mainstream manhood and masculinity, which include autonomy, assertiveness, self-control, independence, and aggression; but we also find introspection, self-reflection, intimacy, vulnerability, and uncertainty as characteristic of Mexican American manhood. Over the long century I discuss, and as the processes of racialization and social exclusion expanded and hardened, Mexican American manhood moved from a public political performance representing democratic ideals to a more internalized engagement with the question of individual subjectivity and productivity. Individuals working to carve out a social position constructed Mexican American manhood as *agentive*, as actively producing and responding to social and political difference and changing historical conditions. This gradual development occurred in tandem with normative constructs of white and other racialized forms of American manhood, yet these developments must be understood within the processes of racialization that affected Mexican Americans. Mexican American men and women sought to integrate themselves into U.S. public life by leveraging familiar and novel ideas about manhood, and while they wielded manhood in different ways, its cultural impact exceeded their control. But in a political climate of exclusion, both in terms of racial status and access to legal and civil rights, Mexican Americans deployed manhood both to combat exclusion and to reflect and create cultural norms.

Focusing on the fin-de-siècle earlier period, scholar Gail Bederman's landmark work *Manliness and Civilization* shows how race in the U.S. was linked to colonial enterprises through the discourse of manhood as a matter of degrees of "civilization." Bederman shows how a rugged, individualistic masculinity (as opposed to the more gentlemanly or effeminate manliness, with roots in Victorian sensibilities) formed part of the expansionist colonial project of the turn-of-the-century United States and how the racialized bodies encountered by U.S. imperial expansion possessed a "primitive" sexuality and aggressive masculinity that was simultaneously desired by white men and needing to be contained. The dialectic she describes, both in its historical time frame as well as its understanding of the processes of racialization, is fundamental to this project. Still, her work operates within a black-white dichotomy in which Mexican Americans do not comfortably fit. Others, like Michael Kimmel, Anthony Rotundo, Amy Kaplan, and Clifford Putney, have shown the powerful force that cultural manhood plays in shaping American society.[29] In particular, these scholars chart the gradual development of male characteristics (such as the gentleman farmer or the frontiersman), whether identifying archetypal formations (e.g. the self-made man) or the reach of a particular men's movement (such as the YMCA), that refined our understandings of manhood as a variable historical cultural concept that intersects with other realms of public life. The forms of Mexican American manhood that I describe are often in conversation with these figures, but evolved separately from their white counterparts. In many cases, Mexican American masculinity was confined, constrained, controlled, and often rooted in reason, the rational, and deliberative action. In contrast to many portrayals of white manhood during the long century, and perhaps as a necessary reaction to racialization, Mexican Americans downplayed the aggressiveness and primitivism associated with white manhood and famously captured in the writings of Jack London or Stephen Crane, for example.

Mexican American manhood similarly questions the exclusionary processes that stereotyped black masculinity, which prompted Philip Brian Harper to ask, "Are we not men?"[30] Mexican American manhood has historical analogues in black masculinity, but the processes of racialization operated in distinct and specific ways. Recalling Nella Larsen's character Irene's remark that "They always took her for an Italian, a Spaniard, a Mexican, or gipsy," U.S. racial binaries frequently did not differentiate within an absolute black-white dichotomy.[31] Yet because of its association with foreignness, Mexican American manhood provided a different response. Whereas black male stereotypes have often seen African American men "as animals, brutes, natural born rapists, and murderers," "stereotypes that were first articulated in the nineteenth century but hold sway over the minds and imaginations of citizens of this nation in the present day," Mexican American manhood has faced different challenges and associations.[32] Other scholars have "elaborate[d] a schema of generative modes by which African American men have historically survived the self-alienating disjunction of race and manhood in American culture" and "how social preoccupations with race, gender, and sexuality inflect not only the writerly record but the larger issue of the social ideal of black masculinity."[33]

Michael Kimmel mentions how racism and nativism bore the mark of gender, as if "depicting 'them' as less manly would make 'us' feel more manly."[34] Amy Kaplan follows up this point in an international setting, showing how "the lament for the close of the frontier loudly voiced such nostalgia for the formative crucible of American manhood; imperial expansion overseas offered a new frontier, where the essential American man could be reconstituted in his escape from modernity and domesticity."[35] For both critics, U.S. anxieties about manhood could be resolved through a nativist response differentiating between "true" American men and the exotic and racialized others against whom they struggled for cultural and political supremacy. While these critics contribute greatly to our understandings of American manhood in the U.S. and imperial contexts, none considers how Mexican Americans' unique position as both familiar citizen and foreign immigrant engaged with, fought, or defined manhood differently from a sense of universalized whiteness.

While the ideas of manhood described by these scholars at least partially overlap with Mexican American notions of manhood prevalent in the same period, most scholars do not pay attention to Latinos generally, and specifically to how Mexican Americans conceptualized a shared, collective notion of masculine public life, an omission which this book seeks to correct. This work amplifies that of feminist scholars of the 1980s and 1990s who sought to dispel the unitary masculinist premise of the Chicano movement in order to recognize Chicana contributions to the movement and to empower Chicanas living with the vestiges of a patriarchal culture.[36] This body of work evolved into what is now known as queer-of-color critique, expanding our knowledge of how sex and gender intersect with other cultural formations.[37] Chicana feminists were instrumental in critiquing the explicit and implicit gender biases that shaped Chicano culture, drawing attention to masculine restrictions and male oppression over women and sexual minorities. More powerfully, these critics and writers helped us realize how multiple, overlapping categories of identity function simultaneously and cannot be analyzed in isolation of each other, a formidable rebuke of the tendency to isolate racial, sexual, or gender differences from each other. This recognition enabled a whole generation of scholars, including myself, to think critically about the multiple ways that gender shapes the lives of people of color. Their work has helped elucidate how gender and sexuality operate to restrict or enable social inclusion, within communities ranging in scale from the intimate to the national. This book draws on the contributions by these scholars in its understanding of how Mexican American manhood distills various and often-contradictory social categories. *Before Chicano* examines manhood not to reify it as central to the project of the Latino subject, but rather to diagnose how it functioned as a key, if problematic, construct of Mexican American public life.

Making Men: Democratic Citizenship as Masculine Values

Manhood is a process inseparable from the legal, political, and social developments of the time, and this study of early Mexican American manhood reveals an engagement with the historical processes of exclusion, a need to define oneself and one's community against the racializing forces that threaten to normalize Mexican Americans as outside or unworthy of U.S. citizenship. It is a reaction to forms of oppression, but it is also a statement of a collective commitment to national ideals and the political process. Nowhere are claims to national belonging more salient than in suffrage, which is often considered the final arbiter of citizenship; a person who has the right to vote is considered a full member of society. At a national level, Mexican American men gained this legal right in 1848; Mexican American women did so in 1920. (It is worth noting that universal women's suffrage in Mexico came much later, in 1953.) Yet for Mexican Americans, legal status as a citizen was hardly a guarantor of social integration; suffrage granted the legal capacity to vote, but in practice access to that right was restricted. Although often in direct dialogue with the legal system and its institutions, Mexican Americans were frequently unable to claim the rights and privileges from the courts or legislative bodies.[38] As a result, both men and women mobilized manhood to advocate for their individual or communal needs, against racial exclusion, but at times also against the needs of other Latinos or recent immigrants.

Departing from a legal viewpoint of citizenship as organized hierarchically from individual to institutions to the nation-state, *Before Chicano* instead treats citizenship as moving laterally across disparate communities through the circulation of texts and ideas in a shared print culture, where the community and the state are equal guarantors of civil rights. Communities found common status not solely in national identity, but in shared cultural norms often articulated around gendered identity. Here, I argue for citizenship as nationally oriented but transnationally derived, a kind of participatory practice both discursive and material that functions to designate inclusion within a local or regional community and as a practice of U.S. nation-building. Rather than resist the nation-state and its exclusionary practices, Mexican Americans prior to the civil rights movement used existing understandings of the U.S. nation and of citizenship to position themselves as agents and producers of national culture.

To engage with U.S. citizenship (a point, as I argue, that was constitutive of early Mexican American manhood) is not to say that such engagements were not critical of the U.S. and of the exclusionary practices that determined social and political rights. Manhood and citizenship represented an attempt to inscribe Mexican Americans within and alter prevailing conceptions of U.S. cultural belonging. The confluence of manhood and citizenship describes social, cultural, legal, and political attachments, and at times emerges as a mode of aspirational citizenship, a desire for social bonds that exceed racial discrimination.[39] For Mexican Americans in the nineteenth and early twentieth century, citizenship provided a means of articulating their own emergence into U.S. national culture alongside the development of a national manhood. However, the conception of citizenship was more expansive than we understand it today. Mexican Americans understood citizenship within a transnational context in which republican or democratic values exceeded national boundaries and the narrative or cultural constructs which sought to represent them. Using "manhood" as a common cultural currency, disparate writers from far-ranging communities began to imagine themselves as a collective and national whole, and these writers mobilized print culture as a part of a broader practice of citizenship.

In its most basic terms, citizenship is a political philosophy describing a relationship between an individual and the political community.[40] "At a minimum, citizenship implies a legally and politically defined status, involving both rights (guaranteed by custom or law) and corresponding responsibilities," and was, at least until the twentieth century, a privileged status extended to a limited number of people, either by de jure or de facto methods.[41] Citizenship rests on the possibility and enforcement of exclusion, of limiting access, and on the legitimation of violence and coercive force. Citizenship is a political identity, as well as a set of rights and obligations that pertain to membership in a nation-state. It is commonly understood as the relationship between the individual and the state: the vertical relations between an individual and the institutions (typically governmental, but not exclusively) that make possible the activities of daily life.

One of the most celebrated philosophers to have written about the United States is the Frenchman Alexis de Tocqueville. Since the first volume was published in 1835, *Democracy in America* has been interpreted as a commendation of U.S. democracy. Tocqueville's writings, based on his travels in the U.S. in 1831, provide a blueprint for the promise of democratic government at a time when the world was experiencing radical change and multiple revolutions. Tocqueville noted how "the government of the Union rests almost entirely upon legal fictions [. . .] only in men's imaginations," a point upon which many have elaborated.[42] He praised the United States' citizenry's ability to understand the relationship between individual and collective sovereignty, between state and federal rights, as among the most laudable characteristics of the country. In contrast, Tocqueville notes, "The Mexicans, aiming for a federal system, took the federal constitution of their neighbors, the Anglo-Americans, as their model and copied it almost exactly. But although they transported the letter of the law, they failed to transfer at the same time the spirit which gave it life."[43] Tocqueville's criticism of the Mexican Constitution of 1824, which he claims left Mexico unable to fully negotiate the tensions between regional and national concerns, accurately predicts Mexico's inability to forge a cohesive central state, but he attributes those shortcomings to a racial and masculinized understanding of political organization, one of "those fine creations of human endeavor which crown their inventors with renown and wealth, but remain sterile in other hands."[44] The tension between these national projects is a secondary concern in his study, but Tocqueville uses the contrast between

Mexico and the United States to point out the importance and intentional fabrication of any democratic project. At the center of his critique of the "fictions of government" is the potential divergence between state and federal law, between the needs of the individual and those of the state, and in this space between the individual and the state, Mexican Americans utilized cultural manhood to inscribe themselves into a national imaginary.[45]

Many of the writers and thinkers discussed in this study were familiar with if not raised in Mexico's political tradition, ideas that informed their political participation in the United States. National citizenship in Mexico developed and shifted throughout the nation's early history, most notably in its founding Constitution of 1824, the liberal Constitution of 1857, and the Revolutionary Constitution of 1917.[46] For much of its national history, Mexico had a relatively weak central state and a large agrarian (and often impoverished) population. From the nation's founding until at least after the French Intervention, "citizenship was continually invoked as the first and foremost need of the nation at a time when the country had no effective central state, had a declining economy, and was threatened by both imperial powers and internal regional dissidents."[47] In its early republic phase, Mexican law (in theory if not always in practice) leaned toward inclusivity in determining citizenship, directed at creating an engaged, patriotic citizenry. The 1824 Mexican Constitution distinguished between "citizen" and "national" as distinct categories of civic participation, with the rights of suffrage and governance vested in the former.[48] Yet, while the nation legally eliminated slavery and caste difference, it reserved public office for wealthy and literate elites. Between the Constitutions of 1824 and 1857, the states determined criteria for citizenship, and presidential election was done by act of Congress. This division tended to concentrate political power among regional elites, and divided power between state and federal rights in a way similar to that of the post-U.S.-Mexican War United States.

These Mexican political legacies carried into the Mexican American culture, but were only one of the characteristics that marked Mexican Americans as different. Perhaps the most easily recognizable difference between the white and Mexican Americans was language, which has historically been used to dismiss Latinos from their role within U.S. national culture. Despite various attempts to the contrary, English is not the official language of the United States, though it has and will continue to be the primary language of communication. In the nation's early days, it was quite common for people to live in multiple languages. The nation's "founding fathers" could speak, read, and write in a variety of languages, including Latin, Greek, and French. Thomas Jefferson claimed to "read Greek, Latin, French, Italian, Spanish, and English of course, with something of its radix the Anglo-Saxon."[49] Multilingualism was a sign of cultivation and education, and it demonstrated the connections between the United States and other democratic states. Subsequent generations seem to have forgotten this aspect of our country's history. Despite claims calling for a multilingual evaluation of American culture, there remains a persistent division by language within ethnic American cultural studies.[50] As Kirsten Silva Gruesz states of a different but related context, "The transnational turn has, with a few exceptions, politely ignored that call [to multilingualism] in favor of methods that compare domestic *English* texts with those written abroad in other languages. The potential of 'multilingual America' is still mostly untapped, but that nascent subfield has even more to do besides recover texts, authors, and the contours of forgotten paths of print circulation."[51] Such linguistic dexterity is a requirement for any study of early Latino culture, and, to access the archives of Latino letters, this study recognizes the bilingualism among its actors as essential to the practices of everyday life.

Nonetheless, for a variety of reasons (institutional, archival, linguistic, etc.), Mexican Americans are frequently left out of accounts of the American nineteenth century. A century and a half after Tocqueville, after the Civil War and the Civil Rights Movement, Thurgood Marshall, the first African American on the Supreme Court, explained how the credit for American democratic values "does not belong to the framers. It belongs to those who refused to acquiesce in outdated notions of 'liberty,' 'justice,' and 'equality,' and who strived to better them."[52] It is in this spirit that Mexican Americans (and arguably Latinos or minorities more broadly) view citizenship, as a developing process. One recurring attribute of nineteenth-century Mexican American manhood is its deployment of ideas of republicanism that circulated in a variety of media and genres, thereby reflecting and creating men as citizens. Throughout the nineteenth and early twentieth centuries, the construction of Mexican American manhood attempts to reinvigorate a communal sense of

democratic potential, which variously takes shape as republican idealism, regional cultural history, transnational citizenship, and sexual cultural politics. Roderick Ferguson identifies "the nation as the domain
determined by racial difference and gender and sexual conformity,"
so that "racist practice articulates itself generally as gender and sexual
regulation" and gendered critique can "approach culture as one site that
compels identifications with and antagonisms to the normative ideals
promoted by state and capital."[53] Writers and thinkers turned to manhood to forge a nationally recognizable Mexican American subject and
citizen from among the scattered Mexican origin groups and in dialogue
with public conceptions of U.S. citizen.

To some extent, democracy itself posed the very challenge to civil and
political obstacles that faced Mexican Americans. It was near impossible to overcome majoritarian rule and control of institutional jurisdiction under the conditions encountered across the U.S., particularly in
the Southwest, the former territories of Mexico. With few alternatives
to the discriminatory legal and social practices, perceptions of manhood were interwoven with notions of citizenship to combat exclusion.
The latter half of the nineteenth century ushered in Women's Property
Acts across many states, guaranteeing women's economic and property
rights to varying degrees, but these rights were repeatedly contested
and occasionally repealed. As political scientist Gretchen Ritter points
out, citizenship "is regarded as a public identity. Gender intersects with
civic identity differently for men and women."[54] Under these conditions,
manhood offered a cultural rhetoric available to both men and women
through which to address social difference and to advocate for political
inclusion across linguistic lines and national origin. In order to exercise
many of the rights and privileges of citizenship, and to be recognized
as an equal member of society, an individual had to qualify as a "man,"
though the standards against which that measure was applied shifted
and varied.[55]

Writing the Nation: Emerging Mexican American Collectivity

The writers discussed here do not fit into easy categorization, and they
work across a multitude of genres and forms not always associated with
literature. In fact, many of these writers would not define themselves as

novelists or, at times, even writers (for Juan Nepomuceno Cortina, for instance, writing was a necessary outgrowth of and complement to his other endeavors, but never a central focus). These texts ask us to reconsider the role of writing, literature, and print culture. In his terrific study of what he calls Latino "textuality," Raul Coronado demonstrates how "the turn of the nineteenth-century Anglo-Protestant world shifted from [a] republican ideology of the common good to liberalism's emphasis on self-fulfillment, [whereas] the Hispanic world would not," as Latinos remained committed to "a nation comprised of constituent groups rather than self-interested individuals."[56] In drawing on the Catholic roots of the modern West, Coronado points to how the family, not the individual, formed the foundational principle of the social contract and social body.[57] In many ways, Mexican American manhood is a political construction of a newly formed social group that emphasized developing collectivity and simultaneously inscribed Mexican Americans as national subjects. For Mexican Americans of the nineteenth and early twentieth centuries, republican ideals presumed the common good over the individual, and republicanism offered an important ideological and political framework through which Mexican Americans could address the limitations and exclusions imposed upon them by democratic rule, even as they sought to perform as members of a national democracy. The focus on the common good never fully dissolved, but by the mid-twentieth century the individual's relation to the collective became a more important focus. Whereas earlier manhood represented transnational republican values, by the early twentieth century those values became embedded within individual labor and the body. Manhood thus provided a language through which to posit the equality of labor and bodies across racial and ethnic groups, and similarly to unify sections of the population. Manhood and citizenship describes the imagined and real relationship between individual and political community; it is both a legal status and an action, the labor and pursuit of political participation.

Because of their long attachment to the geographic space of the Americas in the age of revolution, Mexican Americans—perhaps more than other ethnic groups—sought to reinvigorate the U.S. nation's conception of citizenship with republican values, against the rising populist democracy that had taken precedence throughout the long nineteenth century. In the United States in the age of empire, Mexican Americans drew on this past to animate an expanded and often conflicting sense of citizenship. Somewhat contradictorily, exerting political rights as an extension of republican values within the nation often required "an acknowledgment of the increasingly transterritorial quality of political and social life, and [. . .] a commitment to a vision of citizenship that is multiple and overlapping."[58] On the one hand, manhood facilitated attempts at incorporating or nationalizing Mexican Americans into the United States by expanding conceptions of U.S. citizenship that located U.S. nationalism within other hemispheric, democratic projects. On the other hand, manhood served as a mechanism of social organization, establishing and communicating commonality across disparate groups within the U.S. and as a tangible representation of lived experience that routinely crossed borders.

In the fields of cultural and American studies, citizenship denotes wide-ranging approaches to the concerns of ethnic Americans and people of the Global South, generally seeking to explain the intricate ways individuals and groups form consensus, affiliation, and attachments to one another and to the nation. These models of citizenship further explain the methods through which the rights and privileges of citizenship are enacted and enforced, expanding on T.H. Marshall's influential formulation of the tripartite structure of citizenship.[59] Within cultural studies, studies of citizenship delineate the forms of attachment and group collectivity that enable, limit, or challenge participation in civil life and the polity. William Flores and Rina Benmayor posit a notion of cultural citizenship, where cultural difference offers a source for claiming access to political life.[60] Others, such as Monica Mookherjee, Lauren Berlant, and Alice Kessler-Harris, focus on how gender and sexuality impact citizenship, developing what might be called affective citizenship.[61] David Luis-Brown, Brian T. Edwards and Dilip Parameshwar Gaonkar, Etienne Balibar, Nigel Dower, and John Williams have sought to identify forms of social and political alliances across national borders, as well as the difficulties these alliances pose and the possibilities they offer.[62]

Yet a legal definition of citizenship inadequately describes the demands placed upon the label, and legal structures are shaped by the political and cultural contexts from which they emerge.[63] For Mexican Americans, citizenship was an ongoing and malleable process of civic life, which could influence and be influenced by the men and women who worked to better themselves and their communities. Where legal and institutional laws and reforms failed to address other means of exclusion, notions of manhood could suture the divide between political and social rights. Men and women turned to print culture to disseminate competing understandings of Mexican Americans and to reflect disparate ideas of who they were and how they were part of the nation. To borrow from Jonathan Fox's analysis of electoral politics and social organization, manhood mirrored "how regimes begin to accept the right of citizens to pursue their goals autonomously."[64]

In conceptualizing gender as a critical framework for accessing this Latino past, this book considers manhood as a feature of Mexican American culture that spans time and geographic space. It asks how these interdependent categories of manhood and citizenship are present in and represented by language, in the archival record and in public life, but also how these cultural narratives about manhood operate along a trajectory that is variously transnational, historical, presentist, and proleptic.[65] Conceiving of gender in this way makes visible how individuals utilize recurring notions of manhood to interject themselves within national conversations about citizen and nation. Throughout the nineteenth and early twentieth centuries, manhood—both as a biological and racial category—was a precondition for the practice of many civil rights, legally and culturally. Each chapter of this study identifies and critiques a recurring and prevalent cultural form of Latino manhood.

The cultural construction of manhood both reflected and constituted the emergence of Mexican Americans as a social group. Cultural narratives are both descriptive and instantiative, which not only register their cultural moment by commenting on and critiquing it, but also bring about the creation of new cultural paths and initiate new directions for public expression. In the late twentieth-century Chicano movement, there emerged a paradigm of resistance as a historically-specific development necessary for the advancement of a particular political project.[66] I take up the challenge of many critics who have shown the need to move beyond a resistance paradigm for the fields of both Chicano and Latino Studies. By focusing on an earlier period, *Before Chicano* seeks to remedy the omission of Chicano participation in the national narrative, a corrective to the historical amnesia that frequently marks Chicanos (and Latinos) as an ethnic group. The tendency to obfuscate this past has repercussions in the present. About once each decade—as the media narrative would have it—Latinos supposedly "emerge": in the 1980 census, the 1990s Hispanics consumer market, the 2000 "watershed" moment in becoming majority minority, the 2012 election as voting block, and so on. Each of these periodic emergences speaks to the rising demographic and cultural visibility of Latinos. In today's national imaginary, too often Latinos are regarded as newcomers, as a contemporary phenomenon whose potential is directed into the ever-receding future, perpetually deferred. The postponement of the Latino present generally hinges on the question of immigration and its associated economic and political policy, a connection both troublesome and difficult to dislodge. But Latinos are already here—they have been part of the nation for generations. The danger in futurity, always receding before us, is that it can cause an historical amnesia that ruptures the past from the present. It is not about Latinos becoming (as the 2000 census or the 2012 election would have us believe), but about the ways they always have been and continue to be part of the national story. Historicizing Chicano manhood enables a different kind of future, and *Before Chicano* alters the prevailing understanding of Latinos as newcomers or outsiders, instead showing how they participated as agents—often fraught, regionally conflicted, and internally disputed, but nonetheless—within a developing U.S. nation and as contributors to American culture.

From Mexican Americans to Latina/os: A Note on Terminology

It is unlikely that any of the writers and thinkers I discuss would have used the term "Latina/o" to identify themselves or their contemporaries, since the word's first documented usage was in 1946 (the term became common in the 1990s and officially adopted as an ethnic category on the 2000 U.S. census).[67] I use the term "Latino" anachronistically to indicate the diverse population within the United States who identify as having some connection (familial, cultural, ethnic, etc.) to the Spanish-speaking world, although in contemporary usage the term also includes other non-Spanish speakers. Similarly, I use the term "Mexican American" to refer to those individuals and communities living within the United States who claim a degree of Mexican origin, whether they are first-generation immigrants or fifth-generation citizens of the United States. I do so primarily to draw a historical distinction from the term "Chicano," which developed in the late twentieth century as part of the civil rights movement. However, the utility of "Chicano" in both past and present to represent a politically minded activism is crucial to the field and to our understanding of the people it represents.

In her excellent book on Chicano literary and cultural history, *Chicano Nations*, Marissa Lopez urges us to consider Chicano culture in broader temporal and spatial terms. Lopez seeks to invigorate the term "Chicano" as something more than a historical referent to the civil rights movement of the 1960s and 1970s, and posits that Chicanismo be understood within "a vast network of transnational *latinidad*" and as a critical mode of engaging with U.S. power. Invoking "ambivalence about the nation," Lopez looks outside the U.S. to invigorate cultural nationalism and to animate the hemispheric origins of Chicano cultural life.[68] I share Lopez's desire to reanimate Chicanismo for the future, although I use the term "Mexican American" precisely for its broader historical signification. Less an oppositional politics than an investment in state making, Mexican American manhood before the Chicano movement produced a sense of collective manhood and citizenship that helped define Chicano *and* U.S. culture. The title *Before Chicano* deliberately invokes the historical frame, but also the political promise of the label.

Before Chicano focuses primarily on the archive of Mexican American experience for several reasons. Demographically, nearly two-thirds of the U.S.-Latino population claims Mexican descent, and recent census data states that over ten percent of the U.S. population is of personal or familial Mexican origin.[69] Moreover, the relationship between the U.S. and its southern neighbor was crucial to the project of U.S. expansion. Through war and direct political annexation, the geographic expansion of the U.S. came through the acquisition of Mexican territory during the period this study covers. Latinos have been present in the United States since before the nation's founding, but the end of the U.S.-Mexican War in 1848 marks an important transition for Mexican Americans as a national group. For these reasons, it is imperative to understand the unique historical relationship of Mexican Americans with the U.S. nation-state, even as this study imagines Chicano print culture within a larger national Latino dynamic.

Figures and Forms of Mexican American Manhood

For the most part, the Mexican Americans we will meet in the coming pages did not imagine themselves as recent arrivals, having spent significant portions of their lives in the United States. Yet these writers do not have an established place in the U.S. political and cultural imaginary. They are relegated to the position of outsider, the target of nativist attacks on national purity. In constructing an archive of Mexican American manhood before the Chicano movement, this book brings together a wide array of material from a variety of sources, genres, and discourses across print media. Mexican American culture varied substantially across geographic areas, among groups in dialogue with each other but often espousing divergent regional concerns. These differences beg the question of how to assemble an archive within such a variegated print culture and among communities that did not yet fully conceive of themselves as a unified demographic block, as we currently do. Borrowing from Deleuze and Guattari's rhizomatic notion of the assemblage, this book organizes its archive *radially* around the central concept of manhood; thus the archive becomes a method of ascribing meaning and boundedness to multiplicity.[70] Thinking about an archive radially also helps account for linguistic difference, in that it can organize by assuming familiarity across languages. It also offers a method through which to connect the notion of individual or idiosyncratic archives: rather than canon as common ground, with specific texts unifying a field, we might ask what common themes, ideas, contexts unite seemingly disparate groups of texts, and how these intersect. As shown by these men and women writers, manhood stands in for a wide array of social concerns.

Chapter one examines the dominant depiction of Mexican American manhood, the bandit figure. Unlike most accounts that either villainize the Mexican American bandit or champion him as a figure of resistance, this chapter reinterprets the bandit as central to the U.S. narrative of liberal democracy, disrupting U.S. colonialism and situating Mexican Americans within broader hemispheric social and political movements. Literature about bandits was ubiquitous in the decades following the U.S.-Mexican War and depicted Mexican Americans as inassimilable, but I insert these fictions into a transnational, multilingual archive that more accurately reflects the Mexican American communities it represented. In contrast to most understandings of the bandit as an anti-U.S. criminal, Mexican American bandits developed cultural values that positioned Mexican Americans as U.S. national citizens fighting for freedom and justice—the very republican ideals used to justify national conflict. This chapter proposes the bandit as a figure that "cleaves" Mexican Americans to citizenship, playing on the contradictory meanings of the term as both to sever and to adhere. Cleaving then becomes a way of conceptualizing the relationship between Mexican American manhood and citizenship throughout the nineteenth and twentieth centuries.

Chapter two considers the other dominant thread of late nineteenth-century gendered public identity, one often directed at a middle-class readership—that of the "Spanish fantasy heritage." By Spanish fantasy heritage, I refer to the cultural construct and identity that emerged in the late nineteenth-century to claim a Europeanized heritage for Mexican Americans and others living in parts of the U.S. Southwest formerly under Spanish colonial rule. The fantasy heritage manifested in myriad ways, including architecture, literature, cultural events, and as personal identity. Spanish fantasy heritage distinguished between assimilated or Europeanized Spaniards and the other mestizo, immigrant, or Spanish-speaking populations that came under U.S. control. Focusing on California as a site of cultural conflict, I contend that Spanish fantasy heritage, which coincided with the revision of California's Constitution, responded to the dual nature of American citizenship (federal vs. state); examining cultural accounts alongside government documents about the constitutional convention reveals the complicated ways in which fantasy heritage racialized Mexican Americans. This chapter recovers the work of Mexican exile, politician, and journalist Adolfo Carrillo alongside more familiar Anglo American regionalist writers such as Gertrude Atherton and Charles Lummis to illustrate how Mexican Americans repudiated their social exclusion and of the need for multilingual cultural history.

As agents of political change, Mexican Americans were embedded within both national and global events. Chapter three examines the expatriate phenomenon known as "*México de afuera*," an extranationalist ideology that emerged during and after the Mexican Revolution (1910–1920) through which those fleeing civil war came to see themselves as the last stronghold of an ailing national identity. The chapter interrogates

México de afuera as a structuring principle of Mexican American manhood, an aspect of the ideology previously unaccounted for. Examining the ideology within a broader dialogue of U.S. manhood and citizenship allows us to consider the global dimensions of U.S. national citizenship in the mid-twentieth century, and asks what happens when World War I replaces the Mexican Revolution as the central national conflict for early twentieth-century Mexican American cultural life and manhood. As a structuring force of manhood, México de afuera shifts from an extranationalist ideology into a mode of citizenship that understands civic participation transnationally, what I call "expatriate citizenship." Alongside periodicals, travel guides, and government promotional materials, the chapter centers on Josefina Niggli's 1947 novel *Step Down, Elder Brother* to contend that Niggli offers a way of understanding U.S. race relations both domestically and abroad, staging Mexican American manhood as both national and global citizenship. Through expatriate citizenship, U.S. readers could deliberate on the nation's place as an emergent global superpower and the contradictions posed between exported democracy and domestic citizenship.

One outcome of the extranationalist and expatriate drive of México de afuera manhood was a re-entrenchment in the nation and in familiar notions of Anglo-American manhood. Chapter four turns to a moment in the early twentieth century in which two novels, now widely accepted as part of the Latino "canon" and central modernist texts, were coincidentally written (though unpublished) within a few years of each other. Since their publication in the 1990s, Jovita González and Margaret Eimer's novel *Caballero* (~1936) and Américo Paredes's novel *George Washington Gomez* (~1937) have become cornerstones of Chicano literature and have largely been interpreted as either furthering Chicano movement resistance or espousing an assimilationist position. Here, I argue that the novels create a manhood that addresses a Mexican American middle class, and they rewrite citizenship as non-migratory labor. This figure of manhood urges pragmatic integration through economic cooperation. By championing the economic capacity of Latinos not as laborers but as managers, inventors, and entrepreneurs, these texts engage with early twentieth-century ideals about productivity and the division of labor, critiquing notions of the so-called "self-made man" and refashioning Mexican American manhood as a model for the national citizen. Economic citizenship seeks a place within the structures of capitalism that dominated social life and to dissociate Mexican Americans from ideas of migration and transience that characterized discourses of labor frequently associated with ethnic Mexicans.

Chapter five sutures the pre– and post–civil rights movements—a divide that operates as a historical schism for Latino Studies. Analyzing José Antonio Villarreal's novel *Pocho* (1959, which many have hailed as the first Chicano novel), I argue that the novel is better understood not as an origin point but rather as a node within a longer genealogy of Latino culture. Few scholars have accounted for the novel's troubling depiction of masculinity and sexuality except to dismiss the narrative as chauvinist and misogynistic. Sexuality underpins the multiethnic community's fragile alliances, and this chapter examines the sexuality, homoeroticism, and homophobia within Anglo and Mexican American culture, a depiction that is at odds with some of the stated objectives of the Chicano movement's foundational documents. Read alongside early Chicano movement manifestos and correspondence, the chapter calls for a more historically expansive understanding of the emergence and legacy of the Chicano movement. In these ways, the Mexican American men and women discussed in the following pages speak to the complexities, contradictions, and interplay of race and gender in the United States.

1

Outlaw Citizenship

Mexican American Manhood and Banditry

In the fall and early winter of 1859, the escalating racial tensions between Anglo and Mexican Americans living along the border transformed Juan Nepomuceno Cortina from a longtime resident of the border region into what U.S. public opinion would label a bandit. In a written proclamation issued on November 23, 1859, the rancher, soldier, and occasional cattle-rustler Cortina offered a scathing portrayal of South Texas. He declared that the state was overrun by "flocks of vampires, in the guise of men [who] came and scattered themselves in the settlements . . . without any capital except the corrupt heart and the most perverse intentions." [1] When Cortina chastised the relatively recent Anglo settlers who flocked to the frontier, he indicted them as a parody of manhood—parasitic "vampires" who failed to live up to dominant notions of male public identity. Yet in this proclamation and others, he transformed the meaning of banditry even as he relied on its cultural significance. His words help identify the ways in which Latinos in the nineteenth century sought to imagine themselves as citizens of a U.S. nation, although they often did so by extending the cultural imaginary across the border. Distinguishing between his actions and those of the Anglo men who undermined nation-building efforts in the U.S. frontier, Cortina's proclamations presented a figure of transnational, democratic manhood by situating his actions within a U.S. revolutionary narrative that imagines the U.S. national project as but one of many ongoing hemispheric, republican, revolutionary projects.

Building on the abundant scholarship on Mexican American banditry, this chapter takes banditry as a defining condition of Mexican American manhood through the second half of the nineteenth century and interrogates the options, outcomes, and repercussions of banditry as a particular form of national citizenship.[2] Banditry "cleaved" Mexican

Americans within the nation-state, both from and to their rights and obligations as citizens of the nation. To cleave is at once instructive and paradoxical; it simultaneously suggests both the ability to separate from and to attach to something.[3] It is this dual meaning of the word that so aptly describes the bandit as citizen. In its dual function, banditry becomes a site of debate about the status of Mexican Americans and of the definition of citizenship.

Banditry took multiple forms and claimed numerous political and social ideologies, but here I want to distinguish between two types of banditry: armed resistance (against government and settler forces) and literary renderings of banditry (the cultural formation of specific groups as bandits or outlaws, and their circulation within print culture). In the former, the disparity between powerless Mexicans and oppressive (Anglo) Americans in the borderlands resulted in the use of violence to oppose social injustice. Armed assaults by Mexican Americans against individuals and the state would occur through at least the early part of the twentieth century, but in most cases met increasingly violent retributions by local and federal forces.[4]

While armed resistance and literary banditry are imbricated throughout the media and in the popular imaginary, it is important to separate the two.[5] Armed resistance uses force to combat oppression and often carries separatist aims, but "literary banditry" in Mexican American authored texts served a different purpose—national consolidation. Literary banditry is closely associated with ideals of manhood and citizenship (themselves intertwined during this period) through its juxtaposition of individual subjectivity and state authority. It describes a relationship between an individual actor and the nation-state that engages with the popular imaginary and works toward social inclusion. In this latter sense, literary banditry is more closely aligned with the Latin American bandit tradition, a point to which I return in the second half of the chapter.

Countless Anglo-authored accounts in the popular press racialized Mexican Americans in the interest of U.S. imperialism or as separatist factions, but within multilingual print culture, especially as it was handled by Mexican American authors, banditry serves to model Mexican Americans' incorporation into a body politic. Often, Mexican Americans bandits stood as foils for Anglo American expansion or to espouse violent opposition to the state, but the texts analyzed here suggest how literary banditry could also work to include Mexican Americans as citizens of the United States by locating Mexican American authors within transnational circuits of cultural exchange. In the accounts below, literary banditry becomes a narrative strategy of adaptation, of incorporation, and of inclusion—more an act of patriotic citizenship than an impulse for or an ideology of separation. This revised understanding has implications for banditry as the originating identity of Mexican American manhood and for our understanding of Mexican Americans within U.S. citizenship.

Citizenship, the relationship between individuals and the nation-state, is premised on the mutual obligation between a people and their government, "instituted among men, deriving their just powers from the consent of the governed" (Declaration of Independence). In the United States, where "a 'democracy of print' had become indispensible to political democracy," the relationship between a people and a government is narrated in ways that seek to draw boundaries between its subjects, to both include and exclude its members.[6] Literary banditry serves that dual purpose, presenting the possibility of national inclusion even as it threatens to write Mexican Americans out of the nation, thereby "cleaving" Mexican Americans to a U.S. national project.

This seemingly counterintuitive premise becomes apparent when banditry is understood as a function of citizenship in a transnational context. Banditry articulates a fundamental question of citizenship: do the rights of citizenship derive from natural rights that precede a social contract, or do they emerge from the duties that nationality vests? Accordingly, the writings by and about Juan Nepomuceno Cortina and Catarino Garza in Texas and Vicente Silva in New Mexico cleave Mexican Americans to U.S. citizenship. Each was a historical actor and a subject of historical fiction; each was a prominent, recognizable figure in his respective state and nationally, though each also conducted illicit activities. Multilingual, transnational literary banditry reveals not just resistance or disobedience, but describes multiple scales of belonging. Although these figures operated in disparate temporal and geographic moments, with wide-ranging aims and goals, together they contribute to our understanding of how Mexican Americans sought to expand U.S. national conceptions of citizenship.

King of Bandits: Joaquin Murieta and the Legacies of a Chicano Bandit Tradition

In the shifting geopolitical landscape following the U.S-Mexican War, the bandit figure emerged as metonym for both the population that the nation encountered in the wake of continental expansion and the problems associated with such expansion.[7] The United States strove to reconcile its republican ideals with the realities of an aggressive war, and since "racial arguments [. . .] were invariably linked with republicanism and all that that concept implied," the Mexican American bandit served to represent various racial categorizations.[8] Consequently, for much of the late nineteenth century, Mexican American manhood was nearly synonymous with various forms of extralegal behavior collectively referred to as banditry. Despite—or perhaps because of—this popular characterization of Mexican Americans as bandits, Mexican Americans used banditry as a tropological strategy through which to engage a national public, to move local concerns into the national spotlight. Certainly, U.S. manifest destiny led to the rise of real social and political resistance that was deemed either revolution or banditry, depending on each party's perspective. Rather than face U.S. territorial acquisition as geographic expansion, Mexican Americans who inhabited the U.S. "frontier" encountered U.S. manifest destiny as colonial encroachment. In such conditions, banditry surfaces as resistance against the threats to existing cultural life in the U.S. Southwest.[9]

As a cultural figure, however, bandits are most often discussed as stereotypes, with scholars considering how closely a particular representation adheres to or deviates from the audience's expectations of criminalized Mexican American behavior.[10] Even as contemporary critics acknowledge the nuanced and multiple meanings that the bandit can hold, the bandit's cultural value is largely assessed along a continuum of positive and negative valences within the accepted stereotype and not as agents engaged in national literary cultures and historical change. These studies of historical bandits and the discourses that surround them almost uniformly situate the bandit in opposition to the U.S. nation-state.

In another vein, scholars have found in the bandit a source for an "authentic" Chicano manhood. Américo Paredes states that the Greater Mexican Border hero represented the paradigm of masculine defiance and that the corridos "epitomized the ideal type of hero [. . .] whose first model" had been Juan Nepomuceno Cortina.[11] This concept of the hero as a man with his pistol in his hand defying the nation-state became a central organizing principle of the late twentieth-century Mexican American civil rights movement, which looked historically to the bandit figure as a an earlier incarnation of these ideals.[12] The model of warrior masculinity was a crucial, if problematic, pillar of *el movimiento*, which John Alba Cutler describes as "an often impracticable notion of ethnic identity as essential, and essentially masculine, inheritance."[13] Yet in the late nineteenth century, Mexican American literary banditry was far more complex and ambivalent. Instead of seeing the bandits as static stereotypes or in opposition to the U.S. nation, literary banditry demonstrates how these narratives function as a practice of citizenship and illuminates the reciprocal relationship between manhood and the state. Banditry was integral to Mexican American manhood in the second half of the nineteenth century, providing what Michael Warner has, in a different context, called the "political conditions of utterance," the cultural structure through which to engage the national public.[14]

Any study of nineteenth-century Mexican American banditry would be remiss not to acknowledge the most famous, albeit largely fictionalized, of bandits, Joaquin Murieta. Beginning with the publication of John Rollin Ridge's *Life and Adventures of Joaquin Murieta* (1854), Murieta has circulated as a figure loathed and admired, feared and revered, whose popularity crosses cultures and whose enduring cultural force persists into the present. His story has been told and retold countless times, beginning just five years after the publication of Ridge's tale with an anonymous version that appeared in the San Francisco *Police Gazette* (1859), which included an account of Murieta's supposed 1845 visit to Mexico.[15]

Joaquin's popularity has not escaped critical attention, and numerous contemporary critics debate the fictiveness and the cultural impact of the tale. Joseph Henry Jackson's introduction to the University of Oklahoma Press's 1954 republication of Ridge's original tale ardently argues for the fictional basis of the Murieta legend, attenuating its historical and cultural cache. In contrast, other critics of American Indian and Chicano cultural production have focused on the Murieta legend and Ridge's novel as indicative of larger social issues. These critics see Ridge, a displaced Cherokee forced to flee the Cherokee Nation after intratribal conflict resulting from territorial disputes that ended in the murder of his father and his own killing of another, masking a desire for intra- and cross-racial vengeance.[16] For more recent Chicana/o critics, Murieta has come to represent hybridity of Mexican Americans and serve as a cornerstone of the Chicano movement's cultural nationalism and reliance on masculine, anti-national resistance.[17]

Although Murieta has been canonized within Mexican American cultural history as a figure of masculine resistance, Ridge's original telling shows a much more complicated relationship between Murieta and the U.S. nation. In Ridge's narrative, Murieta develops from a victim of race hatred to a bandit terrorizing the California countryside to a revolutionary organizing a large-scale campaign against the United States. About midway through, Murieta has an epiphany, choosing to harness his bandits for a larger purpose. Murieta gathers his

"fighting members" as he called them, one hundred men, and explained to them fully his views and purposes. "I am at the head of an organization" said he, "of two thousand men whose ramifications are in Sonora, Lower California, and in this State. I have money in abundance deposited in a safe place. I intend to arm and equip fifteen hundred or two thousand men and make a clean sweep of the southern counties. I intend to kill the Americans by 'wholesale,' burn their ranchos, and run off their property at one single swoop so rapidly that they will not have time to collect an opposing force before I will have finished the work and found safety in the mountains of Sonora. When I do this, I shall wind up my career. My brothers, we will then be revenged for our wrongs, and some little, too, for the wrongs of our poor, bleeding country."[18]

As head of a large number of men, Murieta expounds on his desire to rid California of the American presence, reversing statehood enacted just a few years earlier. His actions are motivated by revenge, eager to exact retribution not only for his personal loss but for the "wrongs of our poor, bleeding country," presumably Mexico. Throughout, both Anglos and Mexicans regularly refer to Joaquin's fellow bandits as "his countrymen," locating Joaquin outside of the U.S. nation-state and emphatically dividing Mexican and American.[19] Although Joaquin never lives to fulfill his plan (he is captured and killed by a posse of men led by Captain Love), the novel implies that the majority of the Mexican origin population of California supported his actions, since "his correspondence was large with many wealthy and influential Mexicans residing in the State of California, and he had received assurances of their earnest cooperation in the movement which he contemplated."[20] Anglo Americans who read this would immediately have been alarmed by Murieta's activities and intentions to pursue the national conflict in bloody fashion, and it is this impulse toward separatism and self-assertion that is later taken up by Chicano activists.

Yet according to his statements, he does not intend to replace American government with Mexican or Californio government, but rather "wind up his career" and retire in isolation, partially deflating his revolutionary zeal. Ridge uses the language of governmentality to describe the relationship Murieta had to the "citizens of the whole state" as one of unfulfilled promise and excess, since "so burdensome were the tributes levied upon the citizens of the whole State by the robbers, and so ceaselessly did they commit their depredations that it became a fit subject for legislative action."[21] At other times, the relationship between Murieta and the Americans is rendered as a masculine contest, where one American is willing to "stake my honor, not as an American citizen, but as a man, who is simply bound by justice to himself, under circumstances in which no other considerations can prevail, that [Murieta] shall not be betrayed."[22] Facing death, the American invokes a sense of shared masculine camaraderie and male values that supersede national status, a plea to which Joaquin is ultimately sympathetic.

Ridge's complicated novel demonstrates how even Joaquin, the paradigm of Mexican American banditry, has an uneven relationship to the state and to ideals of resistance, though the latter is privileged in subsequent literary history. As Mark Rifkin points out, "Ridge's novel questions the process by which the country claims to have internalized various peoples and places," but "expresses deep anxiety about and even hostility toward popular insurgency."[23] As literary banditry, *The Life and Adventures of Joaquín Murieta* works both within and against national consolidation, seeking justice while never abandoning its revolutionary cause, though the complexity possible within literary banditry has since been forgotten. Although Murieta stands as the most recognized Mexican American bandit, he is but one node in a network of representations that had material consequences on the lives of Mexican Americans during this time.

Juan Nepomuceno Cortina: Cortina's War to Be Read

Murieta's cultural resilience can in part be attributed to his fictional roots, but several real-life bandits adapted the figure of the bandit to their political ends. In the decade after the U.S.-Mexican War, the border between the U.S. and Mexico was anything but assured, and the U.S. Southwest was, to varying degrees, troubled by social unrest and open conflict between its Native, Mexican, and Anglo American inhabitants. In one effort to settle territorial uncertainty, the United States completed the Gadsden Purchase in 1854 to acquire territory in present-day New Mexico and Arizona for the transcontinental railroad, to secure trade routes to California, and appease Mexican concerns with Indian raids in the area.[24] But the territorial disputes did not end there. Just five years later, events in South Texas would rekindle the racial tensions that persisted since the war, resulting in armed conflict and the involvement of the federal army in an affair that solicited national attention.

Born on May 16, 1824, in the state of Tamaulipas, Mexico, Juan Nepomuceno Cortina moved to what is now Brownsville, Texas, at a young age and lived between Brownsville and Matamoros throughout his adolescence. During the U.S.-Mexican War, Cortina fought under Gen. Mariano Arista in the battles of Resaca de la Palma and Palo Alto, afterwards returning to Brownsville as a rancher and occasional cattle rustler on both sides of the border. In July of 1859, Cortina chanced upon Deputy Sheriff Bob Spears beating a former family employee. Cortina intervened and, after Spears supposedly racially insulted Cortina, Cortina shot Spears in the shoulder. Fearing repercussions, Cortina fled to Mexico, until several months later, on September 28, and leading a group of approximately seventy-five armed men, Cortina stormed into Brownsville to settle a feud with Adolphus Glaveke, a German immigrant and long-time resident of the area who, in collusion with others, sought to despoil the Mexican American community. Anglo American citizens used the raid to appeal to Washington for heightened security along the border, and the local police force, the Mexican military in Matamoros, the Texas Rangers, and the U.S. army under Robert E. Lee were all mobilized to repel Cortina from the area.[25]

The Cortina Wars, as this episode is usually referred to, is more productively understood as Cortina's war to be read. Stories about Mexico, Mexicans, and the newly created Mexican Americans proliferated in both popular fiction and nonfiction in the decades following the U.S.-Mexican War, and Cortina became somewhat of a regional hero, making an appearance in several popular fictions.[26] Yet in his proclamations, Cortina attempts to inscribe banditry within recognizable frameworks of national manhood. In the press and in official and private correspondence surrounding his activities, Cortina was variously described as "robber," "savage,"[27] "brutal," "ruthless," "beastly,"[28] "desperate, lawless, and licentious,"[29] "cold-blooded,"[30] and his followers were "marauders" and "armed banditti."[31] The list goes on, but in short, he was described as a bandit. In his proclamations, however, banditry functioned as a *practice* of citizenship, providing a means through which to speak back to the nation.

Cortina's citizenship status was a hotly contested point of debate. According to Rodolfo Acuña, Cortina "goes beyond the *bandido* model. Unlike the social bandit, he had an organization with a definite ideology and organization [. . .] Cortina was a regionalist who identified with northern Mexico," yet for Cortina, the region included both the U.S. and Mexican sides of the Rio Grande, and his regional interests were in conversation with both national projects.[32] Members of Brownsville's "committee of safety" wrote to President Buchanan arguing, "It is very uncertain whether he is a citizen of the State."[33] They cited the legal battles around his mother's land claim and questioned his permanent residency at the time leading up to the annexation of Texas. Such debates represent opposite political causes, but more importantly emphasize the importance of citizenship as a precursor for the legitimization of his claims. Cortina's actions as a U.S. citizen were even more dangerous because treating him as such tacitly acknowledged the unequal treatment and failure to incorporate the Mexican population. The significance of Cortina and his actions does not rest solely on exposing these injustices, however, but rather on the way he sought to transform citizenship so that it included Mexican Americans.

Days after Cortina occupied the town of Brownsville, the first of Cortina's "Proclamations" circulated on both sides of the border, published concurrently as broadsides in both English and Spanish and in the Matamoros newspaper *El Jaque*.[34] Cortina's proclamations are typically written in the second person, directly addressing both the Mexican and Anglo residents of Texas, the U.S., and Mexico. This rhetorical gesture is an essential part of his literary act, creating the community of readers as active, engaged political beings and urging them to likewise respond. It is "*your* beautiful city," he says, reiterating that he is "*your* humble servant," and that "those guarantees which are denied *you*, thus violating the most sacred laws, are *that which moves me to address you these words*."[35] Cortina's conversational tone locates Cortina in fellowship with his readers, and heightens the sense of shared urgency in explaining the events. Emphasizing their shared involvement in the events transpiring, he implores the readers to take ownership of their part in the events, but does so by issuing not so much a call to arms or to action, but a call to "words."

For many readers concerned with an impending race war (Cortina's raid happened within weeks of John Brown's attack at Harper's Ferry), it was easier to understand the racial tensions of the region as an unfortunate escalation of a duel, a common literary and cultural trope for Southern manhood.[36] Some tried to dismiss his actions as nothing more than a personal feud gone awry. The *Southern Intelligencer* described the raids as "private revenge," a letter from the self-organized "committee of safety" to President Buchanan considered it an attempt to remedy a "private grudge," and the *New Orleans Picayune* contended the "quarrel is wholly a family one."[37] But Cortina's actions and his proclamations explicitly shifted the focus from the personal to the communal and national.

Further undermining the press's characterization of Cortina as outlaw or personal vendetta is a tension about his manhood. The Anglo press acknowledges that Cortina was "lionized by principal citizens there we are told, as a hero"; Cortina's behavior is "formidable and dangerous" and he possessed "extraordinary influence."[38] The *Southern Intelligencer* states that "the man shows great skill as well as courage," nervously noting that "he seems to wait his time and opportunity, and this with a self-reliance and firmness of purpose which may well give a pause," puzzling

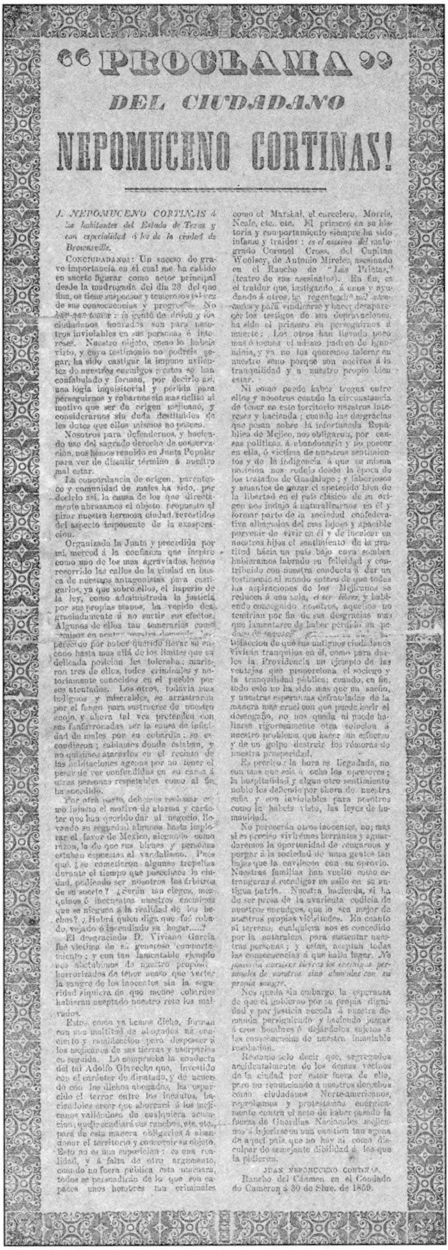

Figure 1.1. Cortina, "Proclamation," Yale Collection of Western Americana, Beinecke Rare Book and Manuscript Library, Yale University.

over the "enigma" of how he maintains his force.[39] The author endows Cortina with many of the masculine ideals then prevalent in the national imaginary—he possesses "skill," "courage," and entrepreneurial acumen to maintain a large military force without the support of the state, but his abilities are kept in check by self-control and commitment to his goals. The author's exhortation to "give a pause," then, considers what happens when a racialized body possesses the very characteristics used to assert heteronormative privilege. Cortina's forces, whose numbers were estimated at anywhere from 100 to 1500 men (a range that speaks both to his actual forces and the perceived threat), posed not only a military threat but an example of his masculine performance, merging what Amy Greenberg has seen as often competing ideas, "restrained" and "martial manhood."[40]

This appropriation of competing manhoods troubled many Anglos. In a letter to Texas Ranger John "Rip" Ford seeking military aid, Mr. Hale complained about the "insecurity of life and property, the stagnation of trade, the *disastrous effect upon our national character abroad*, which this state of affairs has produced."[41] Mr. Hale appeals to his reader's sense of "national character," their perception of integrity, pride, and manhood which Cortina's raids "exposed at every moment [and] in which their lives, fortunes, and honor are to be risked." Mr. Hale quickly moves to highlight the lingering political hostilities underlying the affair, expressing concern that Cortina "appeals to the national antipathies of the Mexicans, and to enmities excited by the last war. It is impossible to doubt that his movements are planned and directed by other minds for some ulterior effect upon the internal politics of Mexico, or the international relations between that country and the United States," triggering either a "reactionist" force in northern Mexico or an international war that would "rally" support for a centralized Mexican government.[42]

It is within this international context that Cortina appeals for national support. In defining the Mexican American "race," Cortina uses the vocabulary of manhood that would have been immediately recognizable as manly to his southern and northern contemporaries.[43] Explaining Texas Mexicans to his readers, Cortina describes them as possessing "genial affability," "humility, simplicity, and docility, directed with dignity," an "irresistible inclination towards ideas of equality," and "adorned with the most lovely disposition towards all that is good and useful in the line of progress," qualities that would ring as manly virtues.[44] At the same time, he demands justice for those that wronged him, warning they may "become subject to the consequences of our immutable resolve"; in short, challenging them to a duel.

Cortina industriously dedicates himself to "constant labor" and paints himself as hard working, unwavering, and invested above all in the prosperity of his fellow men who are also "honorably and exclusively dedicated to the exercise of industry." His bandit manhood is then confident and courageous, not the rigid machismo often associated with banditry, but rather in deliberate concert with a feminized sense of mutual freedom, in "sisterhood of liberty." Cortina readily accepts the label of bandit, stating "If, my dear compatriots, I am honored with the name, I am ready for the combat," but only if qualified by an explanation of its attributes.

Cortina's proclamations and the print coverage of events interpreted his exploits in terms of national manhood, but antebellum notions of manhood were intimately connected to national citizenship, which in its strict association with a single nation-state limited the degree to which Cortina was read. Cortina's sense of national belonging transgressed national boundaries, thereby challenging his readers' notions of both manhood and citizenship. In his first proclamation, Cortina expresses his aim only "to chastise the villainy of our enemies" who "form, so to speak, a perfidious inquisitorial lodge to persecute and rob us, without any cause, and for no other crime on our part than that of being of Mexican origin."[45] Cortina affirms the racial prejudice that dominates the Texas social structure, but excuses his use of violence as emanating from the state's inability to meet its obligations to its own citizens, stating bluntly, "Inasmuch as justice, being administered by their own hands, the supremacy of the law has failed to accomplish its object."[46] He elevates democratic values above national affiliation in efforts to justify his actions and make them legible across national borders.

The failure of the nation-state animates his position as a U.S. citizen, and Cortina's proclamation is as much a declaration of U.S. citizenship as it is a declamation of racial injustice. Cortina imagines himself within the ideals of emancipatory citizenship, as "a part of the confederacy" that champions the rights of its citizens, calling on the government, "for the sake of its own dignity, and in obsequiousness to justice," to come to the aid of Texas Mexicans. His statements bear quoting at length as it sets the terms for a vexed nationalism:

> And how can it be otherwise, when the ills that weigh upon the unfortunate republic of Mexico have obliged us for many heart-touching causes to abandon it and our possessions in it, or else become the victims of our principles or of the indigence to which its intestine disturbances had reduced us since the treaty of Guadalupe? When, ever diligent and industrious, and desirous of enjoying the longed-for boon of liberty within the classic country of its origin, we were induced to naturalize ourselves in it and form a part of the confederacy, flattered by the bright and peaceful prospect of living therein and inculcating in the bosoms of our children a feeling of gratitude towards a country beneath whose aegis we would have wrought their felicity and contributed with our conduct to give evidence to the whole world that all the aspirations of the Mexicans are confined to one only, that of being freemen; and that having secured this ourselves, those of the old country, notwithstanding their misfortunes, might have nothing to regret save the loss of a section of territory, but with the sweet satisfaction that their old fellow citizens lived therein, enjoying tranquility, as if Providence had so ordained to set them an example of the advantages to be derived from public peace and quietude.[47]

For "diligent and industrious" Cortina, it is the failure of the Mexican nation-state that has led Texas Mexicans, perhaps with regret, to "abandon" Mexico and become U.S. citizens. The shift in national affiliation was not taken lightly, but was a calculated risk, lest Texas Mexicans "become the victims of our principles," the victims of national loyalty over self-preservation. In Cortina's words, Texas Mexicans worked diligently to prosper and uphold order and justice, but when circumstances of fate required them to switch national allegiance, they did so willingly. Cortina's sense of citizenship moves fluidly between nations—perhaps a consequence of the war or an early articulation of cultural nationalism—but he publicly states his desire to leave behind ties to Mexico (the "old country") and to "their old fellow citizens" in exchange for liberty, the "advantages derived from public peace," and being "freemen." In Cortina's formulation, Texas Mexicans value democratic ideals over the authority of any single nation-state, crediting the U.S. with republican ideals that fuel their desire to become American. His commitment to the U.S. nation-state would have been complete had Texas Mexicans not been "defrauded in the most cruel manner" and left with no other option than to retaliate and "destroy the obstacles to our prosperity."[48]

This excerpt, like much of the proclamations, is written in long, sprawling sentences, with numerous appositional phrases interrupting the flow of his assertions. The appositions provide useful description and needed contextualization of the events Cortina narrates, but the syntactic breakup of the narrative imparts a sense of dislocation on the reader, one which formally reflects Cortina's own condition of provisional control. At once conversational and disruptive, the text undermines the authority of the written document even as it utilizes it to assert command of the events. Through repeated intervention in his own narrative, Cortina reminds the reader of the failures of the nation-state and interjects on behalf of the Texas Mexican community, calling for new interpretations and new voices.

Casting himself as a champion of justice, Cortina seeks to rewrite the bandit figure as a defender of the rights putatively guaranteed by the state. This literary performance charges banditry with both moral and revolutionary purpose, and transforms banditry into patriotism by revealing a language of rebellion familiar to U.S. audiences. Cortina's proclamations envelop his raids in a rhetoric of revolutionary right that fit squarely within familiar regional nationalist movements of the mid-nineteenth century, including Texas's own independence movement and those of 1850s Mexico, especially the Plan de Ayutla (1854) that called for the overthrow of Santa Anna and set the stage for Benito Juarez's liberal government and Constitution of 1857. The Plan de Ayutla sought to establish a democratic republic "sin otra restricción que la de respetar inviolablemente las garantías individuales" [without other restriction except the inviolable respect for individual rights], but used masculinist tropes in defining national belonging, grounding its claims by "usando de los mismos derechos de que usaron nuestros padres en 1821" [using the same rights that our forefathers used in 1821], the year the Spanish recognized Mexican independence.[49] Where Cortina staunchly defended the "sacred right of self-preservation," he used the word "inviolable" three times in just these two Proclamations: discussing the "inviolable laws"; how "hospitality and other noble sentiments shield them at present from our wrath, and such, as you have seen, are inviolable to us" (notably, the Spanish includes the phrase *"las leyes de humanidad,"* invoking universal humanism over national affiliation, but this line is omitted in the English translation); and "orderly people and honest citizens are inviolable to us in their persons and interests" (in Spanish, "gente de orden y los ciudadanos honrados son para nosotros inviolables"), foregrounding ideological commitment over personal retribution.[50]

At the same time, Cortina's banditry located Mexican American manhood within a tradition of patriotic resistance and national defense reminiscent of the founding fathers and the United States' national origin story. Cortina's proclamations recalls Thomas Paine, who, in *Thoughts on Defensive War*, praises "a point to view this matter in of superior consequence to the defence of property; and that point is *Liberty* in all its meanings."[51] Historians have shown that for Paine, "creating a viable national identity for Americans other than through their customary association with Britain [a competing national presence] was a crucial part of the revolutionary process."[52] Eric Foner states that among Paine's contributions to revolutionary America, "the politicization of the mass of Philadelphians—from the master craftsmen to a significant segment of the laborers and poor—was the most important development in Philadelphia's political life in the decade before independence."[53] Foner holds that this politicization helped mobilize a fledgling nation otherwise culturally indistinct from England, made possible through print culture and the inception of an imagined reading public. However, the bandit narratives go one step further, and the revolutionary process itself becomes a crucial part of the creation of a viable national identity. Cortina's Proclamations make an analogous statement that mobilizes the local populace, composed mostly of Texas Mexicans with a minority Anglo U.S. population, in support of his ideals and in opposition to an absent national government unable to provide for the defense of its borders. In Cortina's narratives, the revolutionary process itself becomes central to Mexican American identity, but elevates democratic ideals above national boundaries.

The Proclamation makes clear that Texas Mexicans are separated by "accident alone, from the other citizens of the city," and that they act explicitly "*not* having renounced our rights as North American citizens."

Cortina and his followers "disapprove, and energetically protest, against the act of having caused a force of the National Guards from Mexico to cross unto this side to ingraft themselves in questions so foreign to their country that there is no excusing such weakness on the part of those who implored their aid" [reprobamos y protestamos enérgicamente contra el acto de haber pasado la fuerza de Guardias Nacionales mejicanas á injerirse en una cuestion tan agena de aquel pais que no hay ni como disculpar de semejante dibilídad á los que la pidieron].[54] Cortina's U.S. citizenship is juxtaposed with Anglo Texans who looked to Mexican enforcement, whose proximity provided a more rapid response to the area disagreements. As Cortina would tell it, his choice for self-defense is a more American action than those who sought the aid of a foreign government, and reframes the threat to U.S. sovereignty not in his assault on Brownsville, but on the Anglo Texans' call to the Mexican National Guard, inviting a foreign army into the country. While Cortina's literary banditry speaks to transnational revolutionary movements, his literary performance of that rebellion reinforces U.S. authority in the region. By reigniting revolutionary discourses, Cortina suggests a U.S. national project still in the making and locates the U.S. within ongoing hemispheric revolutions.

Though Cortina may not have explicitly modeled his proclamations on the founding documents of the United States, the proclamations resound with the rhetoric of republican revolution that situates banditry not apart from but within democratic national projects. Cortina was heavily invested in hemispheric revolutionary movements and was committed to the liberal reforms. Throughout the 1860s, he fought alongside Juarez and against the French intervention, until Porfirio Díaz imprisoned him in 1876. His proclamations need be understood within transnational movements for democracy, both in the U.S. and in Mexico, both against the nation-state but also in cooperation with it. Transforming banditry into an act of citizenship, Cortina's actions resonated with public understandings of national obligation, manhood, and the duties of citizenship. As the Brownsville "committee of safety" put it, many could now "believe him to be the man he represents himself [to be] in his proclamations."[55]

His proclamations transform banditry into claims for citizenship, basing his claims to citizenship on "the sacred right of self-preservation," the natural rights that both precede and derive from national law. Cortina goes to great lengths to downplay the violence in his actions. He is "horrified at the thought of having to shed innocent blood," and reports to be "loth to attack," odd words for a career soldier.[56] He laments the way events were portrayed, stating "it behooves us to maintain that it was unjust to give the affair such a terrible aspect, and to represent it as of a character foreboding evil."[57] Rather than think of the bandit as a figure who operates outside of accepted social order, using violence with disregard for society and its institutions, Cortina emphasizes shared democratic ideals that cross race and nation. As banditry moves from armed resistance to literary representation, it presents the possibility for Mexican American manhood to move from regional conflict to national manhood by imagining Mexican Americans within the American body politic. In his writings, Cortina casts himself as the champion of American democracy and republican virtue rather than a figure of resistance to the nation-state. Elsewhere, Mexican Americans would use banditry in analogous but distinct strategies for national inclusion.

Bandit Societies: Manuel Cabeza de Baca and Vicente Silva

In 1959, José Timoteo López, Edgardo Nuñez, and Roberto Lara Vialapando compiled *Una Breve Reseña de la literatura hispana de Nuevo mexico y Colorado*, what amounts to the first Chicano literary history.[58] This early study calls Manuel Cabeza de Baca's novel *La Historia de Vicente Silva y sus cuarenta bandidos, sus crimines y sus retribuciones* (1896) "el más representativo de los escritores hispanos de Nuevo Mexico, tanto por el estilo como el argumento" [the most representative of the New Mexican Hispanic writers as much for its style as for its argument].[59] Cabeza de Baca's story achieved regional popularity but, unlike the Murieta tale or Cortina's exploits, never garnered a similar degree of national recognition, most likely because the novel is rooted in a specific regional political history not familiar to national audiences and because Silva's factual criminal acts were not easily absorbed into a "social outlaw" model. It was only a half century later that the story was translated into English, but including Cabeza de Baca's *Historia de Vicente Silva* within multilingual American literature highlights how literary banditry presents complex claims to citizenship.[60]

In the 1880s and early 90s, roughly thirty years after the Cortina Wars, Vicente Silva, a saloon owner, embarked on a crime spree involving robbery and murder that terrorized the Anglo and Hispano populations of north-central New Mexico. Like Murieta and Cortina before him, Silva organized the area's residents and outlaws into a criminal network known as the Sociedad de Bandidos, with Silva at its head. But unlike these, Silva's actions were not guided by any clearly articulated moral or ideological agenda; his crimes were committed for personal gain. Valuing self-preservation and aggrandizement, Silva ordered his brother-in-law, whom he suspected of informing the authorities about the gang's activities, killed and the body disappeared. When his wife began inquiring about her brother's death, Silva plotted her death as well, but was betrayed and murdered by his own henchmen. Manuel Cabeza de Baca, the New Mexican Hispano attorney who prosecuted several of Silva's bandits, recorded and novelized many of these actions.

Much of what is known about Manuel Cabeza de Baca comes from critic A. Gabriel Meléndez and from Manuel's niece Fabiola Cabeza de Baca, whose novel *We Fed Them Cactus* has enjoyed some recent critical attention. Born in 1853, Manuel Cabeza de Baca was educated in the Catholic school systems around Las Vegas, New Mexico (the public school system did not exist until 1891). In 1886, he served as a member of the House in the territorial legislature from San Miguel County and was voted Speaker of the House for that term. Manuel held numerous government posts, was a member of the nuevomexicano elite, "quite a humanitarian" who often "cancelled debts of poor people who were unable to pay him for his services as a lawyer," and was a "staunch Republican" who supported New Mexico's admission into the United States.[61]

A descendent of a land grant family in the region, by 1890 Cabeza de Baca worked as an attorney for San Miguel County, prosecuting members of Vicente Silva's crime syndicate shortly after his assumption of the post. As implied by his career choice, Cabeza de Baca was a committed advocate of legal and moral order, highly influenced by Christian values and committed to New Mexican statehood; his politics and sense of communal obligation were driven by a desire to work within the American legal and juridical system.[62] Like much of the U.S. Southwest, New Mexico experienced massive population growth in the last decades of the nineteenth century. Anglo settlers came in droves, and traditional industries like sheepherding collided with the growing cattle, mining, and railroad interests. By the time the railroad reached the town of Las Vegas in 1879, then the largest town in New Mexico, newspapers and political organizations formed to coordinate efforts against social changes. By the 1890s, Spanish print culture was flourishing in New Mexico, and Cabeza de Baca was fully embroiled in its development. As a voice against political corruption by Anglos and nuevomexicanos, Cabeza de Baca founded his own newspaper, *El Sol de Mayo*, which began publication on May 1, 1891, and used the newspaper as a mouthpiece for his political and cultural views.

Specifically, Cabeza de Baca saw *El Sol* as a necessary counterpoint to the ideological dissemination and illicit activities of more radical groups, especially those of Las Gorras Blancas (the White Caps), known for their distinctive white head coverings, which in turn formed as an "activist" counterpart to the Partido del Pueblo Unido (the United People's Party), whose action threatened social disorder similar to what Cabeza de Baca had seen with Silva. According to Gabriel Meléndez, "Las Gorras Blancas were for the most part land grant heirs who were being dispossessed by Anglo-American land companies and speculators who consorted with political rings to wrench control of Mexican and Spanish land grants" and used illegal methods to challenge their disenfranchisement.[63]

But not all residents of northern New Mexico agreed with either the politics or the tactics espoused by these groups, and Cabeza de Baca explicitly viewed his literary endeavors as a moral response. In counterpoint to Felix Martinez's long-running newspaper *La Voz del Pueblo,* which was sympathetic to both the Partido del Pueblo Unido and Las Gorras Blancas (and which, in testament to mutual cooperation despite political disagreement, published *La Historia de Vicente Silva*), *El Sol de Mayo* led each issue with the statement, "La virtud debe amarse, no solo porque es virtud, sino por que como el sol con su ejemplo ilumina las conciencias, con su calor vivifica los corazones, el ser virtuoso consigue elevar a la virtud a los seres que le rodean aunque hayan caido en lo mas profundo del vicio" [Virtue should love itself, not only because it is virtue, but also like the sun with its example illuminates the conscience, with its heat revitalizes hearts, the virtuous elevate those around him to virtue, even though they may have fallen to the depths of vice].[64] Cabeza de Baca openly espoused a moral rectitude that eschewed violence and hoped the newspaper would help sway others to his more pacifist approach. Moreover, Cabeza de Baca billed the newspaper as a "periódico consagrado a los intereses del pueblo de Nuevo Mexico–y organo de la Orden de Caballeros de Proteccion Mutua de Ley y Orden del Territorio" [newspaper devoted to the interests of the New Mexican people— and organ of the Order of Knights for Mutual Aid of Law and Order of the Territory].[65] (La Orden de Caballeros was an organization formed by Cabeza de Baca candidly opposed to the illicit tactics of Las Gorras Blancas and similar groups.)

Despite political and ideological differences, the Spanish language press in New Mexico viewed the press as an essential element in advocating for the rights of the Mexican origin population. In order to reach as wide an audience as possible, a group of journalists formed La Prensa Asociada, a collaborative effort by journalists and publishers to share information. La Prensa Asociada "assumed the role of guarantor of the community it served," functioned as an "antidote to the threat of social and cultural erasure," and "had the immediate effect of enhancing the exchange of information among its membership. A network of *canjes* created by the association improved exchange among member editors and provided nuevomexicano editors with a steady and inexhaustible source of texts from member newspapers in northern Mexico, who in turn reprinted items from other Latin American sources."[66] La Prensa Asociada strengthened the newspapers' reach and scope, and enabled journalists to mediate between the class and social differences by organizing the public in support of shared communal goals.

This unified response was especially important given the hotly contested debate around New Mexican statehood. Though New Mexico became a territory in 1850, it was not granted statehood until 1912. Historically, elite nuevomexicanos had controlled the political sphere, and in the long transition to statehood, they struggled to maintain their power. Many Anglos capitalized on the class discrepancy between elite nueovmexicanos and the working class to argue against statehood on the grounds that New Mexico's working class Mexicans and Native Americans were racially unfit for citizenship.[67] In all facets of his professional and public life, Cabeza de Baca advocated statehood as a means to social equality, but for Cabeza de Baca, violent protest was contrary to that goal. In his history of Vicente Silva, Cabeza de Baca uses an account of extralegal violence to critique illegal behavior within the nuevomexicano community and to challenge the banditry of Las Gorras Blancas and other criminal groups in the area. *La Historia de Vicente Silva* sheds light on the intra-cultural class-based infighting among the nuevomexicanos, but within a transnational tradition of literary banditry, it also communicates a complicated relationship between Mexican Americans and the U.S. nation from a region seeking national recognition.

Much of Cabeza de Baca's narrative of Silva was based on the confession and testimony from the bandit El Mellado that Cabeza de Baca heard as state prosecutor, but the novel is a fictionalized account of Vicente Silva's crime syndicate. It is told achronologically, skipping across a bloody timeline interspersed with accounts of the deaths, deeds, and capture of Silva, his bandits, and their victims. Cabeza de Baca adds descriptive details to enhance readerly interest, inserts dialogue in dramatic moments, and offers authorial commentary on the heinousness of the crimes. In other words, Cabeza de Baca presents the events not as journalistic account, but within a genre of sensational literature and Mexican American banditry.

Yet in Cabeza de Baca's novel, Mexican Americans play all the roles; they are villains, victims, and heroes, bandits and lawmen. Cabeza de Baca shows a broad spectrum of Mexican American society in New Mexico and distances the majority of the Mexican American population from the criminal acts of Silva's syndicate. By distinguishing criminal from lawman, the novel absolves the community of any potential, collective labeling as criminal. Furthermore, Cabeza de Baca's account of Silva seeks to prevent the possibility that other writers may turn Vicente Silva into a Murieta-like popular hero, which as a symbol of anti-national violence might detract from the author's goals of statehood. Silva's violence knows no limits and his self-interest trumps all other social alliances, be it familial or communal. By emphasizing Silva's horrific and bloody crimes, Cabeza de Baca commands a picture of Silva as both abhorrent and an aberration, an outlier to the shared values of most law-abiding nuevomexicanos.

This narrative purpose is made apparent when read within a transnational literary tradition. The bandit is a widely used and well-recognized narrative trope of nation formation in the Mexican and broader Latin

American tradition.[68] During the late nineteenth century, Mexican literature sought to forge a national culture through literary representations of the national landscape, particularly after several failed attempts at national consolidation (such as the U.S.-Mexican War (la guerra de 1847), the Constitution of 1857, and the French Intervention of the 1860s). During the prolonged civil conflict that marked much of the mid-nineteenth century, factionalism was rampant and "endemic banditry disrupted the economy" at large.[69] An industry unto itself, banditry threatened the stability of the central state and signified a failure in the government's contract with its citizens. Attempting to make sense of that rupture, Mexican authors used literary banditry to suture divisions among the citizenry.

In this category famously stands Manuel Payno's *Los Bandidos del Rio Frio*, what Mexican literature scholar Margo Glantz has called no less than "una épica nacional."[70] Published serially in both Spanish and Mexican newspapers between 1889 and 1891, Payno's novel garnered immediate success. It has been continuously in print over the last century and hailed as a prime example of costumbrismo, the novel of everyday life and manners. *Los Bandidos* is a vast, sweeping novel that links together a disparate and wide-ranging cast of characters around the construction of the railroad between Veracruz and Mexico City, the ultimate technological assertion of liberal political ideologies. The sprawling novel centers around three bandits—Juan Robreño, Evaristo Lecuona, and Relumbrón—who turn to banditry for disparate reasons, though each confronts the Mexican nation-state to be absorbed, condemned, or punished.

Cabeza de Baca's novel fits within the tradition of the Mexican literary bandit, a genre widely understood as "a narrative of national redemption [that issued] normative claims about what it meant to be Mexican" and that debated the rights and duties of citizenship.[71] Latin American literature scholar Juan Pablo Dabove argues that a primary function of the Latin American literary bandit was to distinguish between rural spaces and urban centers, where the bandit is "both the product of and the arena for the struggles between the lettered city [*letrado*] and the various social sectors that challenged its dominance [and] in which the opposition between lawful and outlaw violence is the defining feature."[72] Cabeza de Baca's push for statehood sets up a parallel struggle between national center and the margins and, drawing on this genre, his bandit narrative challenges both the intracultural tensions among nuevomexicanos and the national narrativization of Mexican Americans as bandits or outlaws.

Payno's bandits collapse the distinction between state and criminal actors through the legitimization of violence, and *La Historia de Vicente Silva* negotiates a similar tension between state violence and authority while at the same time modeling Silva's absorption into the institutions of government authority. The archive is incomplete and direct influence is difficult to ascertain, yet Cabeza de Baca, a member of La Prensa Asociada, was likely familiar with Mexican literary traditions. Through La Prensa Asociada, Cabeza de Baca had access to the popular serialized novel, as well as other bandit narratives of the Latin American tradition (like *El Periquillo Sarniento*, or *Martín Fierro*), and *La Historia de Vicente Silva* shares a similar nationalizing purpose to the Latin American letrado, demonstrating the nuevomexicano population's position as citizens of the United States and distinct from the outlaws. As a journalist and politician, Cabeza de Baca turned to the bandit narrative because of its history in Latin American nation formation and its uses in narrativizing the relationship between a region's inhabitants and the nation-state.

In Cabeza de Baca's novel of Vicente Silva, there is no conciliatory romance between Anglos and Mexicans, nor any marriage resolution to heal a wounded (national) family structure. Instead, greed and corruption lead Silva to murder his own family members, acts that ultimately cause his bandits to turn against him. Central to Cabeza de Baca's *Historia de Vicente Silva* is the conspiracy and murder of Gabriel Sandoval, brother-in-law to Silva. According to the novel, the philandering Silva, eager to leave his wife Telesfora Sandoval and paranoid about the possibility of her betrayal, plotted to dispose of Gabriel Sandoval and eventually Telesfora in order to clear obstructions between himself and his lover. One of Silva's accomplices sends Silva a letter accusing Telesfora of betraying the group, of having "declarado públicamente todos los secretos que guarda de las picardías que hemos cometido" [publically declared all the secrets she knows about the foul deeds we have committed]. In response, Silva, with characteristic gruesomeness, stabs his wife and "le hundió el puñal en mitad del jadeante pecho, un mar de sangre hirviente brotó de la herida, Doña Telesfora se agitó violentamente y su cuerpo se desplomó sobre el duro pavimento" [he plunged the dagger between her heaving breasts. A sea of boiling blood burst from the wound, she dropped to the ground writhing in the last agonies of death].[73]

Silva also directs familial violence at his brother-in-law, Gabriel Sandoval. Angry with Sandoval, Silva orders his men to lure him to a secluded area and then attack him. The bandits follow his orders, and Cabeza de Baca notes how under Silva's leadership,

> aquellos á quienes se les habia confiado la seguridad de las vidas y propie-
> dades del pueblo del condado de San Miguel; los guardianes de la tranqu-
> ilidad publica; los que habian jurado soportar la ley obligándose á vigilar
> por lós intereses de la comunidad, tratando con el más vil bandido, con
> el mayor enemigo de la sociedad; no para cumplir con sus sagrados de-
> beres, no para enforzar la ley, sino tratando de dar muerte á un jóven que
> ningun daño les habia hecho [. . .] á un jóven incauto que los consid-
> eraba como amigos, que no imaginaba que los protectores asalariados
> del gobierno del condado fueran capaces de dar cabida en su corazon
> á pensamientos malévolos, mucho menos que tratasen de exterminarlo.

> [those to whom the security of the lives and property of the people of
> San Miguel County had been entrusted; the guardians of public tranquil-
> ity; those that had sworn to uphold the law and obligating themselves to
> guard the interests of the community, dealing with the most vile outlaw,
> with the greatest enemy of society; [worked] not to comply with their
> sacred duties, not to enforce the law, but to murder an innocent man,
> [. . .] an unsuspecting man who considered them friends, who could not
> imagine the paid protectors of the county government would be capable
> of evil thoughts, let alone would try to kill him.] (39)

The author juxtaposes Sandoval's truthfulness and honesty with the cor-
ruption and greed of the bandits, made worse by the betrayal of their duties. Cabeza de Baca takes care to distinguish between the character of Silva's bandits and the victims and law-abiding citizens who fought Silva's power. The distinction between these two types sharply divides the characters along a moral binary. For Cabeza de Baca, manhood is a moral obligation and a commitment to justice and community, anathema to

violence. In these scenes, the violence is directed not against an oppressive regime, but turned domestically as an affront to the family. Silva's heinous crime shows his willingness to betray those closest to him and his disregard for any individual or ideal beyond his immediate desire. Here, banditry is self-serving and undermining the stability of the community, and Cabeza de Baca prevents Silva from reinterpretation as a revolutionary figure of communal importance.

Condemning his wife to death, Silva uses as evidence a letter allegedly sent from Telesfora to the state authorities. Facing execution at the hands of her husband, Telesfora pleads with Silva "que crédito merece esta carta" [what credence does this letter merit?], yet the letter seals her fate. Both the written word and the act of reading condemn Telesfora, and Silva orders her to "lee las palabras de esa carta fatal para tí, leelas y averguenzate de ti misma" [read the words of the letter. Read them and be ashamed of yourself] (83–4). Calling attention to the literary reason for her death, the letter falsely justifies the crimes he commits but belies a fear that the written word can be misused, even for immoral purpose. As a prosecutor Cabeza de Baca promoted strict adherence to law, but as editor and newspaperman he cautioned against the power of the written word in shaping public opinion.

Although the characters are motivated by greed, Silva's crime streak ends when Silva's henchman Piernas de Rana (Frog Legs), motivated by a corrupted sense of chivalry, promises, "Si Silva mata á su esposa, por vida del hijo de mi madre que yo le despacho en el momento que él menos lo espere" [If Silva kills his wife, I swear on the life of the son of my mother that I will dispatch him the moment he least expects it] (63). Silva stabs his wife and is immediately repaid with a bullet to the temple. In Cabeza de Baca's telling, a masculine code of honor and obligation to one's community overrides criminal loyalties. Banditry occludes these qualities, but the text opens the possibility for a strong and centralized government to prevent the abuses and corruptions of unethical leadership.

Where in popular genres banditry may exist in opposition or resistance to the nation-state, here Cabeza de Baca implies that it is the absence of the state that allows banditry to emerge, censuring the state for its absence. In the novel, Silva's modus operandi mimics the state's, and "como era el Rey de los malhechores, habia dividido el Territorio en distritos *vandálicos*" [like the King of lawbreakers, had divided the Territory in vandalic districts], and to some "les habian designado los precintos que componen los condados de Mora, Taos y Colfax con permiso especial para traspasar los límites del Estado de Colorado" [he designated a jurisdiction including the counties of Mora, Taos, and Colfax with special permission to cross the border into the neighboring state of Colorado] (93). Silva structures his organization as an administrative hierarchy with groups of bandits given specific geographic areas to pillage, but depicted as a perversion of authority caused by the absence of a strong state power.

To some members of his gang, "el robo era su política, su religion, su creencia, su ambicion" [robbery was their politics, their religion, their belief, their ambition] (93). Cabeza de Baca's narrative cautions against this and urges that a national project can help provide the order and ideology to govern actions. Without such, banditry would continue unhindered. Earlier in the novel, by way of introduction of the titular character, Cabeza de Baca depicts Silva organizing his syndicate of bandits in a tribunal for a member accused of betraying the group. Each member of the group is given a role in the trial, "al *Mellado* [gap-tooth] como presidente, al *Moro* [the Moor], secretario, al *Romo* [the boor] y al *Gavilan*, mariscales [the Hawk, as bailiff], á Silva, fiscal [prosecutor], y á Polanco, defensor [defense attorney]" (16). As prosecutor, Silva accuses gang member Patricio Maes of the crime of treason and produces a note purportedly sent from Maes to the editor of *El Sol de Mayo*, the newspaper Cabeza de Baca began. In the letter, Maes resigns from the United People's Party (the political organization often associated with Las Gorras Blancas) and joins the Order of Knights for Mutual Aid, the counter organization founded again by Cabeza de Baca. Found guilty by a jury of his peers, the gang debated over Maes's punishment. Fearful of his role as a potential informant, the bandits eventually sentence Maes to death by hanging.

While Silva uses the mock trial to justify the use of violence, Cabeza de Baca condemns the actions of the tribunal, using language such as "sed de sangre humana" [bloodthirsty], "despiadado" [merciless], and "bárabaros verdugos" [barbarous executioners] to describe the participants (18). By depicting the bandits as performing the institutional practices of "legal" society (not mocking the judicial system, but representing an analogous version of it, albeit with Silva the criminal as authority figure), Cabeza de Baca's purpose is two-fold. He demonstrates the Mexican American community's ability to participate in the practices of democracy, and concomitantly, their willingness to enter into American civil and political society by showing initiative and developing their own organizations. Additionally, reproducing a tribunal organized by Silva illustrates the risks posed to the U.S. nation by not including Mexican Americans in the national narrative (as a danger both to society and to the legitimacy of existing legal institutions). In the novel, Silva's legal authority is idiosyncratic and justified only by his willingness to use violence for personal gain; when he is ultimately captured, Cabeza de Baca restores authority to nationally sanctioned institutions. The restoration of just society hinges on the bandit figure as the representative of Mexican American manhood.

The second half of the narrative is a case-by-case account of the numerous murders for which Vicente Silva and his bandits were blamed. The events provide the reader with closure, but reinforce the inevitability of the triumph of law and the legal system, through the help of the New Mexican communities, even against the violence perpetrated by Silva and his gang. One bandit, Feliciano Chaves, goes to the gallows described as "habia sido buen ciudadano, buen hijo, buen esposo y buen padre, pero que las malas compañias le habian causado tan temprana muerte. Aconsejó á los padres y madres de familia de apartar á sus hijos de las malas companies" [having been a good citizen, a good son, a good husband and a good father, but that bad company had caused such an early death. He advised the fathers and mothers of families to keep their children from bad company], reiterating the theme of corruption in the absence of the state (113). Chaves, "listo y resignado á morir como un hombre" [ready and resigned to die like a man], states, "May God grant that my blood spilled on this gallows will serve as an example to society, and that with me, the last of the murderers are gone" (114).[74] Following his execution, the narrator interjects, "La ley quedó vindicada" [The law was vindicated] (114).

No crime is more reprehensible to Cabeza de Baca than those that betray those institutions:

Mas se hace el deber de la corte pintar la enormidad de vuestra ofensa para que el pueblo pueda realizarla y ver el peligro que puede amenazarle de aquellos que debieran ser sus protectores. Vos y algunos de vuestros complices érais los escogidos guardianes de vuestra comunidad, encargados de protejerla encontra del peligro; los representantes de la ley y del órden, encargados de enforzar la una y preservar el otro, para la seguridad y bienestar de vuestros constituyentes; portabais la insignia del cargo oficial, la cual constituia vuestra autoridad para restringuir las violencias é impedir el crímen; vuestro era el deber de velar al pueblo mientras dormia, protejerlo contra los malhechores y preservar sus hogares. Pero descuidando esta sagrada obligacion, os tornasteis en sus enemigos, malhechores contra ellos, conspiradores contra la vida de uno que jamas os hizo daño, y á quien debierais haber salvado.

[Moreover it is the duty of the court to illustrate the enormity of your crimes so that the people may realize and see the danger that may arise from those that should be their protectors. You and your accomplices were the chosen guardians of your community, charged to protect it against danger; the representatives of law and order, charged to enforce the one and preserve the other; for the safety and security of your constituents; bearing the official seal that vested authority to restrict violence and prevent crime; yours was the responsibility to watch over the people as they slept, protect them against evildoers and preserve their homes. But disregarding this sacred obligation, you became their enemy, criminal against them, conspirator against the life of one who never did you harm, and to whom you should have saved.] (78–9)

In the portrayal of Alarid, a member of both Silva's gang and a police officer, Cabeza de Baca offers a bitter indictment of Alarid's perversion of duty. Cabeza de Baca criticizes the failure of those who were "the chosen guardians of your community," the "representatives of law and order" who fail to uphold it. Cabeza de Baca chronicles the attempt to root out corruption while at the same time critiquing both the crime syndicate and the U.S. nation's failure to include New Mexico into the national body. Still, his critique of the government and the relative strength of its governing agencies is tempered by a deep faith in its institutions.

In writing the novel, Cabeza de Baca is most concerned with how Silva is remembered, how his narrative gets told, and the communal purpose to which his memory is put. By writing a semi-fictionalized history of Silva, Cabeza de Baca precludes the chance for the bandit to be commemorated as either social outlaw or archetype of Mexican American manhood. Rather, by critiquing the violent tactics of some regional actors in the absence of state authority, Cabeza de Baca uses Silva to galvanize the support of his Spanish readership for statehood and to advocate for the place of New Mexico in the U.S. nation.

"La Batalla Intelectual": Catarino Garza and the Logic of Banditry

Both Cortina and Cabeza de Baca were interested in the bandit as a model for manhood and an entrance into the U.S. state and the benefits of citizenship, but there were others who sought to improve the social conditions of Mexican Americans without rendering literary banditry as a condition of U.S. citizenship. Born in Matamoros, Tamulipas, Mexico, in 1859, the year of Cortina's uprising, the Mexican expatriot and future revolutionary Catarino Garza moved to Brownsville, Texas, when he was offered a position in the commercial import/export house Blowberg & Raphael, in 1877.[75] Like Cortina, Garza came of age in the racially and nationally stratified environment of South Texas and northern Mexico.[76] After several years witnessing social injustice and disparity between the Anglo and Mexican American populations, Garza was propelled to speak up against what he deemed injustice. Garza began working in journalism, first as an op-ed columnist and later launching his own newspapers. He too believed in the power of the press as a vehicle against state oppression, and established several newspapers in the region, including Brownsville's *El Bien Público*, Eagle Pass's *El Comercio Mexicano*, and Laredo's *El Libre Pensador*. Garza's print campaigns often led to civil unrest by exposing racial inequality, but he would become frustrated by the lack of change resulting from his work as a newspaperman.[77] Garza turned to military action, and in 1891, he led an attack from Texas into Mexico against Díaz and members of his regional government, pitting Garza against local and national forces on both sides of the border, creating a familiar scenario. Garza and his group of revolutionaries marched across the Texas border into Mexico, declaring a "Plan Revolucionario" against the Mexican government. For nearly two years, Garza and his followers, stationed primarily in Texas, were involved in skirmishes against the Mexican government. Eventually, Garza was defeated, though he escaped the region, continuing his revolutionary activities and fighting for equality in the Caribbean and Central America, and reportedly dying while staging a jail break in Colombia (now Panama) in March of 1895.

Whereas the other bandit figures discussed earlier turned to print in order to explain the actions of themselves or others, Garza's path was the inverse; his print activities as a journalist eventually led him to become a revolutionary/bandit. This reverse path coincides with his refusal of U.S. citizenship and is evident in the print record he left behind. Garza began but never completed nor published a memoir, written between late 1889 and early 1891, where he eschews the romanticism popular in literature of his day and instead favors a more realist account of his life and activities, claiming "mi pluma no sabe pintar, pero si reproducir . . ." [my pen does not know how to paint, only how to reproduce]. This realist impulse is perhaps a sign of the manuscript's explicit political purpose, yet despite his claims to the contrary, Garza's work is elegantly written, highly descriptive, and playful with language. Like Cortina and Cabeza de Baca, Garza couches his activities in the interests of his countrymen: "Desde que pisé el extranjero suelo en que me encuentro, he consagrado mis trabajos por la felicidad, bienestar, y decoro de mis hermanos exptariados" [Since stepping foot on the foreign soil in which I find myself, I have dedicated my work to the happiness, well being, and dignity of my fellow expatriates]. He, like the others discussed above, invokes republican idealism and describes his newspaper and its actions as "cuyos santos principios eran pregonar la union y la perservación de los derechos de la ciudadanía" [whose holy purpose was to preach the union and the preservation of the rights of citizenship]. In his memoir, Garza moves quickly past the initial events that brought him to the United States and instead focuses on the political machine that dominated South Texas in the late nineteenth century. In doing so, Garza understands himself and the idea of countrymen quite differently, continuing to view himself as displaced and as Mexican.[78]

Garza depicts how citizenship in South Texas was readily handed out to the Mexican immigrants and residents of the region, neither as a benefit of residence, through nationalistic impulse, nor for the privileges it provided, but rather through the machinations and manipulations of the Texan political bosses. Garza describes how Anglo politicians typically ignored the Mexican residents except during election cycles, when politicians would throw a series of parties and recruitment events, speed people through the naturalization procedure, and then direct the new citizens to the polling booth. Once voting ceased, Mexican Americans saw little benefit from or the protections of their newly acquired legal status.[79] Unlike the potential invested in citizenship by Cortina and Cabeza de Baca, Garza considered Mexican American citizenship a means of furthering the Anglo power structure and as a perversion of the promise of democratic ideals. For Garza, U.S. citizenship was an "instrument a sus propios verdugos" [an instrument of their own execution], as it provided a legal structure to limit equality rather than a means to communal improvement.[80]

Consequently, Garza occupies a strange place in understanding banditry and national identity. Although he did not identify as American, he demonstrates the uses to which literary banditry could function in cleaving citizenship. Garza's forces were stationed in Texas, a move that recalls the filibustering expeditions of the nineteenth century, but he also found himself in conflict with U.S. authorities. He directed his military action against the Mexican state, yet in his memoir, Garza details his desire to "elevar en mejor escala social a la raza Mexicana en la primera población de Texas" [to elevate the social standing of the Mexican people in Texas]. For Garza, the best solution for the defense of Mexican Americans lay not with a reformed U.S. state, but with solidarity arising from cultural unity, across national lines. Still, Garza's actions further demonstrate the complicated ways Mexican Americans formulated a sense of U.S. national belonging.

Bandit Legacies

Since the mid-nineteenth century to the present, the bandit has persisted as a recurring trope of Mexican American manhood in countless stories, films, music, advertisements, and other forms of popular culture. At the height of the Chicano civil rights movement, historians Pedro Castillo and Albert Camarillo published *Furia y Muerte: Los Bandidos Chicanos* (1973). Employing Eric J. Hobsbawm's definition of "social banditry" as a global phenomenon of peasant movements, Castillo and Camarillo provide historical accounts for several Chicano bandits that attempt to wrest banditry's critical reception from that of "folk-myth personalities" or "murderous, blood thirsty, thieving outlaws"; instead, they seek to challenge the "limited viewpoints [that] perpetuate prevailing myths and stereotypes, and [threaten] to falsify Chicano history" and insist upon the Chicano bandit as a figure of resistance to the oppressive and racist social conditions that confronted Mexican Americans.[81]

In part, *Furia y Muerte* is a compelling reappraisal of the limited, racializing discourse that framed Mexican Americans as a threat to national stability, and the text helped initiate a surge of Chicana/o activist scholarship. Castillo and Camarillo insist that the Chicano bandit was not an "outlaw, fugitive, and criminal," "were not lawbreakers," but rather "victims of injustice" who refused to submit to the Anglo-American invasion.[82] Their reinterpretation explains the "dichotomous attitude" between Anglo and Chicano communities that characterizes the bandits' reception.[83] Significantly, the text is one of the first revisionist historical accounts by a Chicana/o and provides an important critique of the historiography that regularly criminalized the Mexican American. However, explaining social banditry exclusively in terms of the colonial conditions of the Mexican American inhabitants of Texas, New Mexico, and California, the authors' own historical positions and investments in the Chicano movement limit the interpretive frameworks that prompted the critique of existing historiographical method. Despite, or because of, a desire to revise exclusionary historical narratives, they insist that "the social bandit belongs to the Chicano, not so much as an historical record of events, but as a symbol of protest and rebellion," thereby unwittingly reifying a notion of Mexican Americans as anti-national, against or separate from the national structures they seek to access.[84] Both their reading of the bandit and the ideological apparatus that drove it replicates the very exclusionary structures they sought to remedy. Castillo and Camarillo provide a telling example of the pervasive and persistent rubric under which Chicana/o intellectual history has operated since the late 1960s. From a position some forty years later, what does twenty-first-century Latina/o Studies do with the intellectual history it inherits?

Although literary banditry has historically been regarded as an exclusion to national unity or a deficiency in the normalization enacted by national narratives, it serves a contrary if counterintuitive purpose, providing what elsewhere David Kazanjian calls a "flashpoint" in U.S. history.[85] Through literary banditry, Mexican Americans expanded the meaning of citizenship beyond the categories of legal status, conceptualizing it as processual, an ongoing cultural and political project. When placed within transnational literary and national projects, literary banditry demonstrates how citizenship operated as a discursive practice rather than as statutory right, as a form of manhood that cleaves Mexican Americans into and out of citizenship. Outlaw citizenship began a strategy through which Mexican Americans communicated with a larger national public, but the complexity of literary banditry seen in these accounts gave way to more one-dimensional representations of Mexican Americans as bandits and outlaws so pervasive in the U.S. cultural and popular imaginary.

2

Fantasy Citizenship

Mexican American Manhood and the Shifting Structures of Legal Belonging

What refuge did you find here,
ancient Californios?
Now at this restaurant nothing remains
But this old oak and an ill-placed plaque.
Is it true that you still live here
In the shadows of these white, high-class houses?
Soy la hija pobrecita
Pero puedo maldecir estas fantasmas blancas.
Las fantasmas tuyas deben aqui quedarse,
Solas las tuyas.
—Lorna Dee Cervantes, "Poema para los Californios Muertos"[1]

In one iteration of the popular Joaquin Murieta legend, Murieta and his band of brigands avenge his sister's rape and murder by marauding the California country, showing the gringos no mercy, but sparing the women and children. Murieta hunts down the villain who violated his sister, eventually capturing him and "cortándole por donde más había pecado" [lopping off the place where the villain most had sinned].[2] In this particular version, however, Joaquin is not captured by Captain Love, nor is he wounded by the lawmen. In this version, Joaquin and his loyal sidekick Three Fingers Jack choose death over capitulation and, arm in arm, shoot the other in the head with the cry, "Los mexicanos no se rinden: mueren!" [Mexicans don't surrender: they die!].[3]

This version of the Murieta story was written nearly seventy years after John Rollin Ridge's original tale *The Life and Adventures of Joaquin Murieta* (1854) and nearly as long before Corky Gonzales famously re-envisioned the legend in the Chicano poem "I Am Joaquin" (1967).

Although the tale has been revised countless times in the one hundred and fifty years since the publication of Ridge's novel, the particular version summarized above is part of the collection of short stories *Cuentos Californianos* (~1922), written by expatriate Mexican and California immigrant Adolfo Carrillo (1855–1924). Throughout his lifetime, Carrillo was variously a politically active author, journalist, translator, editor, law student, and government consul. Exiled from Mexico for his opposition of *el porfiriato*, the dictatorial regime of Mexican president Porfirio Díaz, Carrillo would eventually take up permanent residence in California. Carrillo's fiction, although written in Spanish, is part of a broader cultural movement that capitalized on California's Spanish colonial past and the national interest in regional fiction.

This chapter connects the multilingual print culture of the period with state, regional, and national shifts in the legal and racialized definitions of citizenship. In particular, I examine how an exclusionary past of imagined Spanish heritage developed as both an English- and Spanish-language cultural phenomenon and how Mexican Americans engaged with this fantasy heritage.[4] As I use the term here, Spanish fantasy heritage refers to the narratives and cultural practices that emerged in the latter half of the nineteenth century surrounding the Spanish conquest of the current U.S. Southwest, especially in California, that had wide-ranging implications. As a familiar trope of racial and national difference, its popularity would shape how Mexican Americans could publicly conduct and portray manhood. Carrillo was well aware of the fantasy heritage's reach and power, and turned it to his advantage for a Spanish reading public and as a form of Mexican American manhood.

Spanish fantasy heritage constructed a now familiar story of Old Spanish Californios and the Catholic mission past that celebrated the diverse cultural mixing that shaped California and the Southwest. However, the movement also operated as a mechanism of social control that excluded Mexican Americans from social participation by linking Mexican Americans to the fantasy past.[5] This chapter critiques the assimilationist view of Spanish fantasy heritage (typically seen as a white-washing or Europeanizing take on Mexican heritage) and instead identifies ways that Mexican Americans utilized the cultural phenomenon to assert themselves as agents of political change and as part of the social landscape.

Spanish fantasy heritage isolated, alienated, and disempowered Mexican Americans by separating living Mexican immigrants and residents from a Europeanized, imagined past. This cultural movement was not historical coincidence but rather the result of a changing legal and political climate, which collectively enabled Jim Crow-style restrictions on Mexican Americans' political participation. Yet these processes did not flow in one direction, and the multilingual print culture of the period reveals how Mexican Americans responded to the racialization process within the very phenomenon working against them. Mexican Americans capitalized on the familiar cultural landscape to claim a place within and as American citizens, yet such engagement is only visible when American culture is understood as multilingual.[6] While Spanish fantasy heritage took myriad forms, the case of California is particularly instructive in unpacking the relationship of citizenship, manhood, and culture, producing a form of gendered political participation that was simultaneously historical and immediately presentist.

Making a Fantasy Heritage

Beginning in the 1840s, increasing numbers of Anglo or European Americans immigrated from the eastern and southern U.S. to California, shifting the demographic makeup of the state. In the 1880s, following the collapse of the gold rush, the Panic of 1873, the stagnation of railroad speculation, and a post–Civil War economic decline, westward migrants displaced the Mexican origin population that resided there. On the heels of the gold rush, the expansion of the railroad, and the rush to complete transcontinental routes came a demographic and real estate boom, with huge numbers of Anglo Americans moving and visiting from the East Coast and the Midwest.[7] Hubert Bancroft's massive history project institutionalized the Spanish origins of California, romanticizing the role of the Spanish or Californio ranchero within American culture, and statewide, California residents turned to the Spanish mission and hacienda past as both tourist attraction and a recruitment tool for Anglo immigration.[8]

This renewed interest in California's past developed from widespread and wide-ranging efforts to imaginatively reconstruct the history of the American Southwest and proved a pervasive mythos in the American public imaginary, one with material consequences in the lives of Mexican Americans. While Spanish fantasy heritage had numerous regional incarnations, its Anglo California variant can largely be traced through a constellation of three figures crucial to its invention and dissemination: Helen Hunt Jackson, Charles Fletcher Lummis, and Gertrude Franklin Horn Atherton. Many historians, notably Cary McWilliams, attribute the inception of the Spanish past to the success of Helen Hunt Jackson's Native American reform novel *Ramona* (1884). In the novel, the titular character of mixed Anglo and Native heritage falls in love with a Native American shepherd, Alessandro, and flees from the hacienda where she was raised by her adopted aunt. Together, Alessandro and Ramona begin a life together among the Native Californio tribes, but eventually Anglo settlers force the couple and the tribe from their lands, leading to Alessandro's death at the hands of a white settler. Ramona reunites with her adopted brother Felipe, who confesses his love for her, and Felipe and Ramona marry and move to Mexico to begin life anew.

The novel spurred interest in both the Spanish missions and in the pastoral California society that inhabited the region from Spanish colonization through Mexican rule until the U.S.-Mexican War. Using the mission past to disguise a sentimental appeal for better treatment of Native Americans—along the lines of Harriet Beecher Stowe's *Uncle Tom's Cabin* (1852)—*Ramona*'s ultimate success lay more in the reclamation of an imagined past than in evoking real change for the Native and mestizo population of California.[9] Jackson's "tremendously popular novel became for many a boosterist device, rather than a battle cry," and wily entrepreneurs quickly created products and attractions to capitalize on the novel's popularity.[10] For example, in May 1886, less than two years after the novel's publication and one year after Jackson's death, the Rancho Comulos was positively "identified" as Ramona's birthplace.[11] Stimulating both tourism and real estate speculation on a massive scale, the narrative events would be mapped onto the actual landscape; several geographic locales "became the premier sites identified with the novel, places fictional associations where [what] would become for most, more important than factual ones."[12] The romantic invention of California's physical and imaginative landscape as a result of the *Ramona* boom extended far beyond the novel's immediate fame, lasting decades and generations. Inspired by the newly created public memory, Spanish fantasy

heritage manifested across the social and cultural landscape in demon-
strations of public holidays ("Spanish Days"), in the education system
(curricular changes to include the Spanish pioneers), and on the physical topography (in a "mission revival" architecture style), what Phoebe
S. Kropp calls "venues": "physical spaces and building that, if not permanent, persist even while accommodating change, often beyond personal
memory."[13] The success of *Ramona* in California and across the United
States also led to its translation into Spanish and publication in Mexico
in 1888.[14]

This imaginative recreation reaches its full cultural realization
through the statewide celebrations established by Charles Lummis
(1859–1928), founding member of the Association for the Preservation
of the Missions (later the Landmarks Club).[15] One of the chief proponents of Spanish fantasy heritage, Lummis worked as a writer and editor
for the *Los Angeles Times*, famously beginning his tenure there in 1884
(coincidentally, but opportunely, the year *Ramona* was published) by
walking from Ohio to his new position 3,500 miles away. Lummis published prolifically, moving between adventure stories and histories of the
American Southwest, such as *The Land of Poco Tiempo* (1893), *The Man
Who Married the Moon* (1892), and *Some Strange Corners of Our Country* (1892). As the titles suggest, Lummis sought to introduce national
readers to the cultures and geographies of the Southwest, though often
through an exoticizing lens. Lummis capitalized on the growing national
desire for regional fiction and provided his readers with stories about a
romanticized, indigenous, and pre-conquest past, a world that existed
before the arrival of the U.S. as a "civilizing" force. In California, Lummis
found in Spanish fantasy heritage a means to conjoin two distinct social
needs—how to address the continuing "Mexican Question" and the need
to refashion American manhood following, as Frederick Jackson Turner
put it, "the closing of the American frontier."[16] As a young man, Lummis suffered from neurasthenia, that ill-defined ailment connected to
emotional or psychological unrest that troubled many privileged young
white men in the later nineteenth and early twentieth centuries.[17] Like
his childhood friend Teddy Roosevelt, Lummis turned to the outdoors,
the so-called "strenuous life," to remedy the physical manifestations of
the "neurasthenic paradox" and actively styled his professional and personal life accordingly.[18]

Figure 2.1. Portrait of Charles Lummis, "Lummis in 'Wild West' Dress," undated, Security Pacific National Bank Collection/Los Angeles Public Library.

In the preface to his book *The Spanish Pioneers* (1893), Charles Lummis confesses, "It is because I believe every other young Saxon-American loves fair-play and admires heroism as much as I do, that this book has been written."[19] He suggests that "race-prejudice, the most ignorant of all human ignorances, must die out," but more tellingly, "we must respect manhood more than nationality, and admire it for its own sake wherever found—and it is found everywhere." Lummis continues, "We love manhood; and the Spanish pioneering of the Americas was the largest and longest and most marvelous feat of manhood in all history."[20] In the hierarchy of ideology that Lummis outlines, racial identity dissolves before other categories, where even national allegiance gives way to desired gendered attributes. In creating a heroic fantasy past, Lummis minimizes the importance of nationality in favor of more generalizable and what he imagines as more universal qualities of manhood. Recasting conquest as an achievement of universalized manhood accomplishes several goals. First, it divests from colonialism the violence and injustice necessary for subjugating populations; second, it allows an adoption of the Spanish past into a triumphalist U.S. national narrative that often privileged northern European conquest above Spanish colonialism; third, it dispels Lummis's anxieties by claiming his own role in the narrativization of the past as part of an ongoing "pioneering" enterprise.[21]

And while his display of male homosocial equality purports to supersede national designation, in reality the fantasy heritage facilitated the racialization of Mexicans by using "Spanish" to designate certain classes as distinct from a racialized or indigenous Mexican identity. Aligning Spanish fantasy heritage with national manhood becomes a way of simultaneously obfuscating the racial character of California's Mexican origin population and of adopting a triumphant history of conquest in the service of national identity. For Lummis, manhood supplants race and nationality as the ultimate determining attribute of character. In Lummis's account, manhood's prowess is not energized by racial superiority but by acts of conquest. "Admir[ing] it for its own sake," he invests in the Spanish colonial past a historical importance attributable to a triumph of gender that does not divide Anglo California from the region's past, but uses manhood as a way to absorb the Spanish heritage into American Californian history. Such a move emphasizes shared manhood, which allows Anglo Americans to claim the Spanish conquest of California as part of a national history.

Lummis decouples nation and race in favor of an outwardly more inclusive notion of gender, but effectively separates the fantasy past from the living descendants of the original settlers, resulting in what Leonard Pitt has described as the "cult" of Spanish California that produced a "patina of romantic mis-information" and "Schizoid Heritage."[22] The alteration of public memory effectively replaced complex Mexican American racial history with a fictional, idealized Spanish pastoralism. Spanish fantasy heritage further aimed to "drive a wedge between the native-born and the foreign born," creating a schism between established residents and newly arrived Mexican immigrants.[23] Of its many cultural uses, fantasy heritage's distinction between historical Californians and contemporary Mexicans hastened the implementation of racist ideologies into California society, of which, in as early as 1946, historian Ruth Tuck noted, "The *ranchero* period was to spawn a romantic tradition of considerable vitality" that, as "a dressed up version of the Spanish and Mexican occupation," perpetuated a fiction useful in maintaining segregationist policies in California.[24]

The convergence of economic and demographic factors enabled the fantasy heritage; however, the fantasy heritage emerged in response to developments in national citizenship. It is an oft-cited truism that the Treaty of Guadalupe Hidalgo officially transformed the previously Mexican population into Mexican Americans. The 1848 signing of the treaty granted Mexican Americans federal citizenship and the "enjoyment of all the rights of citizens of the United States, according to the principles of the Constitution."[25] The protection under the treaty ostensibly assured the freedoms of the Mexican origin population that the territorial cession following the U.S.-Mexican War re-nationalized in the U.S. Their status "according to the principles of the Constitution" only guaranteed protection under the Constitution, and thus, as national citizens. However, the treaty ignored the question of state citizenship. According to the dualistic character of American citizenship in the latter half of the nineteenth century, only the states had the authority to bestow political rights. With the omission of Article IX of the treaty, it remained to the individual states to designate state citizenship.

One of the crucial consequences in the Treaty of Guadalupe Hidalgo's vesting of citizenship was the intermediary status of Mexican Americans. Laura Gómez points out how *"federal* citizenship was inferior to *state* citizenship [. . .] Federal citizenship extended the protections of the Constitution and provided 'a shield of nationality' abroad, but it did not convey political rights. Instead, political rights stemmed only from being a citizen of a *state.*"[26] Legal scholar James H. Kettner anticipates and elaborates on Gómez's point, stating how the courts defined citizenship according to "the relevance of intent, residence, and so forth aimed at providing a working definition of state citizenship for the purpose of establishing diversity jurisdiction; they did not purport to create general criteria that states were obliged to use in identifying their own members," and "considerable ambiguity thus remained at the heart of this notion of dual citizenship."[27] Consequently, the division between federal and state citizenship enabled the states to bestow and withdraw political rights according to the political exigencies of respective regions. Irrespective of guarantees made by the Civil Rights Acts of 1866, 1870 (Enforcement Act), and 1875, the division between state and federal rights was affirmed in an 1873 Supreme Court ruling known as the Slaughter-House Cases.[28] As a result of the ruling, "while the federal government could and did protect a more narrow list of rights—those traditionally associated with national citizenship, such as habeas corpus or the right to assemble peaceably to petition for redress of grievances—citizens still had to seek protection for most of their civil rights from state government and state courts."[29] It was only after the 1920s that the courts began to incorporate the protections of the Bill of Rights and enforce them at the state level. Thus, state recognition of citizenship was the cornerstone of social inclusion.

Just five years before the publication of *Ramona*, on May 7, 1879, California revised the state constitution that had been in effect since October 13, 1849. Both the 1849 and 1879 Constitutions were published simultaneously in English and in Spanish, and of the numerous changes, Section One, Article II, defining the rights of suffrage (i.e. the recognition of state citizenship), was revised in revealing ways. The original Constitution of 1849 defined the rights of suffrage with the following statement:

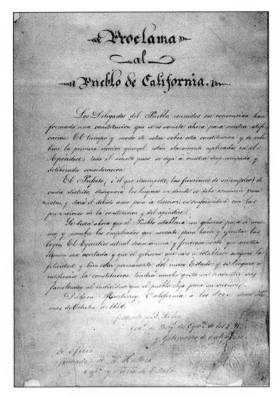

Figure 2.2. "Proclama," Preamble to the Spanish translation of the California Constitution, 1849, California State Archives.

Every white male citizen of the United States, and every white male citizen of Mexico, who shall have elected to become a citizen of the United States, under the treaty of peace exchanged and ratified at Queretaro, on the 30th day of May, 1848 of the age of twenty-one years, who shall have been a resident of the State six months next preceding the election, and the county or district in which he claims his vote thirty days, shall be entitled to vote at all elections which are now or hereafter may authorized by law: Provided, nothing herein contained, shall be construed to prevent the Legislature, by a two-thirds concurrent vote, from admitting to the right of suffrage, Indians or the descendants of Indians, in such special cases as such proportion of the legislative body may deem just and proper.[30]

Adopted shortly after the conquest of California by the United States in the U.S.-Mexican War, the original Constitution provided access for its Mexican citizenry to the privileges of local and state government, or at least allowed former Mexican nationals to assume state citizenship by deferring eligibility to national law. However, the Constitution references not the Treaty of Guadalupe Hidalgo, which ended the war, but curiously rather the Protocol of Querétaro, the exchange of ratifications describing the changes made to the treaty subsequent to its signing. The Protocol of Querétaro (May 26, 1848) intended to assure Mexican representatives that changes to Articles IX, X, and XII of the treaty did not diminish the protections to civil rights and land ownership that the treaty guaranteed. Despite this obtuse definition of citizenship, the California Constitution of 1849 still affirmed the privileges and rights of citizenship for Mexican Californios. The California Constitution of 1849 defined suffrage specifically with respect to "every white male citizen" of both the United States and Mexico, assuming the latter would soon become full-fledged U.S. citizens. This definition complied with existing federal law, and the Constitution even provided a vehicle for the eventual inclusion of California's indigenous population. The right to vote was considered an "entitlement," a privilege of residency that went into effect automatically, and whiteness a legal category necessary for citizenship.

By 1879, the California state legal system had become sufficiently complex so as to require revision to the original Constitution to allow, among other things, more flexibility for the legislative branch to enact change and to regulate taxation. The general population was largely split on whether a constitutional revision was necessary, but eventually the reformers prevailed and enacted changes that further allowed for the state Constitution to be reconciled with federal legal changes following the Thirteenth, Fourteenth, and Fifteenth Amendments. Whereas the Fourteenth Amendment defined citizenship and equal protection under law, the Fifteenth guaranteed the right to vote regardless of race or color. These remain among the most significant constitutional changes and the most important pieces of civil rights legislation until the mid-twentieth century. Since the California Constitution of 1849 explicitly relied upon race as a prerequisite for suffrage, in conflict with national law, members of the 1879 Constitutional Convention sought to redress these issues.

Because of its political importance, the verbatim proceedings of the floor debate over changes to the Constitution were published in *Debates and Proceedings of the Constitutional Convention*. One of the more hotly debated issues at the convention was women's suffrage; the delegates debated for days whether to include in the Constitution the possibility of such, and delegates voiced numerous impassioned appeals on both sides of the issue. Mr. Caples of Sacramento presented arguments against enfranchising women. Caples claimed he was there to "perform a solemn duty, to speak the truth [. . .] to defend the virtue of woman, the honor of man, the experience of mankind, and the eternal decrees of God of the universe." Calling on male chivalry as demonstrable evidence that women are not oppressed, Caples relied on a familiar call for separate spheres for men and women, supporting the idea that female virtue justified the denial of women's suffrage.[31] He even quoted from the *Quarterly Journal of Science* to provide scientific reasoning for a historical tradition of social difference, concerned that voting would be the first step leading to full enfranchisement and, later, the "dirty vile trickeries of primary politics" which would corrupt women.

The debate over female suffrage is particularly revealing because it describes how men understood themselves as men and provides their views on who was qualified and eligible to vote. The debates ultimately had to define what it means to vote, and who was eligible for that privilege. To that end, Mr. Caples, as voice to the anti–women's suffrage faction, defines the rights of citizenship through a syllogistic notion of martial manhood, where "the right to vote, the power of sovereignty, does rest squarely upon the basis of the ability of men to wield the sword."[32] According to this point of view, it is the universal and supposedly exclusive masculine ability to bear arms that justifies limiting suffrage to men. Moreover, the matter takes on signification beyond the ballot; it is a matter of "equality. Not merely the right to vote, because the right to vote carries with it all the co-relative obligations of citizenship."[33] Numerous delegates rebutted Mr. Caples's argument, in both serious and humorous ways, but the reference to the ballot as metonym for citizenship is repeated later on and the point is reiterated when the conversation shifts to racial qualifications for citizenship. Offering the opposite position and basing his argument on the Fifteenth Amendment, Mr. Vacquerel of San Francisco rebuts Mr. Caples's claims that the rights of citizenship "applies to white and black; but sir, I have learned in my youth that there were other colors, and I ask you, gentlemen, where is the word or the law that prevents another color from voting when the people of that color shall have been admitted to citizenship."[34] On the one hand, Mr. Vacquerel defends women's right to vote, but on the other does so to secure white political power and challenge the demographic rise of Chinese immigrants, as evidenced elsewhere throughout his speech. (In fact, Chinese immigration was among the most contested points of debate regarding suffrage, and resulted in exclusionary and racist definitions of eligibility.) Nonetheless, Mr. Vacquerel's remarks reveal that the admission or denial of women's suffrage had implications for other ethnic and racial groups.

When debate shifted to which men should have the right to vote, the Convention ultimately agreed upon the following changes. Article II was amended and the right of suffrage now belonged to "every native male citizen of the United States, every male person who shall have acquired the rights of citizenship under or by virtue of the Treaty of Querétaro, and every male naturalized citizen thereof," and who met certain restrictive residency requirements.[35] In the amended text, the language of "white male citizen" was removed and replaced with "every native male citizen," complying with federal regulations set forth in the Fourteenth and Fifteenth Amendments. Furthermore, for the Mexican Californian, the burden of citizenship is moved from "election" to "acquisition," from choosing to exercise one's rights to previous recognition of those rights. Three decades after statehood, when California's population was increasingly of European American ancestry and included a significant population of U.S. immigrants, the right to vote now carried the burden of proof of citizenship, the rights and documentation of acquired citizenship.

At one point during the Convention, Mr. Beerstecher invokes the distinction between federal and state rights, and reminds the Convention that "the Supreme Court of the United States [holds] that the matter of exercising the right of suffrage was a matter absolutely and exclusively within the supervision of the State, and that the State had a right to decide, had the right to say who should vote at its elections."[36] The strict legal distinction between state and federal rights gave heightened significance to extralegal forms of social control, shifting the ground of social inclusion from institutional mandate to civil society. While the federal Constitution no longer allowed for de jure political exclusion on the basis of race, the demographic shift due to immigration exacerbated existing racial tensions. Spanish fantasy heritage emerged precisely in the moment when these legal developments attempted to manage incompatibilities between racial ideologies and legal status, a concurrence that seems more than coincidental. Recognition at the state level was crucial for the attainment of civil, political, and social rights and as a result, California cultural history became a prime, extralegal site for the racialization of Mexican Americans that circumvented legal frameworks for citizenship. Cultural history, like that created by Gertrude Atherton, could restrict or provide an avenue toward social and political recognition.

Gertrude Atherton's California

One of the central figures in this imaginative reconstruction of history and successor to Helen Hunt Jackson was the author Gertrude Atherton. Atherton was perhaps the best-known fiction writer on California's mission past, at least during her lifetime. Her biographer Emily Leider asserts that by the turn of the century her career was established "on both sides of the Atlantic, and in Europe in the 1920s Atherton's books [. . .] were the most popular of all American novels," while "to many, she seemed the embodiment of California."[37] Much of Atherton's fiction draws upon California history for its source material, and according to California historian Kevin Starr, her fiction was "concerned with the coming of the Americans and their assumption of power after conquest. By the late 1890s Atherton's sympathies lay with the Old Californians, tragically doomed aristocrats who represented the poetry and romance of California giving way to gringo efficiency."[38]

Atherton and her stories achieved national recognition as examples of "local color," what one editor of Philadelphia-based *Lippincott's* magazine praised as the "actual vivid reality" of her California romances and the *North American Review* applauded as the "paradoxical union of romance with realism."[39] Atherton, with entrepreneurial acumen, seized upon the national appetite for regional fiction that had dominated the literary marketplace since Reconstruction. Leider suggests Atherton's turn to California local color emerged out of "a new perspective on the way the rest of the world viewed California and a new respect for the commercial potential of regional fiction," hoping "to turn her study of pre-American California to profit."[40] Atherton self-consciously imagined herself a purveyor of the state's past. Beginning with *Los Cerritos* (1890), developing in the short story collection *Before the Gringo Came* (1894), expanded and republished as *Splendid Idle Forties* (1902), and most fully in *The Californians* (1898), Atherton created an interconnected, imaginative narrative community, what Starr calls "one ongoing saga." Characters appear in multiple texts, as the central focus in one and reappearing elsewhere in brief postscripts to the characters' stories, producing a triumphalist state history that diffuses the violence of imperial conquest and simultaneously rewrites regional history with an eye to national appeal. While Atherton popularized a version of California for the nation in her novels and short fiction, she erases Mexican American males from the California landscape through a nostalgic appeal to a largely fabricated history.

Atherton's short fiction effaces Mexican American manhood either by substituting "Spanish" racial-national characteristics or by killing off Mexican men.[41] In the short story "La Perdida," the old Californio society marry a young girl to an old man, preventing the attainment of her true love, but "such were the law and justice in California before the Americans came" (*Splendid Idle Forties* 319). In "The Bells of San Gabriel," the protagonist, Don Luis de la Torre, is a soldier in the Mexican army, but is nonetheless described as "very good-looking, this tall young Spaniard" (371). The narrative shifts between Spanish and Mexican to discriminate between the Spanish inhabitants of California and the physical nation of Mexico, located somewhere to the South. Sturges, an American character in "Head of a Priest," rescues and elopes with a young Californian woman alienated by her mother and the church. "The Ears of Twenty Americans" begins on the eve of the American occupation of California in 1846, with the hawkish Californio Doña Eustaquia berating the Californios; she decries the men of California as "cowards" and wishes "the women of California were men" (50–1). Soon thereafter, when the American invasion turns to inevitable conquest, Doña Eustaquia concedes, "All is over and cannot be changed. So, it is better we [Anglos and Californios] are good friends than poor ones" (64).

Learning that the Californio men are defeated, she belabors the point, stating bluntly, "I like better the Americans than the men of my own race . . . I shall hate [the American] flag so long as life is in me; but I cannot hate the brave men who fight for it" (69). Doña Eustaquia never relinquishes her dislike for the United States, but when the American captain Russell and the Californio Fernando Altimira compete for the hand of Doña Eustaquia's daughter Benicia (on the battlefield no less) and Russell emerges triumphant, Eustaquia "forgive[s] him for being an American" and "love[s] him like my own son" (126). Atherton's short stories focus on female protagonists living under the yoke of patriarchy, and triumphalist narratives of American conquest override the treatment of Mexican American manhood in her short fiction. Her longer fiction more deeply engages with questions of assimilation and the potential inclusion of "Spanish" Americans in the U.S. nation.

The Californians, set in the decades after the American conquest primarily in Menlo Park, a late nineteenth-century retreat for the affluent just outside San Francisco, follows the young protagonist Magdaléna. *The Californians* differs from Atherton's short stories in assuming a much more realist tone and style. Magdaléna "dreamed of caballeros serenading beneath her casement," but the dreams "had curled up and fallen to dust" as she witnesses the decline of Californio society against Anglo cultural and social pressures.[42] Magdaléna, "an unhappy and incongruous mixture of Spanish and New England traits," finds herself a reluctant participant in the idyllic indolence of the Californio lifestyle, uncomfortable and unable to find satisfaction in the sociality expected of a young woman of her class (*The Californians* 17). Living alone with her father, the oppressively restrictive Don Roberto Yorba, and unimpressed by Californio suitors, Magdaléna eventually falls for an older Anglo male, Mr. John Trennahan of New York, and the two begin a tangled romance. Trennahan and Magdaléna plan to marry, but before they do Trennahan falls for Magdaléna's beautiful yet capricious friend Helena, abandoning a distraught Magdaléna. After learning of Trennahan's lurid past, Helena dissolves the engagement and by the novel's end Magdaléna and Trennahan reconcile, but only after Don Roberto goes mad lamenting the failed marriage.

Unlike most Californio land owners, Don Roberto "was a man of wealth and consequence to-day" who preserved his fortune through careful investment in gold mines, real estate in San Francisco, other ventures, and most importantly in a bank. Yet his pecuniary success was not entirely self-made. Don Roberto strikes a partnership with the "shrewd Yankee" Mr. Polk, who came to California in July 1846 as a midshipman in Commodore Sloat's navy and was complicit in the taking of land from native Californios through usurious lending practices (12).[43] While his "gratitude and friendship for Don Roberto never flickered," Polk nonetheless sees Don Roberto's "boots are a comfortable fit, and I propose to wear them," openly announcing his desire to appropriate Californio manhood (13). As representative of the Spanish conquest of California, Polk's move corresponds to Lummis's own valorization of the Spanish conquest. The friendship is cemented when Don Roberto marries Polk's thirty-two-year-old sister "some eleven years after the Occupation of California by the United States" (15). Polk reciprocates, marrying Don Roberto's younger sister (also named Magdaléna Yorba) and the two men establish a new Californio aristocracy, merging the military conquest of California and its civil society. Atherton's novel inverts the marriage resolution common to fictions of interracial or national romance, beginning her novel with a Californio-Anglo marriage. This make possible the conquest of California, yet the transcultural marriages do not resolve the cultural tension in the region but rather set the stage for the subsequent containment of Mexican American manhood.[44]

Through Don Roberto's and Polk's marriages, California presents the possibility for an inherited European aristocracy and its attendant cultural capital. Atherton turns to the Californio past to preserve a European cultural legacy, embodied in Mexican American manhood and represented by Don Roberto. When his daughter's marriage to an East Coast aristocrat is called off, Don Roberto worries about perpetuating his family, as his desire to see his daughter married is inseparable from his desire to Anglicize his lineage. His fears are imbedded within an apprehension over losing his "Americanness." Even as Atherton valorizes Californio culture, Don Roberto is plagued by the inevitability and the desirability of Anglo assimilation. Without the security of Anglo posterity to complete the "structure of his Americanism," Don Roberto is unable to navigate within California society (101). The death of Mr. Polk compounds his inaction and incapacitates Don Roberto, "afraid to trust himself in the world for fear he would relapse into his natural instincts" of pastoral idleness (348). Within the racial logic of the novel, class status alone protects Don Roberto from his "natural instincts," wealth withstanding the pressures of racialization. Without the guidance of either Mr. Polk's business acumen or Trennahan as future heir, Don Roberto becomes incapable of managing his family and his position in California society. Atherton is sympathetic to the difficulties facing a conquered culture, but she advocates assimilation to combat the threat of racial reversion.

In the final scene, Don Roberto "hanged himself with the American flag" which "had floated above the house of Don Roberto Yorba for thirty years" (351, 339). Through his friendships and professional life, Don Roberto identified with Anglo America and sought to become a recognized, assimilated American, but the novel denies him the possibility of national inclusion, although it leaves open the potential assimilation of his daughter. Roberto dies believing his daughter to be a spinster and overwrought by the lack of a male heir, shattering his dreams of social incorporation. In a desperate act of physical and symbolic integration, Roberto became "no longer so much a man as an ideal" and wrapped himself in the emblem of national unity before removing himself from the California landscape (337). With Roberto now dead, Trennahan inherits his father-in-law's estate and with it the legacy of Californio aristocracy, paving the way for his and Magdalena's racially unencumbered future. Don Roberto never lives to see his dreams of social incorporation; rather, the novel's haunting final image is Don Roberto suspended in death by the American flag, his American dream betrayed.

That Don Roberto hangs himself with the American flag serves as a gesture toward colonization and as an acknowledgment of the tension between Anglo and Mexican American manhoods. His action recalls a story from the U.S.-Mexican War, familiar in Mexican but not U.S. history: that of the "*niños héroes*," the boy soldiers who resisted the U.S. invasion of Mexico City and are memorialized in Mexican cultural memory. Defending their hilltop post at Chapultepec Castle against the besieging American army, six teenage soldiers were killed, but the last wrapped himself in the Mexican flag and leapt to his death rather than surrender. Of course, Don Roberto's suicide is not an act of defiance like that of the niños héroes, but of failure and surrender. The American flag does not incorporate Don Roberto, who "might have been wrought into the tissue of that beautiful delicate web," into the fabric of the nation—he instead perishes as a "grotesque intruder" in his very home (351). In death, Don Roberto fulfills Atherton's purpose, allowing Spanish history to be co-opted for nationalist ends. In the national imaginary, where "the West is imagined as (masculine) epic [and] is as often dismissed as cultureless," Californio manhood provides Atherton with the cultural capital necessary to dispel East Coast claims of western crudity, but is ultimately subsumed under Anglo American manhood.[45] Reminiscent of Lummis's desire for the Californio heritage as American cultural capital, Atherton's depiction of Don Roberto denies that heritage as an explicitly male inheritance. Don Roberto's attempts at assimilation are incomplete, and he must die so that his successors, his daughter Magdaléna and the Anglo male Trennahan, can carry forward the Californio legacy. The land itself is both redeemed and redemptive, but only when under control of a white American manhood; to perform Don Roberto's Mexican American manhood is suicide.

Atherton translates Old California for a national audience by managing racial and class problems through the removal of Mexican American manhood, consequently separating "Spanish as a legal category linked to autonomous identity and individual rights, and 'Mexican' as a racial category linked to insurgent social problems and secret, hereditary alliances with racial otherness," where Mexican Americans become available as a landless, history-less labor force.[46] Atherton dedicated *The Splendid Idle Forties* to the Bohemian Club, a "moral, beneficial and literary association" and private men's club in San Francisco devoted to building fraternal alliances in journalism and the literary arts.[47] Dedicating the book to an all-male organization itself dedicated to the preservation of California and regional literature reveals Atherton's collaboration in the fantastical construction of Mexican American manhood. Relocating Mexican American manhood into a fictionalized past transforms Californios into historical relics, a marketable, consumable product of cultural memory suitable for regionalist fiction. As *The Californians* protagonist remarks, "It is only the living enemies we fear; the dead and their past are beautiful unrealities to the smarting ego" (323).

In a different context, Marita Sturken defines cultural memory as "a field of contested meanings in which Americans interact with cultural elements to produce concepts of the nation, particularly in events of trauma, where both the structures and the fractures of a culture are exposed. Examining cultural memory thus provides insight into how American culture functions, how oppositional politics engages with nationalism, and how cultural arenas such as art, popular culture, activism, and consumer culture intersect."[48] Spanish fantasy heritage provides such an intersection of cultural arenas, and the cultural memory promulgated by Atherton's fiction dissolved the Mexican presence in California even as it glorified a Mexican (and pre-Mexican) past. This was the cultural environment of California during the first decades of the twentieth century. When Adolfo Carrillo arrived in San Francisco in the 1890s, he witnessed firsthand the ascendancy of this myth, and later reworked the California mission tales to organize the Mexican origin population of California toward political enfranchisement.

A Biography of Exile

While Adolfo Carrillo spent over half his life in California, his formative childhood was spent under Porfirio Díaz's dictatorship in Mexico. Forced into exile, his early engagement with an autocratic government shaped his political and literary views. Born in the town of Sayula, in Jalisco, Mexico, in July of 1855, Carrillo was educated in a Catholic seminary in Guadalajara, the state capital. He became involved in newspapers at a young age, publishing *La Picota* in 1877 and shortly thereafter, *La Unión Mercantil* in 1878, both in Guadalajara. Fluent in Spanish, English, and French, he often translated sources for his newspapers. As a writer for *La Unión Mercantil*, Carrillo's attacks on the Guadalajara government quickly drew attention, and he was forced to leave Guadalajara for Mexico City.

Carrillo arrived in Mexico City less than two years after Porfirio Díaz assumed the presidency. Carrillo supported Benito Juarez's Liberal government legacy, and once in Mexico City, he used the newspaper as an outlet to mount a critique of Díaz's newly assumed dictatorship. He continued his assault on the local and national government as editor of Mexico City's *El correo del lunes*, "de los que mayor circulacion alcanzan el el país" [a newspaper with one of the largest circulations in the country].[49] In July of 1885, Carrillo and several other newspapermen were imprisoned for criticizing Díaz, and later that month Carrillo and

Sees Bright Future for Mexico.

Señor Adolfo Carrillo,

Mexican Consul in Los Angeles, who declares that one of the first acts of Carranza, now that he has been recognized, will be to call a fair election in the republic which will be conducted as they are in the United States.

Figure 2.3. "Portrait of Señor Adolfo Carrillo," *Los Angeles Times*, October 20, 1915.

fellow editor Enrique Chavarri were found guilty of "sedicion, insidia, calumnia y faltas a las autoridades" [sedition, deceit, slander, crimes against the state].[50] Sentenced to seven and a half months in prison and a fine, Carrillo's case was upheld by the Supreme Court, which "de una vez concluye con la libertad de imprenta, fijando una jurisprudencia enteramente contraria a la libertad del pensamiento" [definitively did away with the right to free speech, affirming legal precedent against freedom of thought].[51] Carrillo's sentencing and its subsequent impact on Mexican journalism and freedom of speech became a central and recurring theme in his writing.

In the winter of 1886, Carrillo, frustrated by his inability to practice his profession, travelled to the United States.[52] In New York City, Carrillo was an acquaintance and regular guest of deposed Mexican president Sebastián Lerdo de Tejada, who served as his benefactor for a short time, and claimed to have befriended José Martí.[53] Drawing on his intimate knowledge of Lerdo, Carrillo wrote a biography of the ex-president entitled *Memorias inéditas del Lic. Don Sebastían Lerdo de Tejada* (1889), which for many years was thought to be autobiographical. Published in Brownsville, Texas (the future site of much revolutionary activity), the apocryphal biography and purported autobiography was a potent tool to protest the Díaz government and served as an instrument of organization for revolutionary forces for years to come, republished numerous times on both sides of the border as recently as 1978. The biography represented Carrillo's first U.S.-published text that used literature to critique government policy.

Carrillo traveled to Cuba and Europe as a reporter for Madrid's *El Dia* and Paris's *L'Intransigeant*, and also studied law at the Sorbonne, before settling permanently in San Francisco where he founded a printing shop, Voz de Mexico. While the exact date of his entry into California is uncertain, by 1891 Carrillo had established himself in San Francisco after several years perambulating the globe, coinciding with the eruption of interest in California's Spanish colonial past. In 1897, Carrillo published a picaresque novel entitled *Memorias del Marqués de San Basilisco*, which chronicles the adventures of the titular marquis Jorge Carmona during the French intervention and advocates for Mexican cultural integrity.[54] In 1914, Mexican president Venustiano Carranza appointed Carrillo consul of Los Angeles, where Carrillo provided information to Carranza's constitutionalist government on the movements of *los científicos* (former supporters of Díaz), Pancho Villa, and other rebels, as well as reported on U.S. public opinion of Carranza. As a result of charges that Carrillo "no ha posesionado del deber que tiene de ayudar y proteger a los mexicanos" [does not use his power to aid and protect Mexicans], Carranza removed Carrillo from office.[55] His forced resignation as consul was the final straw in a lifelong struggle against state-sanctioned violence. Aged, beleaguered, and insolvent, Carrillo felt betrayed by his country and the revolution to which he had devoted thirty years of his life.

As in his youth, Carrillo again found himself embroiled in national politics, but this time "the partisan divisions in Mexican politics were duplicated in Chicano communities" of Los Angles and, caught between multiple national loyalties, he became the subject, if not the victim, of the very processes of *pochismo* (Americanization) he had previously combated.[56] Carrillo often blurred the distinction between journalism and fiction, and his prose is heavily laden with allegory, allusion, and irony, which his readers frequently misread. His style led to numerous public disagreements and statements asking Carrillo to clarify his outspoken criticism of violence and whether it was state-sanctioned or against the state, a situation that made him unpopular with anarchists and revolutionaries. His termination from office, however, would again force him to reevaluate his relationship to both his home and adopted country. Carrillo would spend the ensuing years traveling through California, collecting material for his next literary project, *Cuentos Californianos*, before his death on August 24, 1926, in Los Angeles.

Carrillo's Cultural Haunting

Gertrude Atherton was not alone in aggrandizing California's Spanish heritage, nor was the deployment of this fantasy heritage confined to Anglo Californian writers. Many novels, like Ruiz de Burton's romantic and romanticized *The Squatter and the Don*, put forth a "political future where the civic ethos of an evolving, educated California citizenry takes as its founding mythos a nostalgic embrace of Californio ranch culture."[57] Adolfo Carrillo arrived in California shortly after the publication of Ruiz de Burton's novels, during Atherton's most prolific period of California fiction. In 1922, after residing for more than thirty years in California, Carrillo turned to Spanish fantasy heritage and published *Cuentos Californianos*, a collection of stories set in and drawing on the state's history. By engaging with this well-worn genre, these tales attempted to translate the state's cultural narrative for Mexican Americans and to rewrite Mexican Americans within it; reading the stories of old California multilingually enables a more complete version of how state history was the site of racial and ethnic competition. Carrillo's use of the Spanish past engaged with state history, both for and on behalf of the state's Mexican origin population. Where Lummis and Atherton saw Mexican American manhood as a boon to U.S. cultural capital and assimilation as the best strategy for social inclusion, Carrillo's stories work transnationally and multilingually for social inclusion and to preserve Mexican American cultural integrity. Within the fantasy heritage, Carrillo challenged the racial and social categories upon which the fantasy heritage depended. His stories emphasize the importance of visibility—of being seen—and de-romanticize the mission past to insert Mexican Americans as central actors in an ongoing state drama, paradoxically linking Mexican American manhood and citizenship through the fantasy heritage.

Virtually the only existing contemporary scholarship on the *Cuentos Californianos* is by Francisco Lomelí. Lomelí reads *Cuentos Californianos* in the context of the Mexican short story, locating Carrillo's fiction in the tradition of "la leyenda novelesca, tan popular en México durante el romanticismo y costumbrismo" [fictionalized legends, so popular in Mexico during the romantic and costumbrismo periods].[58] Lomelí astutely identifies how Carrillo is able to "rescatar en los cuentos una cultura que . . . estaba experimentando el opacamiento por parte de la cultura anglo-americana" [rescue through the stories a culture that was experiencing suppression by Anglo American culture].[59] While Lomelí praises the collection, his focus on Mexican literary traditions misses how Carrillo intervenes in both the fantasy heritage and the cultural myth's connection to citizenship. Carrillo published his collection just two years before the passage of the Immigration Act of 1924, which caused a surge in Mexican immigration even as it limited immigration from other national and ethnic groups.[60] But those immigrants were overwhelmingly admitted as migrant laborers and not seen as contributing citizens of a state or national society. Manhood was at the center of fantasy heritage as Lummis and Atherton imagine it, and I suggest that Carrillo reworked the fantasy heritage to combat social exclusion and to revise the cultural history essential for recognizing the continued and "permanente presencia mexicana."

Carrillo's revisions to the Murieta legend summarized at the beginning of this chapter are particularly instructive, as the performance of manhood functions as "linguistic, legal, cultural, and political repetitions-in-transformation, invocations that are also revocations."[61]

In addition to having Murieta and Three Fingers Jack commit mutual suicide, Carrillo adds numerous biographical details not found else-where: the location of Murieta's home, that he lived with his mother and sister, and the monetary value attached to his capture.[62] In contrast to John Rollin Ridge's original tale and most subsequent versions, Car-rillo rewrites the rape of Dorotea, which catalyzes Joaquin's move into crime, as Joaquin's sister, not his wife, shifting the narrative away from marital obligation and dispelling notions of sentimental politics depen-dent on romantic union. Murieta pillages California carefully, "robando y asesinando a los hombres y dejando en libertad a las mujeres y los niños" [robbing and murdering the men but leaving free the women and children].[63] Noting his differential treatment of the sexes grants Murieta a chivalric sense of compassion, but it also de-masculinizes the Anglo population in a retaliatory move against imperial conquest. Carrillo's Murieta castrates the Anglo assailant that violated his sister, and he sub-sequently attempts to depopulate the landscape of Anglo men.

Removing Anglo men from the narrative enables the tale to establish heteronormative relations between Mexican American males exclusive of extra-cultural involvement. In the fourth part of the story, Murieta attends a dance in honor of the niece of Mariano Guadalupe Vallejo, the factual Californian whose story was famously captured in Bancroft's histories. At the dance, Joaquin meets and falls in love with Lina Solano, "[quien] pertenece a una familia de renegados" y "su tio el señor Vallejo, fue uno de los que entregaron California a los gringos" [who belongs to a family of renegades [and whose] uncle was one of those who delivered California to the foreigners] (*Cuentos Californianos* 41). By introducing Vallejo, perhaps the most famous Californio thanks to a lengthy mem-oir included in Hubert H. Bancroft's multi-volume history of California, Carrillo connects the literary banditry discussed in the previous chapter to the fantasy heritage. Juxtaposing Murieta and Vallejo, Carrillo com-bines the two dominant narratives of Mexican Americans in California state history, merging ideas of national resistance that Murieta symbol-ized with the fantasy heritage that held the potential for social inclusion.

Joaquin, the hero of Mexican American lore, loves Lina blindly, but that love is misguided. Rather than write Murieta as a symbol of resis-tance against the U.S. state, Carrillo depicts him as a tragic consequence of national rivalry. At the same time, he emphasizes the importance of

cultural integrity, here taking the form of homosocial loyalty, in asserting Mexican Americans' place as citizens of the United States. Joaquin's
judgment was clouded by his love for Lina, and he chooses to stay in
California despite Jack's warnings of imminent danger. The romance
endangers the life of Joaquin and his comrades, but the lovestruck Joaquin disregards the warnings of Three Fingers Jack, who "estimaba a su
Jefe con el cariño de hermano" [respected his leader with the love of a
brother] (41). Joaquin discloses his plans to Lina, who betrays him to the
state governor, an action that leads to the dramatic joint suicide. Lina's
surrounds herself with Vallejo and the social environment he represents,
and she is unable to distance herself from that space. Her ultimate attachment to that ideal, and her only partial commitment to Joaquin,
serves as a warning to Mexican origin people not to accept the fantasy
heritage. Carrillo made legible that critique through the popular bandit
figure and adjusted the terms through which Joaquin enters the lore.

In place of the romance of the fantasy heritage, Carrillo invokes homosocial obligation to enable a national brotherhood demarcated by
shared masculine ideals. The story disavows the romance and marriage
resolution as viable options for the reconciliation of masculine authority or as means toward social improvement. The dramatic climax and
self-imposed death emphasize the importance of homosocial cooperation in the face of Anglo racism, as the story unequivocally states that
Joaquin was persecuted "por el solo hecho de ser mexicano" [for the
sole reason of being Mexican] (36). Yet the story's emphasis on homosocial relations also invokes a diasporic ideology of return—the desire
to, as Three Fingers Jack urges, "olivdala y regresemos a Mexico" [forget
her and let us return to Mexico] (41). The hero Joaquin, born in Sonora
but a resident of California, claims both Mexican and American cultural heritage but stands in contradistinction to the class of Californios
here responsible for surrendering the state to Anglo America. Jack goes
so far as to say he prefers "un gringo hecho y derecho, que una de esas
viborillas de charco" [an honest and upright American to one of those
snakes] that would betray his nation (41). Before their suicide, he beseeches Joaquin to return to Mexico, but Joaquin chooses to remain
loyal to his adopted state.

Joaquin, a figure of transcultural power, is martyred on behalf of the
Mexican population of California. By choosing death over repatriation

to Mexico, Carrillo ties Mexican American males to the land, both in the diegetic present and the historical past, and places the burden of social change within the Mexican American community itself. Carrillo's Joaquin defies the threat of cultural dissolution within the Mexican origin community of California at the hands of Anglo society. He instills a sense of collective residence among the Mexican American readership through attachment to geographic space, mediated by a model of manhood that emphasizes tight homosocial bonds. In choosing death at the hands of a fellow Mexican instead of capitulation or death by the American authority, Joaquin remains loyal to the ideals of resistance with which he was associated and serves as a proponent of fraternal allegiance.

This sense of national brotherhood is typical of the narratives of Mexican writers residing in the United States during the first half of the twentieth century.[64] Within the Mexican exile population living in the U.S. emerged an ideology of cultural nationalism known as México de afuera, in which "it was the duty of the individual to maintain the Spanish language, keep the Catholic faith, and insulate the children from what community leaders perceived as the low moral standards of Anglo-Americans. Basic to this belief system was the imminent return to Mexico, when the hostilities of the Revolution were over."[65] I give a fuller treatment of México de afuera in the following chapter, but here suffice it to say that those who adhered to these traditional ideals saw themselves as an extension of a Mexican national project.

Like Mexican American novelists Jorge Ulica and Daniel Venegas, Carrillo utilized popular fiction to communicate with Spanish-speaking, Mexican-origin people living in the United States, founding a print shop in 1897 and the newspapers *México Libre* (1914) and *La Prensa* (1912) in Los Angeles.[66] In similar fashion to Daniel Venegas's *The Adventures of Don Chipote*, Carrillo's earlier novel *Memorias del Marques de San Basilisco* used the picaresque form to engage the Mexican origin population and advocate for the perpetuation of Mexican culture. However, Carrillo's short fiction balances between expressing a desire to preserve cultural integrity and the need to integrate into California and U.S. society. *Las Memorias del Marques de San Basilisco* demonstrates the dangers of foreign influence for the Mexican expatriate and immigrant community and "how those attitudes applied pressure on families to conform to old gender roles and resist the social change that the new American host culture was making imminent"; *Cuentos Californianos* modifies the staunch México de afuera ideology away from the presumption of eventual return in favor of a more permanent Mexican American presence in California.[67] Through his experience as consul, Carrillo was well acquainted with the policies of the Mexican government in the United States. But over the course of his lifetime, Carrillo lived among the Mexican middle-class intelligentsia on both sides of the border, and while only partially effective as consul, the stories seemed poised to make a middle-class cultural argument for the inclusion of Mexican Americans through the California fantasy heritage. After thirty plus years in the United States, Carrillo was more immediately concerned with local issues that determined social inclusion.

Carrillo's decision to write Spanish fantasy heritage myths for a Spanish-speaking audience offered the appeal of national participation but for a Mexican American reading public more heavily invested in life in the United States. The collection's prologue begins with a reference to the "Cuento Californiano" column in *La Prensa del sábado*, a newspaper to which Carrillo contributed several articles and editorials. The stories were eventually collected, but given Carrillo's long-standing work in journalism, it seems very likely that at least some were published in one of the many daily or weekly Spanish language newspapers then in print in California.[68] The Spanish language press was thriving during this period, had significant readership, and had reached a large audience on both sides of the border. Readers in the Mexican American communities of California would have been surrounded by the Spanish fantasy mythos, and Carrillo's stories of old California would both translate that history for their consumption and constitute their participation in it, working against fantasy heritage's erasure of the Mexican population.

Carrillo's choice to enter the genre signals a move toward the establishment of a distinctly U.S.-oriented Mexican American culture in the height of a period still known for its México de afuera ideology. *Cuentos Californianos* could mediate transnational obligations linguistically, as its Spanish-language readers were still engaged with the literature of Mexico, but the content and context of the stories' consumption located Mexicans within the territorial, historical, and cultural United States. *Cuentos Californianos* produced a Mexican American reading public en-

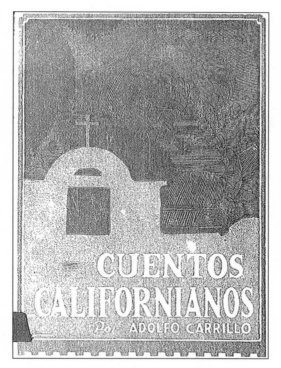

Figure 2.4. Cover of *Cuentos Californianos*, ca. 1922,
courtesy of the Recovering the U.S. Hispanic Literary
Heritage Project.

gaged with the rights of citizenship in Mexico and the U.S. cultural mi-
lieu, demonstrating the necessity of local engagement for the emigrant
community. In many ways Carrillo's use of the fantasy myth prefigures
Aztlán (the Chicano movement ideal of a transnational homeland) in
that it enables de-nationalized, universal claims to belonging, yet his
appropriation of Spanish fantasy heritage is expressly located within the
U.S. and specifically California context.[69] Despite his global travels, this
is not cosmopolitan universalism, but a politically potent localized response.[70] Carrillo rewrote popular fiction to potentially include Mexican
Americans within California's literary economy against the ambiguity
of legal discourse that enabled the state to exclude racialized subjects.
Carrillo relies on the imaginative construction of the citizen-subject in
order to remap those boundaries of civic participation.

Of the nineteen tales contained in the collection, eleven are set in the mission past, seven are ghost stories or contain gothic elements, and all are located in precise geographic locations. Unlike in Atherton's tales, in *Cuentos Californianos* women, Anglos, or priests commit nearly all of the violence; several of the tales describe priests who break their vows by falling in love or who commit crimes driven by greed, de-romanticizing the mission past. The decision to engage with this genre of regional literature suggests Carrillo's awareness of the fantasy heritage in defining state identity and his desire to critique its exclusion of Mexican Americans. The fantasy heritage sought to separate living Mexican Americans from or relegate them to the past, and Carrillo's de-romanticized mission past seeks to expose that false separation. The departure from the otherwise traditional valorization of the mission past culminates in a disavowal of the mission system as corrupted. Additionally, *Cuentos Californianos* asserts the Mexican origin population as descendants of the mission past, largely through the narrative use of ghosts. Carrillo's characters are, know of, or encounter spectral presences in many of the stories.

The sixteenth story of the collection, "Los Espectros [or Ghosts] de San Luis Rey," demonstrates how the mission past haunts the California landscape and how the past affects the Mexican American population. The tale is set at two of California's missions, San Luis Rey and San Juan Capistrano, roughly 30 miles apart in the area now between Los Angeles and San Diego. In her deathbed confession to Friar Pedro Somera, Doña Claudina confesses an illicit, premarital affair with Juan José de La Serna, former prior of the San Luis Rey mission who "escandalizando la comarca con sus francachelas y estruendosas orgías" [scandaliz(ed) the region with his binges and rowdy orgies] (79). The youthful and sacrilegious romance resulted in Doña Claudina giving birth to two children, who were buried alive by Fray Serna in order to conceal the secret of their affair. Doña Claudina dies, and a few years later Fray Serna is hung from a tree by the pirate Rene Bouchard, a French corsair equipped by an unnamed Latin American country to combat Spanish rule. These events fill the first three parts of the story, but in the final part, the narrative jumps forward one hundred years, to the lobby of a small hotel where several "huéspedes norte-americanos" are staying. Over dinner, conversation turns to local folklore; one of the guests, a Hollywood photographer, is determined to find "aparecidos y apariciones" [visions and ghosts], armed with "unos lentes [a que] nada escapa, ni aun los objectos intangibles e invisibles" [photographic equipment from which nothing escapes, not even the intangible or invisible] (81). An elderly man, the only character in the section identified as a native Californian, confirms the presence of ghosts at the mission and recounts the nightly visits of two young children dressed in white and of a young woman, followed by a terrifying silhouette swinging from an old tree. The party ventures out, and by sunrise, the Hollywood photographer successfully captures the ghosts on film. As the guests depart, the photographer triumphantly declaims that "muy pronto aplaudirán en la plantalla la tragedia sin música que acaban de presenciar" [very soon you will applaud on the screen the tragedy without music that you have all just witnessed] (83).

This story about the ghosts of California history haunting the then-present takes as its subject the same mythic California past, but radically reshifts the framework for its interpretation. By rupturing the narrative diegesis and compressing story time, Carrillo forces readers to confront their relationship with the cultural transmission of California's literary history. California's missions are alive in the present, though their spectral presence suggests ephemerality and illusoriness rather than historical reality. The photographer brings in the camera a symbol of progress, but a paradoxical one, as the ghosts "que fueron realidades y no fantasias" [that were reality and not fantasy] would seemingly contradict the scientific knowledge the camera represents (83). Successfully capturing the images of the ghosts, the camera at once affirms and denies the California mission lore; by converting myth into scientific evidence or marketable culture, the camera effectively commodifies the legends. In this tale, "la fantasmagoría [es] transformada en símbolos positivos" [the fantastic (is) transformed into absolute symbols], in parallel to how the mythos of Old California is rendered historical fact through the fantasy heritage. In almost the same breath, however, Carrillo infuses the myth with a new legend, as the image of a ghostly woman in white and her two children are eerily reminiscent of La Llorona, a mythic figure widely familiar to a Mexican cultural readership. Though the North American guests are primarily interested in the ghosts' value as cultural objects, the elderly Californian is a living reminder of the people the fantasy heritage obscures. Consequently, "el efecto ilusionista habia desaparecido" [the magical effect had disappeared], and the myth is exposed as a cultural construction (83).

Carrillo repeats this strategy of linking Mexican American men to both past and present through ghosts in several stories. While the ghost of "Los Espectros" connects history to the present, the story "El Resucitado" recasts a Mexican American male as the ghost himself. "El Resucitado" is told through a first-person narrator whose story is relayed as a found object, the purported memoirs of a Californian named José Palau who experienced the American occupation of California. Born in Los Angeles, Palau became a priest at the San Gabriel mission in 1835, but soon relinquishes his priestly garb in the face of the American annexation. Palau explains his departure from the mission as a response to the "hombres de otras razas, de luengas barbas y formidable aspecto," who offer him "el oro y el moro si yo, José Palau, predicaba haciendo propoganda anexionista" [men of other races, speaking barbarous languages and of formidable appearance, (who) offer gold and riches if I, José Palau, preached separatist propaganda] (51). José Palau is thus rendered the "true," patriotic Californio, placing loyalty above all else.

The loyalty to California is further emphasized by the romance around which the plot turns. Palau further justifies his decision to leave the priesthood by asserting that "en mi cutis había algo del celibata y mucho del sátiro en mi talante habia mas de soldado que de monje" [in my skin there was some of the celibate and much of the satyr. And in my character more soldier than monk] (51).[71] Carrillo charges Palau's self-identity with the sexuality of a satyr and the martial prowess of a soldier, characteristics incommensurate with priesthood, but appropriate to the "feats of manhood" the state requires. His realization of his true character is made clear when he meets Elena Castro, daughter of General José Castro (general of the Mexican army during the U.S.-Mexican War), in the confession booth. Elena "revelomé entonces las intrigas que se movían entre sus hermanos de California para independer la Provincia, or entregarla a manos de un poder extranjero" [revealed to me the intrigues that moved among her Californian brother to free the province or turn it over to the hands of a foreign power], and after Palau absolves Elena of her sins, he then joins her cause (51).

As a Californio first and foremost, Palau's national loyalties are dependent on what he deems the best interests of the Californio people.

Set during a tumultuous period of California history when the government changed hands numerous times, the story is thus of shifting and emerging national affiliations, as Californian, as Mexican, and as American. Palau witnesses Governor Micheltorena's entrance into Los Angeles at the head of an army of *cholos*—the mercenaries and criminals who made up the Mexican-appointed governor's army. Observing the way that Micheltorena's army pillages the town, the next day Palau "colgue los habitos, y ciñendo las espada, fuíme con Elena a refugiarme en la casa de Pio Pico" [hung up my monk's habit and grasping the spear, Elena and I took refuge in the home of Pio Pico], a third-generation Californian and future governor (52). Renouncing his vows and rebelling against the Mexican government, Palau disclaims both the church and the Mexican authority, choosing instead a native Californio political position.

Palau joins an army of horsemen who, as native Californians, are "dispuestos a rechazar a laos audaces invasores" [ready to repel the audacious invaders] (52). On August 18, 1847, a gruesome battle ensues, during which an explosion traps him under his dead horse and he is consequently buried alive. Emerging from the grave three days later, perhaps alluding to Christ's resurrection, the reborn Californio searches for his beloved, only to find her bedded with the American Captain Gillepsi. Palau feels betrayed by both his beloved and the lost cause, having died in the defense of California only to be quickly forgotten. Returning from the dead, furious for having lost his land and his woman, Palau plots his revenge.

Donning his priestly garb once again, this time as a disguise, Palau sneaks into Gillepsi's home to murder Elena. Assuming that Gillepsi would sacrifice his life to defend Elena, Palau, "sentíame capaz de embestir contra todo un batallón" [feeling capable of attacking an entire battalion], nevertheless proceeds with an inflated sense of masculine power (55). Palau takes on Gillepsi, fighting "cuerpo a cuerpo de salvaje contra salvaje" [hand to hand, savage against savage] (55). In the ensuing battle, Elena is murdered and Gillepsi badly wounded, and Palau becomes an outcast and a wanted man. Energized by a speech "exitándolos a que fueran hombres" [rallying them to act like men], Palau equates martial achievement and manhood with success, but his blind rage only results in the death of his beloved (55).

Elena, daughter of a Californio and lover of an American, trading her affection between the two, at least partially symbolizes the U.S., a construction perhaps familiar to allegories of national conquest. While Elena is able to shift her national loyalties, assuming that her former lover has fallen victim to the American occupation, Palau is unable to make the transition. From Palau's perspective, the story takes a decidedly less sympathetic stance toward Americans, but the mere act of writing in this genre suggests Carrillo's engagement with American cultural practices. Palau, both ghost and man, priest and Californian, also represents the conflated and conflicted loyalties that Mexican American Californians faced.

Palau attends Elena's funeral, where in remorseful passion he pleads to the heavens, "Perdonala, Dios, misericordioso, como yo la he perdonado!" [Forgive her, merciful god, like I have forgiven her!] (56). Whether Palau makes this plea as layman or as clergyman is unclear, but in either case Palau does not excuse his murderous behavior, but rather beseeches the heavens to forgive Elena for choosing the American captain. This somewhat perplexing request speaks to the quandary in which Mexican American national status and cultural affiliation was placed. In the story, the attachment to land and place supplants personal and national loyalties, but that attachment was grounded in a fantasy heritage of the mission past. The fantasy heritage made the performance of manhood difficult if not impossible for Mexican Americans, and at one point in the story, Carrillo openly critiques the Spanish heritage myth, stating, "Mas bajo la superficie de ese idilio patriarchal, bullian infernales ambiciones" [Beneath the surface of the patriarchal romance were teeming diabolical ambitions] (51). Unable to cope with his contradictions and left with the broken dreams of state inclusion, Palau seeks "expiación de mi crímen" [expiation from my crime] and, like Joaquin and Don Roberto, commits suicide (56).

Carrillo portrays Mexican American males as agentive—agents of both historical change and their own destruction. The ghosts of Carrillo's fiction function much in the way of what Kathleen Brogan identifies in contemporary ethnic literature, where ghosts "attempt to recover and make social use of a poorly documented, partially erased cultural history" and point to "the degree to which any such historical reconstruction is essentially an imaginative act."[72] The social marginalization of California's Mexican residents took place in part through the creative rewriting of state history, so Carrillo turns to this cultural arena to advocate for social inclusion. Carrillo's ghosts are less about the spectral than about the continuing historical presence of Mexican American manhood. The repeated inclusion of the native narrator as or alongside the ghosts of the mission past emphasizes the presence of Mexican Americans in both historical and contemporary California.

The tale "El Hombre Invisible" illustrates the spectral presence of Mexican American men. The story takes place on San Francisco's Kearney Street in 1902, the same year Atherton published *Splendid Idle Forties*. The protagonist is a Mexican tailor named Pepe Pérez de Perezcano, "tan trigueño, que al verle uno no sabia si era de dia o de noche" [so dark-skinned that upon seeing him one could not tell if it was day or night] (84). Engaged to a German woman named Celendina Ham, Pepe is very jealous and suspects her infidelity. One day a sorcerer from South Asia visits his shop, promising a potion that will make him invisible. Upon taking the potion before bed, "nadie la verá aunque se halle usted presente" [no one would see you until you make your presence known] (84). The sorcerer touts the advantages of being invisible, suggesting to Pepe he could rob a bank unnoticed. Pepe immediately and fiercely protests, "Yo no soy ladrón" [I am not a thief]. Changing his pitch before one of "los hombres honrados," the witch doctor instead promises that the potion will allow Pepe to test Celendina's fidelity, and the tailor immediately accedes. The next morning, having drunk the potion the previous evening, Pepe returns to his store as usual. The first customers come in, and although Pepe offers clothes in many styles ("tengo de todos: franceses, ingleses, y . . ."), the customers leave angrily, appalled by el "sastre tan flojo" [the very lazy tailor] (85). Eventually, Pepe realizes the potion functioned as promised, rendering him invisible. He quickly departs to the home of his "Dulcinea," where his suspicions are confirmed: Celendina and "un hombre peludo" are locked arm in arm. Lamenting "los malditos polvos," Pepe throws himself into the sea, and "como nadie le veía, le dejaron ahogarse" [since no one could see him, they let him drown] (85).

This is one of few stories that distinguish between Californios and Mexicans. Pepe is explicitly racialized here, and his skin color acts as his sole defining physical characteristic. In contradistinction, Celendi-

na's "cabellera color de panocha y ojos de azul celeste" [caramel colored
hair and sky-blue eyes] invoke whiteness (84).[73] In racial terms, the two
characters function as referents for Anglo Mexican relations, portrayed
here as romantic betrayal. The dark-skinned Pepe tries to foster a relationship with his white girlfriend, who has "dado su palabra de casa-
miento" [given her word in marriage] (84). Celendina had promised to
marry Pepe, to convey upon him the legal and institutional recognition
of their relationship. Pepe himself fully commits to their relationship,
more interested in his love for Celendina than his desire for "el banco,"
the promises of wealth insinuated by the witch doctor. Pepe's romantic
attraction suggests the primacy of social relations over pecuniary gain,
yet he remains highly suspicious of the promises previously extended.

Pepe's suspicions are ultimately well founded. He catches his sweetheart in the act of betrayal. Curiously, Celendina's hairy "amante" more
resembles "un oso escapado del Golden Gate" [a bear escaped from
Golden Gate Park] than a lover (85). While the peculiar description of
the lover as hairy carries less overt racial overtones, the comparison to
a bear makes a historical analogy. The bear holds a celebrated place in
California history, immortalized on the state flag and, as part of the Bear
Flag Revolt referenced in "El Resucitado," a lasting symbol of the U.S.-
Mexican War.[74] The nameless man, a symbol of California's "indepen-
dence," intentionally or unknowingly wrests Pepe's lover away, and both
Celendina and the man are oblivious to Pepe's protests. His efforts futile,
Pepe, left isolated and unheard, is left with few options.

His death does not go unmarked, and Pepe's story is still remembered
by "sus deudores, colmando su memoria de bendiciones" [his debtors,
who fill his memory with blessings] (85). The survivors of California un-
derstandably bless Pepe's memory, whose absence allows them to profit
from his efforts. It is not his friends or family who note his disappear-
ance, but those that carry debts unpaid. In the context of the story, this
concluding remark implicates California in bearing the fruit of Mexicans' efforts without recognition, remuneration, or recompense for their
labor, politically, economically, socially, or otherwise. The "polvo" that
transforms Pedro implies more than the literal potion of the story. In
Spanish, "polvo" carries several meanings. Though it literally translates
as "powder", the phrase "hecho polvo" is idiomatic for "to be ruined";
similarly, "morder polvo" is "to be overcome." In "El Hombre Invisible,"

the Mexican male protagonist is rendered powerless by the powder, divested of his connection to state and society. Carrillo recognizes Mexican American manhood's invisibility as social syndrome, the result of cultural displacement. If Atherton conveniently dispenses with Mexican American men by consigning them to history as cultural artifact, Carrillo critiques the cultural relegation and attempts to remedy the displacement. His Mexican male is reminded that "nadie la verá aunque se halle usted presente" [no one would see you until you make your presence known] (84). The story makes available the possibility of social enunciation, the affirmation of Mexican American manhood in California culture.

"El Hombre Invisible" works within models of civic participation that would only emerge in the later half of the twentieth century. Carrillo's *Cuentos Californianos* asked the Mexican origin community to reevaluate its relationship to the state and to cooperate as a permanent ethnic presence. Carrillo's stories present an early effort at organizing cultural belonging by creating an inclusive shared mythos for Mexican Americans against the prevailing exclusionary histories, claiming Spanish fantasy heritage on behalf of the Mexican origin community. He uses Mexican American manhood to create an alternative mode of civic participation, citizenship through cultural inclusion, asserting historic connections to the geographic space and to cross, in Laura Lomas's words, "the gap between the existent and the possible to stress the role of the imagination as a force for creative political change."[75] While others reached beyond national boundaries in crafting modes of citizenship, Carrillo retreats to the region to reconfigure the parameters of belonging. Like Ruiz de Burton, Carrillo "works within existing frameworks of U.S. citizenship (and its accompanying racial hierarchies) rather than challenging such frameworks with a discourse of hemispheric citizenship."[76] Spanish fantasy heritage as a cultural form operates as a particular practice of citizenship, outside of legal and juridical frameworks.

At the same time, in the context of American literature more broadly, Carrillo's fiction reveals his attempt to inscribe the Mexican origin community into state history in ways that do not require assimilation. Reading the stories of old California multilingually enables a more complete version of how state cultural history was the site of racial and ethnic competition. Carrillo's stories openly contest the disavowal of Mexican heritage that the California fantasy heritage attempted, with considerable success, to enact. *Cuentos Californianos* lays claim to cultural inclusion as a necessary prerequisite for California to obtain state's rights and a first step toward the state's eventual granting of political citizenship. The contest over Mexican American manhood in California puts into conversation multiple locations and discursive arenas (national, regional, local) that are collectively and intersectionally formative.

In a different context, Rosa-Linda Fregoso has described the "ways in which fantasy heritage represented the phantasmagoric convergence of racial, economic, and cultural domination in the region."[77] Fregoso examines early Mexican and Chicana/o film history to make a case for the contradictions inherent in cultural genealogies that rely exclusively on Chicano movement models of interpretation and that often neglect conflicting representational politics of early Mexican American culture. What is so fascinating about Carrillo's work is how he uses fantasy heritage itself as the very site to make visible the contradictions of civic participation. Carrillo, who had a vexed relationship to both his home and adoptive countries, is both a participant in and demonstrates the limits of transnational cultural belonging. The cultural objects discussed in this chapter, although informed by Mexican, U.S., and Mexican American cultures, are only legible within a nation-based and regionally specific cultural economy. Including Carrillo in American literary history underscores the need for new interpretive models that account for multiple linguistic and national affiliations obtained across historical moments.

3

Expatriate Citizenship

Manhood, México de Afuera, and Josefina Niggli's Step Down, Elder Brother

The world moves, and the future is already yesterday.
—Josefina Niggli, *Step Down, Elder Brother*[1]

In 1953, Metro-Goldwyn-Mayer released the film *Sombrero*. Starring Pier Angeli, Yvonne de Carlo, Vittorio Gassman, and—most famously—the debonair Ricardo Montalban, the film portrays a trio of love stories set in a quaint and picturesque Mexican mountain town.[2] The amorous entanglements cross class lines and flout inter-village feuds, but the film never fully realizes its ambition to portray Mexico sympathetically, let alone realistically. Full of tropical scenery, stock representations of Mexican characters, and dance numbers worthy of the best of mid-century Hollywood, the film addresses the racial and class complexity of Mexico's mestizo identity, yet tries to remain innocuous in its presentation. It chooses a romanticized vision that refrains from taking an overtly political position, instead giving a panoramic overview that highlights the technical achievement of Technicolor film. For its U.S. audience at the onset of the Cold War, the film offered an escapist fantasy of Mexican life, a relief from the tensions surrounding the communist scare in full force at the time. The film notably divests the revolution-era Mexican village from any association with social upheaval or socialist leanings.

With its light-hearted approach, the film is a far cry from its source material *Mexican Village* (1945) by the author and playwright Josefina Niggli, despite her work as screenwriter on it. Critics largely panned the film adaptation of Niggli's play, with one *New York Times* critic describing it as a "jumbled, tedious blob."[3] Part of its failure is the film's dissociation from its original source, and particularly from the transnational context of its creation. *Mexican Village*, like much of Niggli's work, came

Figure 3.1. Still from film *Sombrero*, from author's personal collection.

out of the lived experiences and cultural repercussions of the Mexican Revolution, a pivotal event in the development of both Mexican and Mexican American cultures. In 1910, after a period of unprecedented economic expansion and the consolidation of power in the hands of a relatively few elite, Mexico erupted into one of the most deadly conflicts of the twentieth century. It is estimated that at least one million people died during the Mexican Revolution, with at least that many displaced— the vast majority of whom migrated to the United States.

The Mexican Revolution has traditionally been seen as marking a crisis in both Mexican political and social life, and subsequent historians have regarded the revolution as the formative moment of Mexican modernity. The conflict and ensuing migration would reshape U.S. attitudes toward its southern neighbor, which directly and indirectly reshaped U.S. immigration policy. Where Mexico and other Latin American countries were omitted from most of the immigration legislation of the early twentieth century due to their importance in agricultural labor, the revolution prompted numerous political shifts to control and absorb the influx of people.[4] These immigrants had a profound influence on American life and on how Mexican Americans related to the U.S. nation-state. While the mid-twentieth century saw a rise in assimilationist movements among Mexican American communities, the earlier half of the century saw a more complicated if contradictory correlation between Mexican Americans, expatriate Mexicans, and the United States.

Departing from the tendency to dismiss Niggli as a local color writer, I suggest her novel *Step Down, Elder Brother* (1947) be understood within a tradition of exile and expatriation.[5] This chapter centers on the expatriate phenomenon known as México de afuera and the ways in which it intersected with Mexican American manhood and U.S. citizenship.[6] México de afuera was an extra-nationalist ideology that emerged during and after the Mexican Revolution through which those fleeing civil war came to see themselves as the true representatives of an ailing national identity. A nationalistic ideology intent on return, México de afuera helped organize Mexican American manhood as it gradually evolved from a focus abroad to a more nationally grounded mode of citizenship within the United States for Mexican Americans. México de afuera posed a challenge because it subverted location and residency in its historic attachment to a separate sovereign nation. But in negotiating the differences between life in Mexico and the lived experience in the U.S., Mexican Americans came to see themselves as embodying the privileges and obligations of U.S. citizenship, distilled through both sides of the U.S.-Mexico border.

As Mexican Americans increasingly negotiated the dual pull of binational affiliations, there emerged a sense of manhood I call "expatriate citizenship." As a type of masculine performance, expatriate citizenship consolidated the multiple national affiliations into a gendered form of political belonging that managed separate and at times competing cultures and differing conceptions about what it meant to participate in a collective political enterprise. Where México de afuera has typically been discussed as by and about men, expatriate citizenship expands political participation to both men and women. Through expatriate citizenship, Mexican Americans debated shared democratic values, sharing a moral responsibility with others outside the nation and in a global context. Expatriate citizenship provided a framework for adapting to multiple national projects; though the distinction between Mexican and American was sometimes fuzzy, it contained a generalized sense of obligation to a broader network of social relations that at once exceeded the nation and was confined by it.[7]

Portraying manhood as expatriate, Mexican Americans were ideally positioned to inform their American compatriots of the multiple obligations to national and global societies, possessing insight into the dynamics between countries pursuing different goals and, perhaps more importantly, the dangers of a state's inability to live up to its ideals. Expatriate citizenship displayed a cultural and civic logic particular to the U.S. context—but saw the U.S. as one among a community of nations and democratic states. The process and the mode of political affiliation acknowledged the seeming contradiction between domestic and foreign, between native and immigrant, but turned such distinctions into political and social strength.

Expatriate citizenship as a mode of political and cultural belonging refers to the conceptualization of a citizen's obligation to and rights derived from a state and how that civic relationship is performed in a variety of publics. México de afuera enabled deep affective and institutional connections to both Mexico and the United States, but Mexican Americans, connected to the national cultures of both, were increasingly invested in their status as U.S. residents and citizens.[8] This was different than the emotional attachment to a nostalgic Mexico famously captured by the Mexican crooner Jorge Negrete ("México lindo y querido") since Mexican nationalistic ideals, often with the (hopeful but unlikely) intent of return, gave way to U.S. political activism and engagement. Expatriate citizenship became a way of infusing U.S. social and political life with a transnational perspective and more global agenda on issues such as civil rights. The writers, thinkers, and activists described in this chapter maintained their connections to Mexico and Mexican culture in the U.S., but those connections increasingly structured their political lives within a U.S. nation-state.[9] Expatriate citizenship reflects how domestic issues are informed by global events, shaped by and for local and national matters.[10]

As Mexican Americans sought to reconcile overlapping or conflicting national agendas, they developed a gendered political belonging that portrayed men as the strongest defense of civil society within a specific national context. In the print culture of the period, democratic values were often associated with manhood, linking ideas such as equality and freedom with masculine attributes like fraternity and brotherhood, although the discourse itself was open to both men and women. Informed by the ideas of expatriate citizenship, Mexican American men and women actively participated in these debates as ethnic Americans contributing to the country's political discourse. This conception of expatriate citizenship emerged alongside articles covering U.S. politics, government policies, and international events from a U.S.-national point of view. Moreover, it stands in contradistinction to the rhetoric of aggressive, overly sexualized masculinity common in white manhood at that time, which scholars such as Gail Bederman or Clifford Putney have described, and also stands apart from the rhetoric of white manhood abroad described by Amy Kaplan or Kristin L. Hoganson.[11] In part, this requires a logic of accumulation, or a logic of accretion, where the fragmentary archive allows only glimpses into the lives and writings of Mexican Americans, yet collectively amasses hundreds of thousands of artifacts that speak to prolonged and sustained engagement with the U.S. national project.

Thinking of México de afuera in this way, not solely as an extranationalist ideology but as a method of public participation informed by transnational political developments, illuminates how Mexican Americans saw themselves as U.S. citizens and how they engaged with U.S. social and political life, especially during a period when the U.S. began to conceive of itself as a global superpower. Mexican Americans operated on the fulcrum between rights and privilege, between supposedly inalienable legal guarantees of membership and the enactment of those rights that manifest instead as a kind of tenuous privilege. Participation was often rooted in a sense of "being a man," yet for many México de afuera writers, that shared investment was limited by a strict disciplining of gendered spheres. Niggli, responding to this shared sense of displacement and reinvestment, used this form of manhood to assert the rights of citizenship (for herself and more generally, Mexican Americans) that had previously been only available to men.

México de Afuera and the Politics of Exile

During the first half of the twentieth century, the U.S. confronted a surge in immigration and changing demographics. Whether it was the migration of southern blacks to the U.S. North, or from southern Europe to the U.S., "the masses of immigrants flooding America's cities [. . .] threatened to wash over American manhood and dash their hopes for self-making," so that "racism, antifeminism, and nativism fed off these fears, as though by excluding the 'others,' gender identity could be preserved."[12] The interwar years also saw a rush of nativist backlash, often in social Darwinist form. The 1910s and '20s saw the publication of Madison Grant's *Passing of the Great Race* (1916), Lathrop Stoddard's *The Rising Tide of Color* (1920), and Homer Lea's *The Day of the Saxon* (1912), as well as the blockbuster success of D. W. Griffith's *Birth of a Nation* (1915). Within this flood of immigration and against the tide of immigrant backlash, Mexican Americans worked to represent themselves as part of the United States.

México de afuera, as an extra-nationalist ideology of return, enabled civic participation for those living outside the boundaries of the Mexican nation-state. In the great upheaval of the years during and following the Mexican Revolution, a significant portion of Mexico's educated and intellectual class fled the political persecution and violence of their home country for the U.S. These people would settle across the United States, in the metropolitan hubs of New York, California, and Texas, with many taking up residence in towns just north of the Mexican border. These immigrants maintained a strong association with Mexico, both through economic ties and affective connections. Many of the immigrants arrived from conservative Mexican circles, bringing these ideals into Mexican American public life, and these immigrants came to see themselves as the arbiters of Mexican cultural values.[13] As part of this assumed role, they developed cultural venues and performances, and established newspapers and other print media to circulate ideas of what they, individually and collectively, deemed proper Mexican culture.

Through print culture, exiles can indirectly but nonetheless intimately experience national participation, what Juan Bruce-Novoa called "vicarious participation in a Mexican national project, even when that project was no longer the official one of a country going through rapid change."[14] Spanish-language newspapers in the U.S. and newspapers in English for the Latino community provided a crucial vehicle for the articulation and maintenance of cultural values. In part, the Mexican Revolution enabled a renewed sense of unified national identity by forging a collective national consciousness in favor of democratic reform, ideas that carried over into the U.S. México de afuera print culture. As the exile population gradually became integrated into existing Mexican American populations and mainstream U.S. life, they brought with them the knowledge of diverse forms of civic participation and gendered belonging. They would regularly publish creative and opinion pieces alongside current events and advertisements, fiction and poetry sharing space with news reports and political stories. Readers consumed these simultaneously, and they fast became a primary means of cultural production and a substantial force in the creation of Mexican American communal values. This is not to say that the ideas presented were uniform, and there was a broad scope of political and social values, ranging from religious and conservative to nationalist to left-wing anarchist. What remained consistent across the broad spectrum of values presented was the distinct sense of nationalism, even as that nationalism took different forms and differing attachments to the U.S. Alongside the conservative thread running through México de afuera was a concern with the rights and responsibilities of an individual to both place and country.

Newspapers and magazines were published in both Spanish and English, but often the linguistic difference served as a marker of which community the papers served. For example, *La Revista Mexicana,* founded in 1915, and *La Revista Ilustrada de Nueva York,* founded in 1882, sought to translate the illustrated magazine format popularized by leading periodicals such as *Harper's Weekly* for a Latino audience.[15] The Spanish-language weekly *La Prensa* (~1912–24), *La Opinion* (1926–present) in Los Angeles, and the daily *La Prensa* (~1913–62) in San Antonio were more oriented toward the immigrant communities and recent arrivals, and included essays as well as close coverage of current events in Mexico.[16] In contrast, *La Voz del Pueblo* (1889–1924) in New Mexico (see chapter one) or the earlier *El Clamor Público* (1855–59) were directed at more long-standing, permanent Latino communities. Nicolás Kanellos, a prolific chronicler and scholar who helped shape the current field of Latino literature, distinguishes between the immigrant press (written for newcomers) and the native press (intended for long-standing residents), stating that immigrant literature writes in the language of the homeland and "reinforces the culture of the homeland while facilitating the accommodation to the new land."[17] This literature—short stories, serialized fiction, journalism, often later published in book form—gradually developed into a political and social ideology not of return but of permanence, interrogating the ideals and adopting the language of the U.S.

Countless stories of immigration emerged among those who travelled, were exiled, or eventually relocated to the United States during these years. These stories of immigration intersect in important ways with stories of the Mexican Revolution, which forms its own genre or period in Mexican literary history.[18] Perhaps the most famous example of a novel of the revolution is Mariano Azuela's *Los de abajo* [*The Underdogs*], published serially in 1915 in the newspaper *El Paso del Norte* and which chronicles the exploits of Demetrio Macias as he fights in and is subsequently disillusioned by the Revolution. Azuela's novel is considered the first in the genre, with other famous works such as those by Martín Luis Guzman or José Rubén Romero to follow, and many critics consider the genre's last entry to be Agustín Yáñez's *Al filo del agua* (1947). These novels circulated widely in Mexico and in the Spanish-reading communities in the United States. Many have subsequently been translated into English, and provide a useful counterpoint to the stories of México de afuera.

In the United States, portrayals of the revolution evolved into stories of exile and immigration, such as the Colombian Alirio Diaz Guerra's *Lucas Guevara* (1914), often considered the first Spanish-language immigration narrative in the United States, or Conrado Espinosa's *El Sol de Texas* [*Under the Texas Sun*] (1927) that narrates parallel stories of successful and failed integration into the U.S. nation. Among the more well known of these stories, many of which have been recovered and/or republished over the last two decades, is Daniel Venegas's serialized novel *The Adventures of Don Chipote, or When Parrots Breast-Feed* (1928). Venegas warns of the perils of immigration and, from his perspective, the damaging cultural effects of exposure to American life. Like Espinosa and Guevara, Venegas describes how the journey north to the United States perverts men and highlights the dangers of the modern metropolitan industrial centers. Having experienced the abuses of the American immigrant labor system, the men return to Mexico, but not to warn their Mexican compatriots of the difficulties of such migration: "Instead of returning to his own great land to tell the God's honest truth about what happened, he twists [the story] around when he returns, recounting stories to others and riling up all those that will listen."[19] There is little integration between the Mexican and American characters in Venegas's story, as the interactions between the protagonist and Americans end with the protagonist unable to sustain himself and morally corrupted by the "loose" American value systems.

The plot supports Venegas's exile position, neatly summarized at the beginning of his novel:

> We don't want to deny that a few compatriots may have made something of themselves in the United States, but they, like a needle in a haystack, are the minority. But the majority go to the United States only to waste all of their energy, get abused by the foremen, and humiliated by that country's citizens, so that, as soon as our countrymen reach old age, they are denied even the right to work in order to feed their own children.[20]

The novel thus explicitly portrays U.S. culture as a corrupting influence, offering the shield of Mexican nationality as a palliative to the perceived degeneracy. Still, the "sueño del retorno," that dream of returning to a homeland, is mediated through a desire for full integration into the United States that pivots on the possibility of citizenship, denied by "that country's citizens" who choose to exclude and exploit Mexican origin peoples.

Mexican expatriates who espoused an ideology of México de afuera frequently retained their status as both citizens and nationals of Mexico, but even such staunch adherence to previous nationality slowly eroded and evolved. Various nationalities and nationalisms interact within a nation-state, changing the composition and ideology of both.[21] Citizenship denotes legal status within a political community designated by birth or through naturalization, demands allegiance, and typically offers the protections of the state. Nationality also denotes allegiance to a particular political community (often congruous with citizenship), and while it may signal a specific legal status, it can be more generally understood as a social category of affiliation, an affective state or a sense of belonging. Nationality implies an attribute describing a relationship to the State, whereas citizenship invokes rights and responsibilities given to nationals of a State. Nowhere is the distinction between nationality and citizenship more pronounced than in the issues around immigration.

When an individual immigrates, they are often required to renounce citizenship in their former nation in order to accept that of their current home state. However, the renunciation of citizenship from a former nation-state is not necessarily equivalent to the renunciation of one's nationality. Frequently, individuals retain national affiliations long after they officially renounce citizenship. Still, in the contemporary legal environment, the terms have been rendered nearly synonymous legal categories, with few exceptions. In the U.S. context, official status as a U.S. national is now restricted only to the outlying territories of American Samoa and Swains Island. Previously, Puerto Rico fit under this category (until March of 1917 when the Jones-Shafroth Act granted Puerto Ricans citizenship), as did Guam, the U.S. Virgin Islands, and the Philippines at different moments in history. While the usage of nationality as a legal category still exists, it was far more prominent in the early twentieth century. However, as a marker of ethnic or cultural identity, the distinction between citizen and national remains a powerful determining force. Often, it is out of this fissure between citizen and nation that U.S.-based categories of ethnicity emerge. Even the U.S. Department of State recognizes that "nationality is a status that is personal to the individual," cannot be determined by parental consent or demand, and must be intentionally forfeited.[22] Thus, somewhat vaguely, U.S. law continues to acknowledge that an individual may be a national of more than one country.[23] Expatriate citizenship is also distinct from dual citizenship commonly associated with multiple nationalities. In the latter, individuals maintain obligations to two nation-states that hold roughly equal weight in terms of legal status; as I use the former, national obligation is directed toward one country, but movement, mobility, and cultural exchange are unconstrained.

Bridging the gap between the novel of revolution and the immigration novel is Luis Pérez's *El Coyote, The Rebel* (1947). His narrative of the revolution generically lies somewhere between fiction and autobiography, and Pérez retells the events that led him from San Potosí, Mexico, where he was born in 1904, to a career as a high school teacher in Los Angeles. Before his immigration to the United States, Pérez served as a child soldier in the Mexican Revolution, an experience that he recounts with a straightforward approach appropriate to the child protagonist. In a lighthearted and almost conversational tone that seems at odds with the severity of the events, the novel covers the experience of the revolution, yet it was only published in the United States several decades later by Pérez, by then an American citizen. As Lauro Flores points out in his introduction to the republished edition (2000), the novel retains an optimistic tone and seems committed to adaptation and acculturation into life in the U.S., somewhat at odds with the disillusionment found in the work of many México de afuera writers.[24] In fact, the novel's final scene involves the character undergoing the process of naturalization.

The protagonist Luis Pérez is very eager to gain U.S. citizenship, most immediately for the possibility it affords of joining the ROTC unit at the public high school, membership that he sees as both necessary for and demonstrative of recognition as a national member. The protagonist links education to citizenship, stating, "One of my greatest desires was to take my second citizenship papers on or about the same time I would graduate from high school."[25] He reiterates the point a few pages later, saying citizenship "represented one of my very greatest desires" (*El Coyote, The Rebel* 163). The novel leaves unresolved whether the protagonist will marry his sweetheart, as perhaps expected in romance or other popular fictions, instead choosing to end the novel with a scene of naturalization, or "one of us" (165). Admission to the United States involves a "very rigid examination of the Constitution" and a ten dollar fee, after which the novel thus ends buoyantly, with "the climax of a perfect today, and the beginning of a new tomorrow" (165). For Pérez, the path to citizenship seemed burdensome but desirable and attainable, an endorsement of the legal processes unavailable to so many immigrants.

Citizenship in the Native Press and Beyond

Pérez's experience was perhaps atypical, but this brief reading of a few paradigmatic examples of México de afuera identifies how the extranationalist ideology inscribed Mexican Americans in opposition to or as transient members in the U.S. nation. Still, these texts do not represent the range of experience captured by the term "México de afuera"; other writers expanded the reach and possibility of México de afuera. One of the more successful and active of the native press was *La Crónica*, published in Laredo, Texas, by Nicasio Idar and his family beginning in 1909 and continuing through most of the subsequent decade. It had broad influence and circulation among the Mexican American communities of the U.S. South, though the Idars were neither immigrants nor exiles, but rather long-term residents of South Texas.[26] Idar was born in Point Isabel, near Brownsville, Texas, was a member of numerous mutual aid organizations, and was deeply connected to the region (his daughter, Jovita Idar, became an early leader of the Mexican American women's rights movement). Idar and his family organized on behalf of the U.S. Mexican-origin population, taking on what José Limón calls a "campaign of journalistic resistance," eventually marshaling a large conference known as the Primer Congresso that brought together numerous civic groups in order to strategize on how best to advocate for the Mexican American community and its rights.[27] Through *La Crónica*, the Idar family became champions of anti-segregationist policies and specifically of discrimination in the school system, offering alternative school models to combat Mexican American exclusion.

In one of the "discursos" that came out of the Primer Congresso Mexicanista, J. M. Mora notes that "en la Fraternidad se encierran todos los deberes del hombre" [in Fraternity there is inscribed all the duties of man].[28] As was common in the nineteenth and early twentieth century, civil rights were entwined with a conception of manhood and the imagined affiliation across gendered belonging. While one might make a case for the universal claims propelling "los deberes del hombre," in the patriarchal culture of tejanos such civil liberties often split along gendered lines. Still, the phrase inevitably recalls Thomas Paine's influential pamphlet of the same name. Unlike Paine's *Common Sense*, which spoke directly to the U.S.-revolutionary context, *The Rights of Man* responds to the French Revolution to take up democratic ideals in a more abstracted, global context. Of concern here, to borrow Paine's words, are the principles and practice of government and how they became accessible within gendered language of citizenship.

Some years before the Primer Congresso, the Idars' newspaper called for a particular form of citizenship for and from the Mexican origin community. From the very beginning, those involved in the conflict understood that both countries and their citizens were mutually implicated in the struggle. An editorial observed, "En el espiritu de esos principios va envuelta la hermosa y eterna verdad: PROGRESSO; porque bajo las condiciones existentes en este Estado, envuleve un germen que dará por fruto los sagrados derechos del hombre y del ciudadano, y porque en la fuerza de la Instrucción y de la Unión, descansa nuestro porvenir" [Wrapped up in the spirit of those principles is the beautiful and eternal truth: PROGRESS; because beneath the conditions of this State, lies a seed that will give fruit to the sacred rights of man and citizen, and through the force of instruction and unity, lies our future].[29]

Although authorship of the editorial was never ascribed, one of the Idar family members or an associate who represented the newspaper's political views likely wrote the piece. The author draws on Mexican political ideals in order to advocate within a U.S. context. Calling for cross-border solidarity, the writer implores his audience (imagined as "los mexicanos en general, ciudadanos o no, de este [U.S.] país" [Mexicans in general, citizens of the U.S. or not]), "Tenemos el deber de instruirnos y unirnos [. . .] instruídos y unidos, sabremos conquistar la justicia y el derecho, seremos factores componentes de un pueblo libre de intereses unidos y reciprocos" [We have the right to educate and organize ourselves [. . .] educated and unified, we will know how to conquer justice and right, we will be crucial pieces of a free people with united and reciprocal interests]. For the author, manhood and citizenship were firmly intertwined, public aspects of a national and political character. In his conception of citizenship, the writer imagines an intellectualized man, one who conjoins practicality with idealism:

No viviran eternamente en un amorfismo intelectual, lucharan contra las tinieblas enervantes de la ignorancia, buscaran la luz para fortalezer el cerebro, desarrollarán la fuerza de sus brazos en las lides del trabajo, y una vez armados de tan exaltadas cualidades varoniles, quedrán cenidos dentro el circulo de los mas aptos; se sobrepondrán, obtendrán completa representación politica y social.

[They would not live in amorphous intellectualism, but would fight against the weakening forces of ignorance, searching for light to strengthen the mind, they would put the strength of their arms to work, and at once fortified by such exalted qualities of manhood, would land within the circle of those most capable; thus situated they would obtain complete social and political representation.]

The full attainment of either characteristic, of political empowerment and social participation, would be achieved by the intellectual pursuit and acquisition of manly virtues, in each case mutually dependent conditions of public life. Echoing something like W. E. B. Du Bois's notion of the "talented tenth," the author centers on the laboring individual who finds inspiration from the "light" of knowledge that then leads to the "circle of those most capable." The idealized man proposed here would rise up from within an embedded community, and using such knowledge and ability could achieve political representation. The author describes that, despite the fact that "vivimos en un atmósfero envenenada por la pasíon animal" [we live in an atmosphere poisoned by animalistic passion], many people of Mexican origin hold public office, federal jobs, and prestigious commercial posts and that "tenemos los privilegios, garantias en la vida privada y pública, iguales derechos que los demás ciudadanos" [we have the same privileges and guarantees in private and public life as other citizens].

The author offers unity and social organization as the best avenue to full social access, saying that the only way to combat racism and exclusion is "dentro de la ley y con el derecho legítimo de ciudadanos que nos asiste, como lo hacen las otras razas" [within the law and with the legal rights of citizenship to help us, like other races do]. Here, the confluence of manhood and the discourses of citizenship imagine an avenue to social progress and public life. The connection only makes sense within the United States, where "seria indigno de un hombre honrado predicar doctrinas nocivas contra el pais en donde ha nacido y que reconoce como patria o que le da albergue y protección [. . .] hacemos lo posible por gobernarnos en conformidad con los sublimes derechos que nos concede la Constitución de este pais" [it would be undignified for an honorable man to preach harmful doctrines against the country where he was born and that he recognizes as homeland or that offers him hospitality and protection [. . .] we do our best to govern ourselves according to the sublime rights that the Constitution of this country endows]. Contrary to the understanding of Mexican Americans as immigrants or temporary residents uninvested in the nation, native Spanish-language newspapers demonstrated a deep commitment to the political structure of the United States. The political allegiance comes out of birthplace, choice ("que reconoce como patria"), or out of the refuge that the United States provides. The author alludes to a self-discipline that aligns with the political values of the United States and the desire for political belonging regardless of nationality.

The evolution of México de afuera into a mode of citizenship was not exclusive to the native press. *La Revista Mexicana*, an illustrated magazine aimed at exiles and refugees of the revolution, devotes a three-page spread translating a speech by 1916 Republican presidential candidate Charles Evan Hughes, which includes a full-page portrait. A former governor of New York, Hughes was a respected progressive thinker, later Secretary of State (1921–25), and influential Chief Justice of the Supreme Court who tended to support civil liberties (1930–41).[30] He narrowly lost the election that year to the incumbent Woodrow Wilson, but in later roles would become tremendously influential in American public life.[31]

The speech reprimanded the Wilson administration for not upholding the promise of the U.S. democratic values through its ineptitude regarding consular and diplomatic appointments. In Hughes's opinion, one ambassador (Herrick to France) served as "la personifcación de valor, de la templanza, de la habilidad para obrar, entre la confianza y el afecto del mundo entero" [the personification of bravery, of self-restraint, a strong work ethic, with the trust and admiration of the whole world], yet was removed because of political infighting. It was "inexcusable de sacrificar el interés nacional ante componedas de partido. Fue un sacrificio lamentable de una reputación internacional" [inexcusable to sacrifice national interest for party interests. It was a regrettable sacrifice to a national reputation].[32] Hughes "propongo que hagamos de nuestras agencias en nuestras relaciones internacionales, algo digno del nombre americano" [proposed that we make the agencies of our international relations worthy of the American name] and laments the current tensions with Mexico.[33] Implied is a comparison between state affairs in and with Mexico and the global context in which the U.S. finds itself during World War I. In this election speech, Hughes attempts to unify the nation (both Anglo and Mexican Americans), downplaying if not outright dismissing segregationist and imperialist agendas. Hughes regrets the current state of affairs in Mexico, blaming the U.S. for abstaining from diplomacy and cooperation and instead relying on military and political intervention, expressing "un hondo sentimiento de humilliación [a deep feeling of humiliation]. He calls the Mexicans "conciudadanos" [fellow citizens] and reprimands the Wilson administration for invading with no clear purpose (a rhetoric familiar still today regarding the role of the U.S. in global stability).

Hughes further accuses the Wilson administration for meddling, not just by failing to recognize the Huerta administration (then sitting president of Mexico) but for actively striving to unseat him, openly condemning the administration for intervening militarily and politically, asking "con que asombro deben de haber visto los mexicanos que asumíamos sus derechos para manejar sus asuntos interiors" [what disdain must the people Mexican have had when we took over their right to manage their own internal affairs].[34] Here, Hughes is referencing the Tampico Affair and subsequent occupation of the Mexican port of Veracruz by the U.S. Navy in 1914.[35] The emphasis on the Tampico Affair and subsequent occupation of Veracruz became a test case for U.S. intervention abroad, both hemispherically and globally, and in his speech, Hughes calls the occupation a "mascarada de política internacional!" [a masquerade of international politics].[36] Hughes's critique of Wilson's interventionist agenda under the guise of the Monroe Doctrine (in Spanish) decenters the U.S. perspective on international affairs within the context of a U.S. presidential political contest. In doing so, it educates its Spanish-language readers about their own participation in U.S. political life and the implications that such participation has for their networks in Mexico.

Hughes invokes the Democratic Party platform of 1912, which stated that government action need "recognize the equality of all of our citizens, irrespective of race or creed, and which does not expressly guarantee the fundamental right of expatriation. The constitutional rights of American citizens should protect them on our borders and go with them throughout the world, and every American citizen residing or having property in any foreign country is entitled to and must be given the full protection of the United States government, both for himself and his property."[37] The official position of the Democratic Party offered a broadened sense of U.S. citizenship, one with domestic and international protections, a point that the editors of *La Revista Mexicana* keenly observed. Hughes was committed to Progressive reform and the increased role of a centralized administrative state in shaping American social life; he would later cement his legacy as champion of Progressivism and civil rights through his support of the New Deal policies. His stance on liberalism and individual rights were at once familiar and a useful entry point into U.S. political debates. That his speeches were translated into Spanish and became a model for manhood details the ways in which Mexican Americans engaged with U.S. political life.

A New Constitution and Constituting New Men

Perhaps unwittingly, Hughes's own position overlaps with emerging developments in Mexican political life. In its expression of U.S. citizenship, the print culture of Mexican expatriates exhibits a concern for social rights and racial equality, borrowing from the ideals fueling the revolution and that circulated during the Mexican legal revision resulting in its Constitution of 1917. At the same moment that the U.S. was implementing contradictory policies restricting immigration and enacting protections for immigrant Mexican workers due to labor shortage during World War I, Mexico was undergoing a project of political and legal change that included the development of a new constitution.[38] Approved on February 5, 1917, under the administration of Venustiano Carranza, the *Constitución Política de los Estados Unidos Mexicanos* substantially revised the earlier federal Constitution of 1857 that governed national life for decades. Whereas the 1857 Constitution established many of the basic rights for its citizens, the Mexican Constitution of

1917 was the first in the world to lay out specific *social rights*, in addition to those of equality and suffrage. The Constitution allowed for private property, but took particular care to inscribe rights for the indigenous, poor, and socially marginalized, an outcome of the nation's ongoing revolution. These social rights thus further enabled full participation in civic life, including codification of the right to free, state-sponsored education (a radically progressive move at the time) and the right to free labor, a reaction to the debt peonage system in effect previously. The Constitution of 1917 restricted the power and reach of the Catholic Church in public life, and also redistributed land among the Mexican population, out of the hands of wealthy hacienda owners and foreign investors, nationalizing certain mineral rights and natural resources. It also sought to regulate maximums on daily labor and to set fair wages for all workers. Within the lengthy first chapter, which describes "las garantias individuales" [individual rights], are the privileges pertaining to Mexican citizens. One article lifted restrictions on individual mobility, assuring "todo hombre tiene derecho para entrar en la República, salir de ella, viajar por sus teritorio y mudra de residencia" [each person has the right to enter the Republic, leave it, travel through its territories and move their residence."[39] Additionally, the Constitution of 1917 changed the requirements and mechanisms for naturalization, allowing for *jus soli* (right of the soil), which is now regularly (and often pejoratively) described in the U.S. as the "birther" option, whereby citizenship is obtained by birth within the territorial jurisdiction of a nation. These terms, among others, sought to dissolve the old feudal system and establish a new, democratic structure of government.[40]

The same concerns for social rights and citizenship found in the Mexican Constitution of 1917 informed the debates in the newspapers and press in the United States. The issues raised in the drafting of the Constitution of 1917 surfaced alongside those in U.S. political debates, and México de afuera's negotiation of multiple nationalities provided a model for a developing U.S. globalism, placing the achievement of democratic ideals in a global context. The debate over the Mexican Constitution and the desire for social rights spoke readily to the concerns of the U.S.-based Mexican-origin communities, for whom access to those rights was continually in jeopardy. Regarding the New Mexican State Constitutional Convention, one columnist explicitly links manhood and citizenship, stating that both political parties "represent the ideal citizenship of Colfax County, both as to manhood and ability."[41] Given the familiarity with oppression and the suppression of political rights that so many Mexican immigrants endured, they entered U.S. public life ready to critique the abnegation of those rights and demand their instatement. Rafael de la Huerta writes that laws should be structured to "poder rescatar, los dones de todo ciudadano que se precie de serlo: Libertad, Justicia, y Ley" [be able to rescue the gifts of every citizen that claims to be one: liberty, justice, and law].[42] These accounts attempt to inscribe the various inalienable rights inherent in the figure of the citizen, and the privileges issuing thereof.

Adjacent to an article advocating for the establishment of "Agrupacion Protectora Mexicana" [Mexican Protection Groups] to protect against racial violence, such as an incident of a savage beating of a Mexican in a pool hall (in which the Mexican was assaulted because "en su casa no se permitia jugar a los mexicanos" [in my house Mexicans aren't allowed to play]), Feliciano Perez writes, "Instruccion civica es el conjunto de conocimiento que debe tener todo ciudadano, ya respecto a los derechos que le corresponden, ya respecto a los obligaciones que debe tener para con la sociedad en que vive y para con los individuos que forman esa misma sociedad" [Civic education is the body of knowledge that every citizen should have, with respect to the accompanying rights, with respect to the obligations he should have with the society in which he lives and with the individuals that form that same society].[43] Perez imagines a society connected by a mutual investment in civic life, united by the obligations that derive from equality before the law. His notion of society extends beyond the Mexican American community, but is limited by society's inability to legislate against racial violence.

Others were more critical of the U.S.'s support for social injustice. The Los Angeles newspaper *Regeneracion* reports that in commemoration of Mexican Independence Day, the Los Angeles school system honored President Díaz (whose regime the U.S. supported) through a system of programs and celebration. According to John Kenneth Turner, who writes against the institution of chattel slavery in Mexico, these programs "constituted a blow to freedom, to common decency, to the general idea of political progress such as has seldom been dealt through the public institutions of a republic. [No one] having any respect for his revolutionary forefathers and their Declaration of Independence, revering the principles upon which this [U.S.] republic is supposed to have been founded" would consent to the celebration of such despotism.[44] Turner's editorial, published less than two months before the first violent conflict of the revolution, reveals a tension in U.S. perceptions of their southern neighbor. On the one hand, Mexico was the site of significant foreign investment for U.S. businessmen, for which the U.S. supported the Díaz regime. On the other hand and at the same time, the inequality created by the Díaz regime enabled a critique of Mexico as slaveholding, undemocratic, and "barbarous." This inconsistency created an uneasy partnership between Mexican revolutionaries and anarchists and U.S.-based, left-leaning activists.[45]

In "An Open Letter to the President of the United States of America," published simultaneously in English and Spanish in the expatriate newspaper *La Prensa,* the author harshly criticizes the U.S. for, "vaunting avarice and vaulting ambition," allowing its greed to sustain injustice in Mexico.[46] The columnist reminds the reader of the United States' own relationship to the hemisphere, subtly critiquing the interventionist and colonial processes that enabled the current situation. The columnist makes global assertions of nations that develop as "a virile force capable of assertion" in response to tyranny, where "every nation and every people will of necessity, shape its welfare." Mexico exposed herself to foreign investment

> all the time feeling that the integrity of her institutions and her rights of sovereignty were sufficiently guarded by the comity of nations and the treaty pacts existing between the Republic and other Powers, whose nationals might find domicile or hospice within her borders. It was never surmised nor contemplated that the hour should ever arrive when those who had come from other countries in search of material gain, [had] sought and obtained the benefits of our resource without the burdens of citizenship.[47]

The column exposes how many who entered Mexico in search of financial gain reap the privileges of economic gain without submitting to the obligations that such belonging requires. The article relies on global ideals of democratic citizenship that proffer equality before national law and under the assumption of mutual recognition among "the comity of nations." Deferring to a notion of Westphalian sovereignty in which international law extends equally to each nation, the author rebukes those who separate their civic duty from their desire for personal financial gain. The author stops short of indicting foreign investment and capital accumulation, but insists civil responsibility takes precedence over those practices, exposing a hypocrisy between universal civic duty and the reality of its national materialization.[48]

One of the most famous and visible proponents of México de afuera was Nemesio Garcia Naranjo, who would be found guilty of breaking neutrality laws for his vociferous critiques of U.S. political figures. Garcia Naranjo wrote "El Otro Centenario" for San Antonio's *La Prensa* on September 18, 1921, which was republished a few weeks later in Los Angeles's *El Heraldo de Mexico* (October 4, 1921). Garcia Naranjo stresses independence as a national trait, lauding how despite numerous attempts to subjugate the nation, "nuestra nacionalidad cumple sus primeros cien años, dueña de sus destinos" [our nationality turns a hundred years old, master of its destiny].[49] In a moment of centennial patriotism, Garica Naranjo promotes "la unión entre mexicanos y mexicanos," between Mexicans of all types, races, and citizenship, calling to all, "hay que ser hermanos" [we must be brothers], and as brothers "podamos lucir la fraternidad soñada por el Liberatador" [we can achieve the fraternity dreamt by the founding fathers].[50] The fraternal call with which Garcia Naranjo hopes to inspire would motivate a unity of all Mexicans—exile, immigrant, and native—an idealized end in itself, but such desires were undermined by the contradiction that was yet unresolved. This call to brotherhood sought to unite all Mexicans and México de afuera would lay the seeds for community organization, but its orientation toward Mexico limited its practicability. Garcia Naranjo asks for a return to a nostalgic and somewhat idealized past, desiring "la llegada de un momento sublime como el de 1910, que dará margen a muchas explosiones brutales, pero qu determinará la resurrección de la Pataria que nació hace un siglo" [the arrival of a sublime moment like in 1910, which gave rise to many brutal explosions, but that would enable the resurrection of the homeland that was born a century ago].[51] Speaking from the U.S. about Mexico, Garica Naranjo pleads for a return to peace and order, and for the promise of the nation-state as the guarantor of individual rights and social stability. In an essay covering the centennial celebrations of 1921, Garcia Naranjo decries how past atrocities are being used to justify current injustice, how the memory of conflict "se ha recordado para declarar lógicos los modernos saqueos del constitucionalismo" [is recalled to declare the logic of the contemporary pillaging of constitutional rights].[52] At stake here, as in many of the other writers I discuss, is the desire for the confluence of national identity and the rights of citizenship in order to achieve social equality. But here, that argument turns on the feasibility of memory to mobilize the present, a hope that sustained many living in exile but did little to achieve real gains in their social rights. Alas, the promise of the return was never fulfilled, and for Garcia Naranjo and most of his fellow México de afuera writers, Mexico would continue to exist as only an imaginary promise of a better future.

Josefina Niggli and the Limits Of México de Afuera

The writers associated with México de afuera had a widespread and lasting influence on Mexican American culture and the conception of expatriate citizenship, but the impact of the phenomenon extended beyond tightknit Mexican American cultural circles. U.S. writer Josefina Niggli's novel *Step Down, Elder Brother* draws on this expatriate ideology but reaches for new audiences and offers a way of understanding the complicated confluence of manhood and citizenship that shaped Mexican American national cultural life. For Niggli, manhood departs from the idealism of México de afuera, from universalized discussions of liberty and civil society, and instead invests in the practical matters of constructing social relations across class and national lines.

Niggli was writing in a moment when Mexican modernism had reached its zenith, and the vogue for all things Mexican, often depicted as romantic primitivism (arguably like in the film *Sombrero*), was a national phenomenon.[53] Yet unlike those American Modernists (the so called "last generation") who fled to Europe in the years around the World Wars attempting to escape and repair their disillusionment with modern American life, critics label Niggli's work as local color and provincial, and overlook her expatriatism.[54] American modernist writers saw in their travels an antidote to their cynicism toward American democracy and the possibility to reflect critically on their home. While this is in part true for her novel, Niggli's experience, and Mexican American expatriate citizenship more generally, served a slightly different purpose. It was not about leaving or fleeing one's home, but about entering into it, examining a national space refracted through global obligation for the specific social circumstances at work there. Expatriate citizenship consolidated nationalist forms of gendered belonging.

Yet as a writer, Niggli maintains an uncertain presence in both Latino aand American modernist literature, a status that comes as much from her fiction as from her unusual biography. Niggli was born in Hidalgo, just outside Monterrey, Mexico, in 1910, the same year the revolution began, to a Swiss Texan father and an Irish-German American mother. Three years later, because of the violence affecting the region, she and her family moved to San Antonio, Texas. She would move with some frequency between northern Mexico and Texas, later to the University of North Carolina where she earned an M.A. in playwriting, to Hollywood where she worked as a screenwriter, and ultimately back to North Carolina where she taught drama until her death in 1983. This complicated biography makes her difficult to claim according to standards of indigeneity or mixed-race popularized by both José Vasconcelos and the essentialist ideas of the Chicano movement. Niggli's perambulations more closely align her with the exiles and native writers who propagated México de afuera.

Regarding her writings, critical accounts, such as Elizabeth Coonrod Martínez's thoroughly researched biography or Gloria Anzaldua's description of Niggli's border consciousness, most often describe Niggli as a "local color" writer of "folk drama," and as a writer who sought to complicate U.S. understandings of Mexico beyond the "barbarous Mexico" prevalent in the early century.[55] Certainly, Niggli self-consciously styled herself as a more nuanced spokesperson for Mexico and its people. These and other critics offer compelling and insightful readings of Niggli's work that grapple with her own identification as well as the content of many of her works.[56] Niggli is most often associated with drama and folklore, and certainly the film adaptation of her successful novel has been lumped into the local color category as a depoliticized account.[57] In their discussion of the film, William Orchard and Yolanda Padilla identify how the Mexican American community's idea of itself was beginning to shift and evolve, and under the control of Hollywood studios, "the story of Mexican Village's adaptation into *Sombrero* reveals how the dominant culture of the United States worked to suppress references to the revolution in the cultural production of Mexican Americans; it also reveals how Mexican Americans themselves repressed aspects of their community as a new political image began to form."[58]

Critics—Niggli's contemporaries and continuing to the present—praise the novel for its depiction of Mexico: the Mexican city of Monterrey, Mexican indigenous practices, Mexican post-revolutionary class structure, etc. The novel was reviewed in the *New York Times*, where Charles Poore gave it a positive if tepid review, providing "some memorable insights into Mexican life."[59] Immediately (including in Poore's review), critics focused on the novel's depiction of Monterrey and its inhabitants. Martínez praises Monterrey as the "star" of the novel "in its historical transition immediately following the Mexican Revolution" and for Niggli's "geographic precision" in its portrayal.[60] Monterrey was established in 1596, making it among the oldest settlements in North America, but it rose to prominence centuries later as a link between Texas and the Mexican capital and as an industrial hub both urban and frontier. Because of its proximity to the border, it was a site for foreign investment and U.S. capital throughout the *Porfiriato* and post-revolution. As such, it is a useful test case for U.S. economic expansion into Mexico that parallels similar moves being made during the early twentieth century across the hemisphere in the Caribbean and in Latin America. Monterrey provides a site through which U.S. readers could deliberate on their own nation's place as an emergent global superpower and the contradictions posed between exported democracy, its attendant rise of capitalist economies, and multifaceted citizenship.

In Niggli's time and beyond, the city represented the challenges of transnational commerce and culture. Juan Mora-Torres has shown how Monterrey and the larger surrounding region in "Northern Mexico became a permanent zone in which the economies and cultures of two nations that were in many ways worlds apart engaged each other."[61] Monterrey's temporality is oriented to the future, shedding the weight of its revolutionary past and casting itself as a site of progress and industrialization. The progressive image of Monterrey found in Niggli's fiction has a factual counterpart, as various civic organizations sought to market the city as such. For example, the *Monterrey Greeter*, a promo-

Figure 3.2. Cover of *The Monterrey Greeter*, 1938, from author's personal collection.

tional booklet published by the Asociacion Mexicana Automovilistica [Mexican Automobile Association] touted the city's proximity to the U.S. as an invitation for tourism, as well as its modernized infrastructure, including the Pan-American Highway system.[62] The pamphlet is mostly informational, including statistics on industrial production, e.g. "annual tonnage shipped" or the "number of sewage connections," and advertising for the city's businesses, but like the novel, it promotes the city's commercial potential as a dialectic between past and present, one that capitalizes on its history to tout its progress.

For scholar Emily Lutenski, the novel locates authentic Mexican-ness in the its "spatialization" of Monterrey, where "Mexican identity is a spatial category" grounded in residency within a specific national space. Lutenski states, "In retheorizing the Mexican as a geographical category, Niggli grants herself access to this contested terrain: she is not [. . .] a Chicana, but she is, indeed, a Mexican, emerging—like the crops in Santa Catarina—from the Republic."[63] Yet if "spatialization" becomes the grounds for nationality, surely Niggli lays equal claim to her own status as American or Mexican American. The problem of categorization is partially resolved by reading Niggli as a late example of the exilic tradition, providing a bookend to México de afuera. I suggest that rather than reading the novel as only about Mexico, it should be considered a novel about Mexican American culture: an allegorical take on the binational experience of early-twentieth-century Mexican American life. The novel meditates on the challenges of migration, the change in social status for its characters, and the possibility of integrating immigrants into a nation, as much for those residing north of the border as for their neighbors to the south.

Despite being bilingual, Niggli chose to write in English, a choice indicating her intended audience. By Kanellos's definition, immigrant literature like México de afuera is written by first-generation migrants, in the language of the homeland, but by writing in English, Niggli sought entry into U.S. literary markets as a U.S. writer. (Certainly, by the time of Step Down, Elder Brother's publication, she had made a career for herself as a U.S.-based writer and playwright.) In subject matter and in her personal life, she never fully detached from her connection to Mexico, but wrote as an American writer with familiarity of U.S. literary histories. Step Down, Elder Brother depicts the drama surrounding a wealthy family in Monterrey, and so stylistically, it recalls the work of Edith Wharton in its depiction of characters struggling with the obligations and privileges of upper class life in an urban setting, or even Louisa May Alcott's dramatization of social restrictions on women. Yet in both of her novels, Niggli chooses a male protagonist through which to tell the story, a decision which locates her within the tradition of the immigrant novel that typically follows a male's journey from Mexico to the U.S.

The novel's concern with history, and more precisely historical memory, is paramount here, although the narrative tension is provided by the class antagonisms between the Vasquez de Anda family and the conflicts their desires bring. The family confronts inherited class restrictions as impediments to their own personal fulfillment, and these are ultimately resolved through various romantic reconciliations (and fallouts). In these ways, the novel fits in with some of the prevailing Mexican cultural concerns following the revolution, the discourses of mestizaje and the re-forging of class structures. The plot itself is rather convoluted, worthy of a contemporary remaking as a telenovela or TV mini-series. The novel centers on the upper-class protagonist, Domingo Vasquez de Anda, eldest son of the family and next in line to inherit the family's real estate business. As the elder brother, Domingo is expected to take responsibility for his siblings and their actions, an obligation he shirks: "It would seem that everything in this house is my responsibility. I want none of it"; nonetheless, as a dutiful son, he assumes these obligations.[64] Domingo's younger brother Cardito (a law student) impregnates a family servant, Serafina, which triggers a fatherly instinct in the older brother to shelter the younger. One of the Vasquez de Anda sisters, Sofia, has fallen in love with another employee of the family, the chauffeur and salesman Mateo, and the two conduct an illicit romance that is eventually exposed and results in marriage. Of all the characters, Sofia (a wonderfully wrought, elusive character) is the most self-aware of class distinction, and uses that knowledge to transcend the shackles of history that would otherwise restrict her life. These affairs dramatize the class dynamics at various levels and between nearly all of the characters.

Domingo has two passions in the novel: medicine and the city of Monterrey. The former is displayed mostly as a frustrated desire to help others, his family and those living in the city of Monterrey, and marked by bitterness that he was unable to pursue this calling due to the insistence of his Uncle Agapito, the "stern elder brother," a position they both share (*Step Down, Elder Brother* 124). His passion for his native town emerges in detailed accounts of the architecture, geography, and topography of the city. As future patriarch of the family, Domingo is expected to enter the family real estate business, which he rebuffs.[65] Domingo never fully recovered from a dissolved romance with an American girl, which left her "North American and he was Middle American (5). All this changes, however, when he meets a mysterious photographer's assistant, Márgara Barcenas. Márgara's past is clouded in constant perambulations across the globe due to her father's unknown role in the revolution. Much of the novel's suspense comes from the mystery surrounding the Barcenas family's connection to the Mexican Revolution, which Domingo desperately searches to unravel.

Because of his interest in the history of the revolution, Domingo is literally handed a visual representation of the masculine heritage from the revolution, "a graphic history of the revolution from nineteen hundred to nineteen hundred and forty" known as the Casasola Collection (81). The collection captures Domingo's imagination, as "there was a something about these photographs that lighted up a memory and yet the memory itself was too nebulous for capture" (81). In the collection of photographs is one of Domingo's grandfather (with whom he shares a name) standing with the German ambassador during a centennial celebration in 1910. The collection of images from the revolution becomes the final authority on the subject, providing the clue Domingo needs to unravel the mystery of Márgara's father (eventually revealed to be an aid to the deposed and brutal Mexican president Victoriano Huerta) and connecting the novel to Niggli's Hollywood career through its visuality.[66]

It is the graphic collection of photos of the revolution that poses the biggest threat to the safety of Márgara and her father. Domingo warns her, "Wherever Mexicans gather together in a group you will find copies of it [the collection]. Even if you went to San Antonio, or Denver, Los Angeles, or New York, there would still be copies of the Casasola collection. Every man who ever fought in the revolution wants to own that series" (191). According to the novel, the Casasola collection, found across the United States, comes to represent the revolution, or at least the memory of it, seized upon by Mexican Americans as both nostalgic history and justification for their departure from the country. But for Niggli, the memory of the revolution is a stumbling block of history, an impediment to full incorporation into U.S. society and life. It is a recurring, simmering presence that threatens to disrupt the status quo, the possibility of growth, rendered here as romantic attachment or masculine attributes.

The Practicality of Expatriate Manhood

According to scholar Claudio Lomnitz, one social consequence of the Mexican Revolution was the "giddy realization that a new state was being shaped and the concordant sense that a new citizen, even a "New Man," needed to be molded for the occasion."[67] As a figure of manhood, Domingo serves as a liminal character, tethering the traditions and stability of older generations with the independence, class mobility, and commercialism of the younger, characteristics often associated in the novel with American influence. For example, the father of Domingo's betrothed (not Márgara but the daughter of another wealthy Monterrey family) hears a rumor of a servant's pregnancy and naturally assumes that the child is Domingo's. He has no problem with his future son-in-law's promiscuity, stating he "would not want my daughter married to anyone less than a true man" (263). Here, at least for the older generation of the novel, "true manhood" is synonymous with sexual conquest and virility, attributes stereotypically associated with masculinity in both the U.S. and Mexico. Yet Domingo did not commit the indiscretion, nor is he particularly interested in sexuality. Instead, Domingo considers himself and is in fact recognized as a "man with brains, not brute force," championing a more introspective, intellectual, and thoughtful manhood (321). Domingo and Mateo, his working class employee, serve as foils to each other, offering opposing ways to reconcile their manhood by channeling the ideals of México de afuera.

For many characters in the novel, chief among them Agapito and Mateo, "practicality" is a virtue and a mantra. The novel explicitly links pragmatism and social development: "This was the 1940s, the age of the practical man, of social progress" (326). In contrast to Cardito's "unpredictable" nature (143), even Serafina, when determining her unborn child's future, claims that she should be responsible and raise the child, that "one must be practical about these things" (142). Recalling the association between practicality and idealism in "Esfuerzo Supremo," practicality is defined as a necessary masculine attribute and requisite for success in the increasingly commercialized space of Monterrey. As a move away from the utopian ideals of liberty and equality, practicality signals an understanding of shifts in historical circumstance; it moves away from the vitriol, zealousness, and idealism of the revolution and instead privileges levelheadedness and a commitment to existing social structures. The novel suggests not economics but predictability and reliability as defining qualities of manhood, because they stand in contrast to the zealousness that justified so much violence just decades before.

Practicality fuels social mobility, most apparently in Mateo. In part, Mateo, like "other men who had built Monterrey into an industrial power," is characterized as "completely ruthless," possessing a raw strength that the more pampered, "delicate, overbred" upper classes cannot compete against (316). The threat of that savagery is tamed by his practicality. Mateo echoes the narrow vision of Uncle Agapito and his quest for financial gain, yet curbs this desire by stating "ambition is of no worth if it is not practical" (97). For Mateo, practicality is a virtue, for whom "every peso contains one hundred centavos" that only come into existence through "work, hard work" (98). Mateo is described as loyal, "ambitious, practical, and in love with the power of land" (228). Mateo's desire to sell real estate is more than utilitarian, moneymaking ambition. For Mateo, real estate signifies a connection with land, with history, and with the authority that comes from it to anchor oneself into place and society. As he explains it, "To own ground, I could think of nothing more wonderful than owning a piece of ground" (225). To Mateo, cultivating land, as a farmer or as urban development, is "like being God" (225). Domingo supports Mateo's ambition, installing him first as his chauffeur and then quickly promoting him to salesman, which he explains as an "office investment," reminiscent of the kind of patronage seen in George Bernard Shaw's *Pygmalion*. Domingo is torn between wanting to help Mateo succeed and his own attachment to the inherited class structures, which in this case threaten to view individuals as a commercial interest. He remains skeptical of Mateo's suitability for inclusion among the Monterrey upper class, but gradually concedes that his individual accomplishments speak more forcefully than inherited class positions.

Part of what Domingo finds so discomforting is how Mateo embodies "all of Uncle Agapito's philosophy—all of Monterrey's philosophy, rolled up in a paragraph. In a sentence really [. . .] no room for dreams" (98). Passion, the frustrations of which Domingo has internalized and repressed for years, are to be subsumed to practicality, and desires are left for recreation, as pastimes. Domingo dreams of pursuing his passions, recklessly abandoning social convention, but he is bound by these duties. Despite his desires, he is painted as logical, a thinker, intelligent: his fiancée Veronica says he is "always looking for the reasons behind an action" (83). Later, he worries that his emotional attachment to Márgara would make it so that "no application of cold logic would be possible" (67). Such rationality serves as a counterpoint to the "barbarism" and savagery associated with revolutionary Mexico. Domingo is ever preoccupied, somewhat rhetorically, by "thinking of history, Veronica, and why men do the things they do" (83).

There is a persistent sense that the revolutionary zeal has faded and the idealism that fueled it is no longer relevant to the lives of the characters. One character, a general in the Mexican military, proclaims this loss of idealism, how he "shall be sorry to see their generation disappear. We'll never have another that is so—innocent" (102). Domingo realizes the growing influence of the U.S. and its capitalist ideals, wondering "why it never occurred to him before that the children of Mexico were passing, and in their place were coming the new adults represented by Mateo Chapa: the practical men who achieve their objectives without bothering with the nonsense of childish plans" (102). The novel expresses a lament for an alternative mode of being that is fading, of a passing existence focused not on profit and the connection to the northern neighbor but of art, self-improvement, and fickle fancy. Still, the distancing from the revolution is seen as a sign of progress for the "frontier city" of Monterrey (104).

Among the Monterrey elite with whom Domingo associates, history, and in particular the revolution, is a recurring topic of conversation. During one such nostalgic trip to revolutionary Mexico Domingo "suddenly felt himself cut off from [the men]. The names they spoke [. . .] were only history-touched names to him, but to these men the names were labels for three-dimensional beings who moved in the shadow world of the past that was not his past" (82). Despite the long-standing economic and social bonds that shape these kinship networks, the relationship to history and continuity can no longer sustain them. Those that cling to the past seem lost to Domingo, playing with shadows in a world far removed from the novel's present. Discussing the major players of the Mexican Revolution, Domingo states, "These men are dead. They only touched the fringes of our world. What they did was evil, but we can't help that, and we should not be asked to pay for their evil" (190). The novel disavows the importance of the revolution, despite the prevalence of the Mexican Revolution in popular national and expatriate memory. Approaching mid-century, when the novel was both written and takes place, the memory of the revolution is already a relic fading from memory. Memory itself becomes unstable, and the characters have difficulty representing history, confronting its fragility as it faces an ever-encroaching future.

By the end of the novel, Monterrey's social world has been upended and new alliances are forged across class lines. Sofia marries Mateo, happy in her new position as head of household, and Mateo successfully leads the Vasquez de Anda real estate firm. Serafina relocates to a nearby village, where she gives birth to a healthy boy, Catarino, though she dies tragically in childbirth. Cardito, seemingly ignorant of his brother's sacrifices, is free to pursue his dreams of education and law school. The romantic resolution is partially undone by Domingo and Márgara's storyline, which concludes with a dramatic chase to the U.S.-Mexico border. Márgara's father Bárcenas (who is a trained doctor, only adding irony to Domingo's frustrated ambitions) delivers Serafina's baby, but then, in what can best be described as post-traumatic stress disorder, Bárcenas takes the baby and flees to Laredo in a panic. Bárcenas unwittingly reenacts his previous flights and goes "back in his mind to the early days so that all he wants is escape," condemned to repeat the past (362). Learning of his irrational flight, and making clear they "did not want to be faced with a charge of illegal entry to the United States," Domingo and Márgara rush to stop Bárcenas before he reaches the border (366). They reach the border, steps behind the crazed Bárcenas, but unable to overtake him. Traversing the border in search of her father, they hear emanating from some nearby revelry an old song of revolution (thought to be "Adios Mamá Carlota," a motif repeated numerous times throughout the novel). The song is punctuated by a gunshot, for the memory it recalls drives Bárcenas to take his own life.

All the other characters in the novel are firmly grounded in place and time, but Bárcenas floats freely temporally, historically, and geographically. He is the novel's exilic figure, fleeing the revolution after having been, we later learn, falsely accused of complicity in Huerta's violence (363). His original expulsion from Mexico led him across the globe, to London, Los Angeles, Denver, Oklahoma City, Dallas, Brooklyn, Paris, and elsewhere, before returning to Mexico.[68] What ends his exile, returning him to Mexico and Monterrey, is that "here there is progress. Here there are eyes to the future, no languishing memories of the past" (190). After decades of exile, Bárcenas longs to return to his native land, a sentiment familiar in the writings of México de afuera. When at last he returns, he remains unable to fully separate himself from the past, which haunts him as a prolonged paranoia that culminates in this frenzied flight to the border. If the dream of the expatriate is to return, Bárcenas demonstrates its impossibility. The imagined past no longer exists.

A meditation on the past, and its potential futures, is a recurring theme throughout the novel, a point on which numerous characters remark, and the novel plays with the idea of temporal displacement. In the final scene, Márgara mourns her father's death and Domingo secures the child, and the text concludes with a dispute over what future might be allowed, and where. Margara wants to flee to the U.S., but Domingo refuses, saying that he and the child must remain in Mexico. Unlike Márgara, who "never had a country [but is] only a name written on the pages of history," he insists that the child be raised in a national environment tied to geographic space, emphasizing national specificity as imperative in the construction of history (373). Yet nationality only functions in its attachment to a specific national territory, outside of which Domingo fears will lose its power. This is a familiar trope of México de afuera, one that is disturbed by the novel's treatment of history. Where the novel earlier offers the aphorism that Mexicans only believe in two things, "peace in the cemetery, and wealth from the lottery," Catarino inspires in Domingo a faith in "the future of our children" (374). The future here is important both for its potential for individual achievement and for disconnecting from the encumbrances of the past. Domingo earlier scolds his uncle, "The past is dead. You are standing still now, and the city is flowing forward without you" (354). Márgara and Domingo are unable to reconcile their different views on the future, and the novel separates them at the end. Márgara heads into the United States, while Domingo returns with Catarino to Monterrey, rationalizing his decision as a debt owed to the child, "a debt greater than any promise made to you, than a man can make to any woman. It is a debt to the future, from me who have failed in the present" (373). Márgara spent most of her life fleeing with her father, desperate to escape his past. Yet finally freed from his past, she chooses to go to the United States, where she sees her future. Indicating the rush of time forward, the novel repeatedly ignores the burden of history, instead orienting itself to the present and future.

Despite the divergent paths Domingo and Márgara choose, Niggli seems aware of how each nation is inexorably linked to the other, dramatized by their blind groping as they strive to negotiate the cliffs along the border: "She had forgotten him in her desperate attempt to reach her father, just as he had forgotten her in his anxiety for the child. But his hand on her arm fastened them together, held them back when they both wanted to run, linked the each to the other in a bondage neither wanted" (366). The two are forever linked, each pushing the other forward, yet with mutual history forever binding them together. Domingo demands that the child be given a choice to his future, adamant that "he'll be what he wants to be, not the product of a plan" (372). In the context of México de afuera, his insistence on individual choice suggests the incompatability of old ideas with the current world. The individual takes precedent over communal obligation, yet regardless of his desire for a free future, Domingo cannot completely detach himself from the past. Despite his unwavering love for Márgara, Domingo chooses the baby Catarino, since "there is no love so great as the love of a man for his son," even if the son is not biologically his own (372). Domingo's decision to remain, his renunciation of romantic resolution, may be read as a failure on his behalf, an unwillingness to relinquish the privileges of his position. Domingo pleads with Márgara to remain, but she adamantly states that she can't live in Mexico: "'It is not my country. The customs here are strange to me. I don't understand them.' She gestured with her chin toward to the International Bridge [leading to the U.S.]. 'That's my world across the river'" (371). Márgara better understands the need to imagine their future in the United States, a point lost on Domingo, whose lingering patriarchal attachments cloud the possibilities of a unified future. But Domingo's dilemma, caught between a desire to begin anew in the United States and an obligation to remain in Mexico, is also a recognition of the historical and impending movements between these spaces.

The novel's treatment of Monterrey and the surrounding region offer a narrativization of what Mary Louise Pratt has called a "contact zone," the "social spaces where cultures meet, clash, and grapple with each other, often in contexts of highly asymmetrical relations of power."[69] While her theorization of the contact zone is best remembered for the idea of cultural interaction, it is also "intended in part to contrast with ideas of community that underlie much thinking about language, communication, and culture."[70] For Pratt, the contact zone was as much about cultural movement between distinct communities that may have more or less in common. Monterrey and its inhabitants that star in the novel exist in a contact zone with the U.S. and Mexico, caught in the current of separate nationalisms. The future that Niggli imagines is one unhindered by the demands of expatriate nationalism, but rather invested in the immediate temporality and geography of the present. Her characters proclaim, "We are the frontier and if we stretch out our hands, we can touch the future" (241). Niggli's novel of the revolution is at least as much about its aftermath, especially for those expatriates like herself that were attempting to make sense of their status as U.S. residents and citizens, situating México de afuera as a U.S. cultural movement. Reading Niggli as an expatriate writer inverts this debate about the border and residency. Domingo's claims to futurity, made in a novel written in English for a U.S. audience, reorient the Mexican American community toward the U.S. nation-state. Niggli writes in a tradition of exile, but for a U.S.-based Mexican-origin population. In the inverse reading I suggest, Domingo's return to Monterrey remains connected to the land and its inhabitants, minimizing the dream of return in favor of connectedness between spaces.

Niggli capitalized on her popularity to present Mexican American manhood for a U.S. audience beginning to imagine its relation to Mexico in terms of migration and flow. Practical manhood forces a recognition of the limits of universalized, utopian idealism often found in the discussion of citizenship, where manhood here is a phenomenon of place, influenced by its connections and attachments to multiple nationalities. Expatriate citizenship provides a blueprint for how Americans could relate to the state in an increasingly global climate, a kind of mirror warning of the dangers of racial and class stratification and the failures of social incorporation. Expatriate citizenship helps elucidate how Mexican social and legal developments and its conception of citizenship travel to the United States. In contrast with the idea of México de afuera as a distinct and unified community, the novel critiques its utility for Mexican Americans. Niggli offers a counterpoint to the uses of history that we see in many of the writers of México de afuera, but is nonetheless continuing in that tradition. For Niggli, Mexico provided a national cultural identity separate from the territorial attachments to her place in the United States, enabling a "practical" manhood connected to but critical of U.S. democratic capitalism. In the next chapter, I examine how ideas about citizenship and manhood were further connected to ideas about work and labor in the early twentieth century.

4

Economic Citizenship

Labored and Laboring Manhood in Américo Paredes's George Washington Gomez *and Jovita González and Eve Raleigh's* Caballero

On October 28, 1929, after a decade of sustained growth and prosperity, the U.S. stock market dropped more than 13%, followed by another 12% decline the next day, marking the start of the Great Depression, the deepest and longest economic contraction in the nation's history. Over the next several years, U.S. stocks, as measured by the Dow Jones Industrial Average, would lose over 80% of their value, not to return to their pre-crash values until the 1950s. Thousands of banks would shutter their doors, and millions (an estimated 25% of the U.S. workforce) found themselves without jobs. The economic crisis affected the nation at a scale previously unimaginable and shook to the core the nation's faith in its political-economic system. Critics debate whether the stock market crash precipitated or was a symptom of larger structural problems with the U.S. economy, but the crash nonetheless signaled a turning point for the U.S. economy that invited larger questions about the stability of capitalism and democracy.

From 1929 until the end of World War II, the nation, reeling from the economic collapse, undertook prodigious and unprecedented measures to remedy the breakdown. For turn-of-the-century white men, "in place of the scramble for wealth, men were advised to return to more stately and Protestant virtues, such as industry, usefulness, and thrift," characteristics that recalled earlier ideals of self-sufficiency and the value in manual labor.[1] As poverty skyrocketed, the kind of wealth generated by financial markets seemed at odds with and even a feminizing influence on the republican virtues of simplicity and hard work. The presumed health and progress of the American economy on which American manhood depended took a direct hit during the Great Depression. Like in other times of great national upheaval and change, this period saw a rise in nativist sentiment, and many of those affected by the economic collapse—jobless, destitute, and hungry—tried to salvage their dignity by shifting the blame onto and seeking solutions through the exclusion of racialized others. At the nadir of economic decline, the *New York Times* reported on "several vexing social problems growing out of the presence of Mexicans and Spanish-Americans" that prompted proposed legislation to deport them, since "a great deal of bitterness against these people has developed since the Depression. If they have been employed, they have been accused of taking work which rightfully belonged to natives, and of lowering living standards by working long hours for small wages" (rhetoric about immigrants and American industry still prevalent in contemporary discourse).[2] Employers now refused to hire "foreign" workers on which they had previously relied; many Americans sought to deport Mexican and Mexican American workers in hopes that it would free up jobs and create economic opportunity, alleviating the tremendous pressures all workers and families faced. In a moment of transnational cooperation, the Mexican government, in efforts led by President Lázarao Cárdenas, actively recruited Mexican nationals, particularly those with experience in agriculture, incentivizing their return through land and capital. These efforts successfully reduced the number of Mexican Americans living in the United States; between 1929 and 1936, anywhere between 500,000 to 1.5 million Mexicans and Mexican Americans (many of whom were American citizens) repatriated to Mexico, either voluntarily or through forced removal.[3] While the repatriation movement reversed the post-revolution immigration trends into the U.S., Mexican Americans who remained in the U.S. faced a difficult situation.

As historian David G. Gutiérrez has shown, there was a "growing sense among many U.S.-born Mexican Americans that the recent arrivals represented an economic threat. Despite cultural affinities Mexican Americans may have felt toward immigrants from Mexico, as their numbers grew, many Mexican Americans began to worry that the recent arrivals were depressing wages, competing with them for scarce jobs and housing, and undercutting their efforts to achieve better working conditions."[4] Moreover, the growing number of Mexican immigrants contributed to the racialization of Mexican Americans as temporary and disposable working-class and unskilled laborers, since "most Americans did not recognize any meaningful distinctions between a Mexican born in Mexico and a Mexican born and raised in the United States. Mexicans and Mexican Americans, however, were well aware of the many regional differences that had long characterized Mexican society."[5] Mexican Americans found themselves caught between a rock and a hard place, in the midst of a national economic retraction and rising hostility toward immigrants that threatened their place in the nation. By one account, the political and economic climate of the Depression "forced many [white] men to abandon their faith in the marketplace as certain to confirm their manhood," requiring them to redefine masculinity to favor inner qualities over monetary success.[6] While such sentiments may have been true for white American men, the historical conditions of Mexican Americans, including their racialization as "foreigners," presented different challenges not easily remedied by performing these masculine attributes or behaviors.

This period produced two important Mexican American cultural texts, both written in Texas at the height of the Depression, although they did not see publication until the 1990s. As part of the nationwide effort to recover the cultural production of Latina/os in the United States, scholars discovered and reissued Américo Paredes's *George Washington Gomez* (1990) and Jovita González and Margaret Eimer's (writing under the pseudonym Eve Raleigh) collaborative *Caballero* (1996). These texts join the works of Josefina Niggli, Maria Cristina Mena, María Elena Zamora O'Shea and still-emerging others as fictional narratives written by Mexican Americans during the interwar period, a time of significant social change in Mexican American communities. Although Paredes's and González and Eimer's texts are relatively recent additions to Mexican American literary history, they provide powerful accounts of Mexican American life in the early and mid-twentieth century, especially in the state of Texas where they were both written.

Paredes and González and Eimer imagine a productive Mexican American participatory manhood, within the nation and within norms of citizenship. The two novels represent national citizenship based on local organization and political cooperation. Other forms of masculine behavior, such as the bandit or the expatriate, were unsuitable to the Depression-era climate and could not constitute the premise for citizenship; rather, Mexican American manhood during this period relied on economics to position Mexican Americans as productive citizens. Linking manhood and citizenship, Paredes and González and Eimer deploy Mexican American manhood to conjecture how communal collaboration and economic activity can underwrite local and national development. Rather than depend on the state to bestow citizenship (which requires legal declaration of competence defined by intellect, race, gender, or otherwise), these authors make civic and economic participation itself the precondition for citizenship.

Downplaying "the heroic mode of cultural resistance" or the "mythic hero of the corrido tradition," *George Washington Gomez* and *Caballero* replace the near-century-long association between Mexican American manhood and extralegal violence with community-wide economic participation.[7] As Alicia Schmidt Camacho observes, "Economic development doubles as a project in subject formation," and, as in these texts, one that is inseparable from the gendered constraints placed on it.[8] Here, I examine minor or marginal characters in their capacity to authorize alternative social relations as a condition of manhood that complicates dominant national narratives during the interwar period. The novels' authors held disparate views about the political climate in which they wrote and the direction Mexican American culture was heading; nevertheless their novels reveal a similar position for Mexican American manhood—that of economic citizenship made visible through a strategy of marginalization. Economic manhood embodies pragmatism, frugality, industriousness, discipline, and independence as virtues and as prerequisites for political participation, directly intervening within national discourses about masculine virtues that were seen as the province of white men. Either as a call for gendered equality (as in *Caballero*) or a lament for the passing of patriarchal authority and the influx of national U.S. culture on Mexican American culture and society (as in *George Washington Gomez*), both texts make claims to national citizenship through participation in the marketplace that draw on but do not exactly reproduce broader, mainstream cultural ideas. These qualities not only serve the economic interests of Mexican Americans, but also undercut racial assumptions about the ability and transient nature of the Mexican American working class. This alternative manhood underwrites Mexican American claims to U.S. citizenship and their place within American cultural history as productive citizens.

In identifying this figure of Mexican American manhood as economic citizenship, I draw upon historian Alice Kessler-Harris's work on women's rights. In her excellent analysis of how gender influences social policies, Kessler-Harris demonstrates that "achieving the formal political equality guaranteed by suffrage did not pave the way to economic equality."[9] Despite the formal guarantee to vote, the policies that governed the marketplace, suffused with concerns over a woman's status as national citizen, found ways to keep women, particularly married women, confined to the domestic space. Kessler-Harris uses the term "economic citizenship"

> to suggest the achievement of an independent and relatively autonomous status that marks self-respect and provides access to the full play of power and influence that defines participation in a democratic society. The concept of economic citizenship demarcates women's efforts to participate in public life and to achieve respect as women (sometimes as mothers and family members) from the efforts of men and women to occupy equitable relationships to corporate and government services.[10]

For Kessler-Harris, economic citizenship conjoins the legal structures that govern access to equality in the workplace and market with the social and cultural ideas that expect women to act in particular ways. In working toward economic citizenship, women sought to secure not just equality in the workplace, but also to transfer that power to their personal lives and the public domain, where gendered ideologies circumscribed political participation.

I borrow Kessler-Harris's term "economic citizenship," but offer a revised definition of it. Here, economic citizenship similarly refers to the conjuncture of gendered labor and political participation, but by focusing on Mexican American manhood, I reframe it within the context of transnational labor flows and as responding to Mexican American patriarchal culture. Economic citizenship in a Mexican American context distinguishes between transitory labor of immigrants and the economic participation of long-established Mexican American communities, whose social incorporation was too readily dismissed through association with migrant labor. Reflective of lived conditions and imagined (but not imaginary) social relations, Mexican American economic citizenship counters social discrimination through the possibility of economic integration and advancement, and offers a counterpoint to the increasing marginalization of Mexican Americans as unskilled or transitory laborers.

Changing Conditions of Mexican American Labor

The form of manhood these authors developed was in many ways a response to decades of economic development and migration patterns on both sides of the U.S.-Mexican border. These novels were produced in a moment when the Mexican American population as a whole, influenced by powerful community leaders and organizations such as the League of United Latin American Citizens (LULAC), shifted toward more accommodationist or assimilationist positions with mainstream white American society.[11] Among a generation of pre–World War II Mexican Americans that fostered assimilation, Mexican American culture (speaking Spanish, for instance) was a private matter to be practiced at home and kept separate from public life. This attitude emerged from an early twentieth-century social landscape that was dramatically shifting, and Mexican Americans were forced to denounce earlier violent tactics, most notably seen in the Borderlands War and the failed Plan de San Diego of 1915.[12] The assimilationist impulse was an attempt to preserve Mexican American cultural integrity, property rights, and the safety of a community unable to resist the organized state violence of the earlier decades. In order to avoid conflict, Mexican American leaders during this period urged cultural assimilation, but as John Alba Cutler explains, assimilation "is really a negotiation of cultural change and dynamism taking place on other terms."[13]

While native and immigrant cooperated during the 1920s and at times during the Depression, the economic collapse intensified the divide between Mexican Americans and Mexican immigrants. A combination of disparate but connected events—including political and social unrest in Mexico, the arrival of increasing numbers of European Americans from the U.S. Midwest into the U.S. Southwest and especially Texas, and the

increasing commercialization of agriculture—actively worked to racial-
ize Mexican Americans as newcomers, as recent immigrants suitable for
temporary unskilled labor separated from the forces of production and
devoid of social power. The need for Mexican American labor rose with
the departure of African Americans to northern and coastal cities as
part of the Great Migration.

In the first half of the twentieth century, a large percentage of Mexicans and Mexican Americans living in Texas worked as sharecroppers
or migrant workers with little economic power. While many Mexican
immigrants considered established Texas Mexicans as cultural traitors,
many Mexican Americans similarly disparaged newly arrived immigrants along common nativist grounds. Frequently, Mexican Americans feared that the influx of Mexican labor would threaten their own
job stability.[14] It is worth remembering that many white Americans did
not—and do not—distinguish between Mexican Americans and Mexican immigrants. "Mexican" was simultaneously a racial and national
term that lumped both groups together as non-white. Labor was socially
stratified along an "agricultural ladder" that separated sharecroppers,
tenant farmers, and landowners, and white owners increasingly leaned
on Mexican migrants to provide farm labor. As these labor practices developed, Mexican Americans increasingly found themselves providing
labor for wealthier whites. Still, their role as cheap labor was not always
welcomed. For example, the *Weekly Labor Herald* in Corpus Christi,
Texas, an official union organ affiliated with the American Federation of
Labor (AFL), railed against commercial farmers who sought to open the
border for Mexican laborers, claiming "there is no need for agricultural
workers in this country at this time, as there are now approximately four
million migrant workers in the Unites States, who have difficulty eking
out a bare existence."[15] Organized labor groups in the United States worried that the influx of Mexican immigrants would undermine job opportunities for those already here.

Economic manhood returns to an older natural rights theory that an
individual's relation to the state emerges from property, from individual
ownership and the state's defense of the individual's right to it. Found in
the writings of John Locke and Thomas Paine, the idea that the right to
work enabled public participation was a cornerstone of American political thinking. Correspondingly, Kimmel asserts that "the making of

the American working class was the making of a distinctly white, male, and native-born class," which would have excluded Mexican Americans by denying them the right to work.[16] Through the end of the nineteenth century, Mexican Americans and the comparatively few Anglo Americans worked out a "peace structure" whereby U.S. expansionist policies could be achieved through accommodationist strategies, rather than outright hostility. By the turn of century, technological progress in transportation and agriculture (such as irrigation, refrigeration, and rail systems) began displacing the deeply rooted ranching culture. These changes in the primary modes of production exacerbated racial tensions that had, until then, been managed through various compromises. In 1904, the completion of the railway between South Texas and other rail networks in the U.S. ushered in an influx of Anglo American immigrants from the U.S. Midwest, South, and elsewhere. By the 1920s, the economics and demographics of the region set the stage for significant social change in terms of who controlled Texas society. As David Montejano has demonstrated, farm owners developed new forms of labor controls so that "the farm working class was firmly tied to the land through the use of 'nonmarket' criteria and sanctions, including violence and coercion. Such labor controls set the context for a striking segregation of the races."[17] This sudden shift in both the real economic conditions and the social clout of Mexican Americans, precipitated and aggravated by immigration from the Mexican Revolution, created tensions between Mexican and Anglo Americans and divisions between Mexican American groups.

In his analysis of South Texas, historian John Weber has shown how Texas relied on cheap, migrant labor to grow a rapidly expanding economy that concentrated wealth and capital in the hands of largely white, domestic immigrants from the U.S. Midwest. Weber shows how, "during the first half of the twentieth century, these migrants helped build a thriving agricultural economy that relied on the introduction of outside capital and the availability of migrant workers coming across the border from Mexico."[18] The social conditions that emerged out of this exploitative labor market took advantage of the precarious position of the refugees fleeing unrest in Mexico, but also undermined the power of Mexican Americans living in the region, who began to compete with new immigrants. These economic conditions advanced, cutting away at the social position of Mexican Americans. Consequently, in a climate where all people of Mexican heritage were presumed to engage in unskilled agricultural work, with little access to the mechanisms of capital necessary for the practice of political rights, Mexican Americans were precluded from participating in a public life grounded on economic citizenship. Simply put, since Mexican Americans were presumed to be migrant laborers, grouped as expendable, transitory, or fungible, there was little social ground for political power.

A former Mexican province, an independent republic, a Confederate state, and, since 1865, unable to fully locate itself as either a western or southern state, Texas occupied a perhaps unique position in U.S. geopolitical developments. This unusual history complicated the more familiar racial binary through which U.S. race relations were understood, and the state's racial configuration, especially as it reacted to the pressures of im/migration, challenged the intersection of race, class, and "whiteness" in a social hierarchy. As labor historian Neil Foley explains in his study of multiracial Texas, in a climate where "the overwhelming majority of Texas whites regarded Mexicans as a 'mongrelized' race of Indian, African, and Spanish ancestry" (a far cry from the romanticized fantasy heritage found elsewhere), social possibility was circumscribed by exclusionary racial logics.[19] This was part of a larger trend that saw, by the mid-century but especially after World War II, increasing discrimination against both Mexican immigrants and Mexican Americans workers.[20]

For Mexican American women, racial exclusion was compounded by gendered limitations on political participation. These novels were written at roughly the same time that the first generation of girls eligible to vote in federal elections came of age (women's suffrage became effective at the federal level in August of 1920 after obtaining the necessary state ratifications). Somewhat surprisingly given its often-conservative leanings, Texas ratified the proposed amendment early on, adopting the legislation on June 28, 1919, a full year before its ratification as part of the Constitution. Without economic autonomy, the ability to exercise other forms of citizenship (e.g. voting, which, in Texas, required a poll tax between 1902 and 1966) and social rights is difficult if not impossible.[21] In light of woman's suffrage, these novels offer a further glimpse into manhood's detachment from the foundations of citizenship; yet the reactions and retrenchments that the passage of the Nineteenth Amendment produced indicate a still-contested status for women's ability to exercise full citizenship.[22] Even as Mexican Americans fought for racial equality at the local and national levels, internal differences persisted as to the extent women should participate in Mexican American cultural and political life.[23]

For Paredes and González and Eimer, who utilized familiar genres in the service of Mexican American national inclusion (bildungsroman and romance, respectively), gender is a contested site in scripting national belonging.[24] Critics such as Shelley Streeby, Amy Kaplan, June Howard, Nina Baym and Doris Sommer, for example, have shown how genres (sensational, realist, naturalist, sentimental, and romantic literature, respectively) play an important role in the narrative of nation building by disseminating, rehashing, and reinventing narratives of national culture.[25] Within these familiar genres, the underlying conditions and possibilities of economic citizenship circumvent assimilation as the sole means of social integration. To do so, the authors rely on minor or marginal characters to inform and critique the central characters. Though these minor characters are often overlooked, they allow alternative masculinities that critique mechanisms for social exclusion— both the practice of seeing all Mexicans as temporary residents and the patriarchal forces that limit social opportunity. Attending to the marginal demonstrates the conflicted and often contradictory nature of Mexican American manhood before the late twentieth century, and the ways in which manhood served as a contentious representation of social belonging.

Working toward Manhood: A Coming of Age Story

Although written in the late 1930s, Américo Paredes's novel *George Washington Gomez* remained unpublished for over fifty years. Since its reissue, *George Washington Gomez* has assumed canonical status in Chicana/o literary history. Variously praised for its depiction of the process of Mexican American subject formation, albeit a fractured and incomplete subject, or as an artifact of Texas Mexican society amidst chaotic social changes in the wake of multiple transnational conflicts, the modernist novel is a moving and unsettling account of a young boy's struggle to become a "great man who will help his people" in the face of institutionalized racism.[26] While the novel differs widely in content and genre from *Caballero*, *George Washington Gomez* shares a vision of Mexican American manhood as economic citizenship behind its protagonist's troubling narrative of assimilation. Here, masculine prowess is tied to economic success, and self-making—the achievement of an independent, autonomous, politically potent self—could be had through economic liberation. In the novel, wage discrepancy caused by the Great Depression is dismissed since "everybody knows that a Mexican family can live on two dollars a week with things as cheap as they are nowadays," and Mexican Americans "can't expect to make as much as [the Anglo American] Johnny Mize. His standard of living is higher than yours. He needs more money to live on. You can do with less" (*George Washington Gomez* 200). This passage, focalized through an unnamed farm owner and listed among a number of anonymous observations about the economic conditions of the Depression, exemplifies attitudes of racial difference rendered in economic terms. Economic power was synonymous with self-governance and independence, qualities affixed to cultural norms about manhood. The independence afforded by economic stability and middle-class status was not available to most Mexican Americans.

George Washington Gomez describes the life of the eponymous character, nicknamed Guálinto, raised by his mother and Uncle Feliciano in the early twentieth century South Texas town of Jonesville-on-the-Grande, a fictionalized version of Brownsville. When Texas Rangers murder Guálinto's father Gumersindo, the family moves to Jonesville to escape the violence of the Borderlands War. The aspiration to lead his people weighs heavily on Guálinto and largely determines his fate as he moves through the various institutional and cultural apparatuses that shape his future. At novel's end, Guálinto ultimately chooses to abandon his South Texas community, renouncing his childhood alliances and his name (assuming the Anglicized moniker George G. Gomez, taking on his mother's maiden name Garcia as a middle initial) and spying on his childhood friends as an Army agent assigned to border security.

Son to a Mexican father and Texas Mexican mother, Guálinto straddles the border both biologically and culturally, producing what Ramon Saldívar has famously called a "checkerboard of consciousness." Explicating the process by which a subject is interpolated within a culture or nation, Saldívar argues that since Guálinto is "formed ideationally as a mirror image of the Anglo-American subject and against the traditional Mexican subject, Guálinto becomes the precursor of a new middle class, partially assimilated and wholly alone, the quintessential buffer between Anglo-American and Mexican American modernity" and opting "for the non-heroic path of Americanization and assimilation."[27] Guálinto limits his vision of economic independence to a homosocial, masculine world, acceding to the masculine privilege that enables his success. By masculine birthright and a tacit sense of primogeniture, he is the one destined to become a "leader of his people," without consideration for his sisters or their desires or abilities (40).[28] In the American ethnic context, the bildungsroman novel—a novel of education that typically follows a male protagonist coming to maturity as citizen-subject—is intertwined with racial overtones and questions of assimilation about a minority protagonist finding his place within the U.S. racial hierarchy.[29] However, *George Washington Gomez's* pathway to social incorporation exceeds Guálinto's own journey and describes a community in flux, one grappling to reposition itself vis-à-vis national debates about Mexican Americans, understood through economic manhood and citizenship.

While the bildungsroman emerged in Anglo American literature, among the Mexican American population of South Texas other forms of cultural expression dominated. Until roughly the period when Paredes composed his novel, the corrido was the predominant cultural expression for Texas Mexicans. As narrative ballad, the corrido is a verse form intended for performance or vocal recital. In its content, the border corrido (specific to the region in which Paredes lived) focuses on "the concept of the local hero fighting for his right, his honor, and status against external foes, usually Anglo authorities, [which] became the central theme of this balladry."[30] In her study of queer Chicanidad, Sandra K. Soto sees in Paredes's fiction "rich material about the construction, maintenance, and dissolution of corrido masculinity, which is to say that it gives masculinity historicity," an important node of Mexican American historical manhood.[31] Steeped in the folkloric tradition of South Texas, Paredes established his professional life (and to a large extent the academic study of minority folklore more broadly) with an account of the corrido as the primary vehicle of cultural expression for greater

Mexico in the authoritative *With His Pistol in His Hand* (1958). According to Paredes, "The ideal type of hero of the Rio Grande people [was] the man who defends his rights with his pistol in his hand."[32] Yet following the Mexican Revolution and the Borderlands War, armed violence proved increasingly detrimental to the Texas Mexican community, as state-sanctioned retribution exacted a murderous toll on the Mexican American population. Consequently, the corrido's social force waned as the Mexican origin community diversified and became more internally stratified between class and national (U.S.- vs. Mexican-born) origins. In *George Washington Gomez*, Paredes grapples with both the social changes facing the community and their related impact on cultural expression.

Though saturated in the corrido tradition, Paredes turned to the novel to communicate the conflicts affecting the Mexican American community. Like González, Paredes chose to write a novel in English, addressing a double audience that reaches beyond his immediate locale. The conflict between an insulated Mexican American culture and national participation in Anglo society is captured through the fusion of these literary forms, what Leif Sorensen sees as "illustrat[ing] the failures of the totalizing models of subject formation encoded in both the corrido and the bildungsroman."[33] This conflict, like Saldívar's "checkerboard of consciousness," leaves the novel at an impasse that relies on the corrido hero, but the novel turns to other forms of manhood to realize alternative possibilities.

George Washington Gomez's Multiple Manhoods

Imagining that the text found publication shortly after it was written, a contemporary Anglo reader might have found the narrative a successful bildungsroman of U.S. assimilation. Against other novels of assimilation, Guálinto/George's narrative education is complete; he journeys from ethnic individual to assimilated national subject, although at the cost of his original communal affiliation. George succeeds in Anglo society and suppresses any underlying revolutionary fervor, downplaying (and internalizing) U.S. racialization in favor of national citizenship, "doing what I do in the service of my country" (302). While his actions in the fifth and final part of the text are portrayed as traitorous and inimical to South Texas Mexicans, George's actions are predicated on an understanding of economic citizenship.

Upon hearing of George's return to Jonesville, his old friends Antonio, Elodia, El Colorado, Arty Cord, and La Gata organize a gathering at La Casita Mexicana, a restaurant owned by Antonio and Elodia. The meeting reveals itself to be a meeting of "the executive committee of Latins for Osuna," supporting Mexican candidates for the city government (292). When the group asks George, "a good speaker," to "get the people really fired up" in support of their cause, George refuses because he is "down here on assignment for the company I work for. They won't like it if I engage in local politics" (293). When repeatedly pressed to reveal the name of his company—he is later revealed as a first lieutenant in counterintelligence for Army border security, a de-facto border control agent—George evades the questions before claiming he is a lawyer for a real estate company based in Washington. The friends press him further, accusing him of being in the FBI. George demurs and maintains secrecy, dismissing the cross-examination in one word: "business" (293).

While George admits that "getting the Mexican out of himself was not an easy *job*," it is through economic gain that he achieves "success" (283, emphasis added). He disregards his former friends as "clowns playing at politics," suggesting that their interests would be better served if they "get rid of their Mexican Greaser attitudes" (300). Implicit in his comments, while derogatory and self-deprecating, is a belief that national channels of economic improvement (at all costs) hold the most promise for improving Mexican American social standing. As an agent of the nation-state, George references the inevitability of national integration for the local population. While George's adoption of economic citizenship is detrimental to his community, other characters use a similar strategy while adhering to different beliefs. *George Washington Gomez* proposes several models of Mexican American manhood—in Guálinto, Feliciano, El Colorado, and Juan Rubio—that compete for representation or seek inclusion either communally or nationally. What these characters' manhood share is an appeal to economic citizenship, made visible through marginalization.

While critics read Guálinto as assimilationist because he turns to institutions for personal economic gain without regard for the network that enabled his success, the novel does not fully embrace assimilation.[34] The text is internally inconsistent, even as it presents a strategy of national inclusion. The characters rely on economic citizenship to represent the Mexican American male, but in ways that would have been familiar to a national Anglo readership and that appealed to the Mexican American community's aspiration for national inclusion. Collectively, multiple protagonists rather than a single hero develop a shared ideology of manhood and undergo the process of developing collective identity, decentering the corrido hero as the foundation for Mexican American masculinity.

The historical context illuminates the divergent visions of civic participation. After the passage of the Immigration Act of 1924 (roughly the time in which the novel is set), protectionist "economic arguments posed by pro- and anti-immigration forces were underpinned by very similar assumptions about the racial characteristics of Mexicans" and they "claimed that 'Mexicans' [Mexican Americans] as a whole did not have the education or cultural understanding to meaningfully participate in a democracy."[35] Historian Clare Sheridan shows how claims to whiteness were insufficient to combat the exclusionary practices of the time.[36] In the first third of the twentieth century, Mexican origin peoples were racialized to provide cheap labor and subsequently suffered widespread poverty. This contributed to a protectionist position that claimed that, as a group, Mexican Americans were unfit for civil participation because "the practice of citizenship required autonomy and independence of mind, and thus, economic independence."[37]

Guálinto serves less as an isolated hero of the national bildungsroman than as the fulcrum that tethers networks around which new social relations are produced. Focusing on homosocial relations instead of "a modernist desire for a singular, unified subject who functions as the single representative of his group," Paredes's corrido-influenced strategy circumvents Anglo stereotypes that threaten to relegate Mexican Americans to roles as non-participatory citizens.[38] In contrast, Guálinto's closest male relative, his uncle Feliciano, presents the possibility for Mexican Americans to find a middle ground between hostility and identification with Anglo exclusion, what José Limón suggests offers a "radical hope" against his nephew's betrayal. For Limón, Feliciano provides a different set of values, an "exemplary figure for ongoing social life for Mexican Americans."[39] Once Feliciano brings his family into town and establishes himself within Judge Roberts's political machine, he works hand in hand with Juan Rubio in executing the Blues political strategy and managing El Danubio Azul saloon. Together, they learn to work within what David Montejano has termed the peace structure in South Texas, however unstable or dissolving that structure might be in the late 1910s. Feliciano succeeds at his job, partly out of determination to survive, partly out of his own ingenuity (he invents the political party's slogan, "arriba los azules"), and partly because "he had what some people called a manly presence" (47).

Feliciano manages to broker a livelihood in Anglo-dominated South Texas, a decision that Limón sees as more practically accommodationist than assimilationist, with the potential for upward mobility without abandoning cultural ideals. Yet Feliciano is never quite able to leave history in the past, and never fully embraces his decision to leave his pistol behind him, always lamenting the passing age of armed resistance, "a revolver and a bottle" longingly beside him (237).[40] Feliciano faces hard decisions in order to care for his family, but ultimately chooses to work within the colonial Anglo order to secure his family's safety. His success in Jonesville models manhood and teaches his nephew the importance of economic citizenship. Still, he never fully comes to terms with his distrust for and dislike of Anglo Texans, suggesting a future of separate spheres for white and Mexican American relations.

Feliciano first confronts the decision to depart from revolutionary manhood through his encounter with Juan Rubio, a marginal character present throughout the narrative. In the opening pages, as a young revolutionary traveling with a band of *sediciosos* (revolutionary Mexicans and Mexican Americans), Feliciano witnesses how the borderlands violence impacts Mexican American solidarity. Feliciano's group of rebels captures a travelling Anglo peddler and his Mexican peasant assistant, later revealed as Juan Rubio. This scene, part of the novel's opening sequence, sets the tone for the text's dissociation of violence from masculine potential. During and in the wake of the Borderlands War, violence leads only to further social disintegration. The novel recounts in vivid detail the violence out of which Feliciano and Juan's friendship begins; in doing so, it privileges violence's impact on the Mexican community, intra- over interracial conflict. While "a Border Mexican knew there was no brotherhood of men" among Gringos and Mexicans, the novel implicitly acknowledges the importance of social cooperation among Texas Mexicans (19). Lupe, Feliciano's brother and leader of the rebel faction, orders Feliciano to kill Juan, but Feliciano opts to stage Juan's death, deceiving his brother in order to save Juan. This decision marks Feliciano's first rupture with patriarchal authority, defying his brother and superior officer in a gesture against traditional familial and military forms of authority. Feliciano's ruse replaces the family bonds of Border Mexican custom with social collaboration and affiliative belonging, catalyzing Feliciano's movement into Anglo society. Juan, unnamed yet "one of ours," permits the possibility for the development (27). Feliciano and Juan part ways only to reconvene serendipitously in Jonesville-on-the-Grande.

Throughout the novel, Guálinto benefits from his uncle Feliciano's economic acumen. Himself a displaced refugee of the Borderlands War, Feliciano navigates the economic and political climate to achieve what Guálinto sees as only moderate success, but given the disadvantages Feliciano has faced, these are nothing short of a triumph. Through hard work, discipline, a bit of guile, and some luck, Feliciano builds himself a prosperous business, leaving him "well off" (190). Feliciano demonstrates a form of business savvy by hoarding gold coins "the backward ranchero way" since he never fully trusts financial institutions, and is able to increase his property by purchasing "land from the old Gringo who rents to me now" (192). Over the years he set up multiple savings accounts to prepare for the future and for Guálinto's education. Feliciano is by no means a financier, but his distrust of market capitalism (itself a sign of his ability to adapt) sets him apart from the majority of his community and allows him to "come out ahead in the end" (193). In doing so, he offers Guálinto a chance at a quality of life approximating the middle class, the elusive American dream, but it is a vision grounded in the physical land and agricultural labor that ties him to the local community. Guálinto ultimately rejects it. Even Guálinto/George's decision to assimilate and disavow his connections to the Texas Mexican community emerges from a sense of economic citizenship. George has to assume a position as racially "unmarked," severing his ties to both his community and his past, in order to push past the limitations on economic possibility.

As national economic trends impact South Texas, Guálinto's own masculine maturation comes to a head when the area feels the effects of the Great Depression. When the Great Depression hits Texas (it is referred to in Spanish as "la Chilla," the cry or wail), economic change prompts Feliciano to treat his nephew as "a man now, and it's time we talked about things like one man to another" (191).[41] Guálinto learns of Feliciano's plans to weather the economic storm, retreating to his farm and sharing with those less fortunate than the family. When Feliciano mentions that he may resort to "peddling vegetables," Guálinto is aghast, "reddened" with shame by the possibility of his family becoming working class laborers. Under these conditions, he insists, "I want to get a job and help out. I've been a burden to you long enough [. . .] I'm a man already, Uncle! You said it yourself, I'm a man," and asserts his own capacity as a worker (193).

In contrast, Juan Rubio embraces that possibility. Juan, who "doesn't say much," undergirds Feliciano's prosperity, and Feliciano "depend[s] a lot on him, though" (39). Juan and Feliciano's relationship enacts a homosocial partnership aimed toward mutual advancement. Relegated to the narrative margins, Juan's presence recurs throughout the novel, emerging at key moments in both Guálinto's and Feliciano's development. The story is rarely focalized through Juan, but his opportune involvement in the text facilitates the others' progression, even as he labors silently in the background. Juan, steadfast, loyal, and hardworking, enables the novel to inscribe Mexican American manhood around a discrete work ethic, though that work ethic is both communally derived and oriented.

Juan patiently achieves economic independence through farm labor and the gradual acquisition of land. The importance of property rights marks the mixing economic and gendered citizenship and is a foundational principle of American citizenship. Procurement of land establishes Juan as a productive member of both Mexican American community and Anglo society, like Gabriel in *Caballero*. While toiling the land, Juan informs Guálinto of his uncle's revolutionary past, changing the course of Guálinto's life. While for much of the novel Guálinto wrestles with Feliciano's alleged cowardice during the racial conflict, Juan affirms Feliciano's bravery, restoring Guálinto's faith in his uncle and in a Mexican cultural past. This prompts Guálinto to pursue a college education, and provides the cornerstone for the novel's perplexing narrative rupture between parts four and five. Paired with Juan Rubio to mend a fence, Guálinto recognizes Juan's ingenuity and ability, commenting, "He's more intelligent than I imagined" (276). Acknowledging Juan's competence at labor that leaves Guálinto having "never felt so tired and sore in all his life" underscores a burgeoning respect for the farmhand and invokes a nostalgic work ethic attributed to previous generations (277). The normally trenchant Juan confesses to Guálinto that Texas Rangers murdered his own family, and that he himself was nearly the victim of sedicioso violence had Feliciano not interceded. Juan functions as an informant, though an informant not between cultures but between history and the narrative present. The novel does not reveal the details of Juan's confession, but "Juan talked for a long time, longer than he had talked to anyone in years" (278). The narrator's statement enables cross-class and transhistorical communication through homosocial alliance, and the novel poses listening as a transformative act that generates communal cohesion from otherwise marginal members of the community.[42] One can only speculate as to the exact content of his monologue, but Juan's declamation of historical and familial events singlehandedly enables Guálinto to pursue his education.

Juan lives on to establish a stable and productive life for himself within the Mexican community, steeped in the knowledge of but not subservient to historical violence. Juan, who for Feliciano "has been like a son to me these past few years . . . [and] will continue to work both parts of the farm," replaces Guálinto as surrogate child and inherits the farm (301). Juan values Feliciano's bravery not as "a being of heroic proportions," but in his dedication to everyday life and the sustenance of his family, despite the omnipresent threat of death should his former involvement in revolutionary activities be discovered (265). Here, Paredes inscribes a different form of heroism, one that imagines manhood free from "the restrictions of patriarchal social forms [that] accentuate the crucial centrality of the *non*heroic (not to be confused with the *un*heroic) agents of history for subsequent political courses of action."[43] Neither kinship nor genealogy dominates masculine performance, but his economic and social success remains firmly rooted in the geography of his people, metaphorically and literally as a farmer. Juan's attachment to the land, as opposed to Gualinto's disgust for agricultural labor, embeds their community within historical continuity and provides an economic resource that instills Mexican American manhood within a growing national commercial agriculture.[44]

Yet Juan and Feliciano's activities are never autonomous from other economic activity. In parallel to Juan Rubio, Juan José Alvarado, better known as El Colorado, models a different mode of economic participation. El Colorado serves as surrogate paternal influence on Guálinto and assumes the role of protector, mediating between Guálinto, "the friend and protégé of El Colorado," and any potential conflict. El Colorado supports himself through work and supplements Guálinto's leisure activities, providing him with spending money for recreation and entertainment, generously offering, "Any time I got money we both got money" (215). Confident in the "future ahead of you," the redheaded Colorado (like Gumersindo) encourages the predictive burden that is Guálinto's fate to be "leader of his people." El Colorado explains, "We will need you here in Jonesville. Men like you and Orestes and me and Antonio Prieto. Our people will need us here. It's time we quit being driven like sheep by the Gringos" (250). El Colorado's diatribe against Anglo racism very clearly delineates social belonging along racial lines, between "our people" and "Gringos," but it also reinforces El Colorado's vision of a future Jonesville-on-the-Grande populated by a male homosocial community, the collective efforts of an alliance of educated, working class Mexican Americans.

El Colorado praises Guálinto's ability to debate, to articulate the conflicts that plague their lives, an attribute that Guálinto peremptorily dismisses as "just getting rid of some of the anger inside me" (250). Rather than minimize the lingering racial violence, El Colorado affirms Guálinto's feeling, claiming that all Mexican Americans in South Texas are "full of anger inside. All of us are, but you can speak out about it. You have that gift. You can get people to listen" (250). By El Colorado's analysis, what distinguishes Guálinto from his companions is his unique ability to make others listen, to promote dialogue in defense and not at the cost of the Mexican community. Guálinto's "gift" is not only the ability to speak, but in getting others to heed his pronouncements. "Listening," as opposed to merely "hearing" (the perception of sound), requires not only the lending of one's attention, but implies some degree of participation on behalf of the listener.

El Colorado endeavors to channel Guálinto's talent into a sense of communal progress through economic achievement. He demonstrates the shared trauma of poverty by recounting personal events from his own abusive childhood and his determination to enact a Horatio Alger-type rags-to-riches story. In defense of economic citizenship, El Colorado gives the "longest speech he had ever made to anyone in his life," and perhaps this is Guálinto's true talent, his real success—not to get others to listen as their leader but to get others to talk, to forge alliances and to imagine a future, acts of transformative listening (253). Rather than be constricted by the poverty in which he was born, El Colorado

> learned to wash and delouse myself. I sewed the seat of my own pants and I went to school without breakfast if I had to. But I stuck to it. I failed again and again till I almost grew up to be a man and I still was in school . . . What do you think all that makes me feel like? Laughing? Oh, I'm always joking and acting dumber than I really am, but I'm not laughing inside . . . Sometimes I get to thinking and I say to myself, 'Who the hell am I? Just a poor damn Mexican that's worth less than a dog in this cursed country. I won't ever get nowhere, I don't have a change, I was born behind the eight-ball, that's all there is to it.' And it makes me feel very sad. But by God, it isn't very many times I feel that way . . . I'm going to be one [a successful accountant], whatever it costs me. I'll show these bastards. (252)

Discipline and ambition drive El Colorado, and he refuses to capitulate to the racism and inequities in which he lives. In the face of institutional and societal racism, he eventually succeeds in the modern economy as an accountant. The self-reliance El Colorado demonstrates would seem a familiar form of manhood in the fin-de-siècle United States.[45] Both financially and emotionally independent, the reliant self that El Colorado enacts is never fully separate from the community in which he is engaged and is offered in the service of "our people [who] will need us here" (250). El Colorado repeatedly emphasizes the collective emphasis of individual achievement; individual success, while important, is only one step toward communal representation.

His achievements come with great personal sacrifice, but induce in him an appreciation for social integration of the individual and community within Anglo society. Able to advance despite monumental structural obstacles, El Colorado enters the arena of citizenship through capitalism. As a "bookkeeper for Acme Produce, Inc. and . . . a public accountant on the side," he regulates the exchange of capital across cultural lines (289). When George returns to Jonesville, he learns it was El Colorado who financed (two of Guálinto's childhood friends) Antonio and Elodia's restaurant that houses a community meeting, a new Casita Mexicana that is "a much better place, and it's the real thing too" (287). El Colorado's success improves his community's, and although less is known about George's other friends, the novel states that Orestes was "now a registered pharmacist working for the Jonesville Drug Store," "Francisco López-Lebré had got a degree in dentistry . . . [and] had finally made it," and that another of Feliciano's farm hands "had a job in town with the City" (289). While El Colorado enters into market capitalism through the service industry and Juan Rubio through agriculture and property ownership, both model the potential of Mexican American national inclusion through economic independence, made legible through viable alternative manhood. Mexican American manhood functions as a practice of citizenship that exhibits civil participation.

El Colorado's desire for economic citizenship replaces the possibility of the traditional family or romantic attachment, but is not unconflicted. He problematically treats women as sexual objects to alleviate either a bodily need or the stress of employment. For El Colorado, "There's no such thing as love [and] I've never wanted a girl except for one thing, and girls won't give it to me. They want marriage, that's what they want. But hell, I don't need girls for that" (254–5). Instead, El Colorado turns to prostitution on the Mexican side of the border to satisfy what he sees as purely biological, self-indulgent urges. Sexuality does not function in the reproduction of a social order, but rather offers another form of economic exchange, and his own economic manhood cannot surpass the masculinism of the patriarchal society in which he was reared.[46] El Colorado thus recalls how Mexican American men sought democratic racial equality while failing to imagine accompanying equality of gender.

Collaborative Labor in González and Eimer's *Caballero*

Separate from the versions of manhood in *George Washington Gomez*, *Caballero* uses economic citizenship to appeal for women's rights and economic inclusion. Writing within and against these social conditions, Jovita González and Eve Raleigh's historical romance chronicles the life of Don Santiago de Mendoza y Soría and his ranchero family as they struggle to cope with the widespread social and political changes following the Anglo occupation of Texas. Incorporating elements of the sensational and the sentimental, and set during the American invasion of Texas in 1846 in the aftermath of the U.S.-Mexican War, Don Santiago sees his family and influence disintegrate under cultural pressure from the Americanos. Each of his children confronts the cultural and imperialist pressures of the American arrival, breaking with tradition and departing from the patriarchal family unit. Santiago's relentless adherence to patriarchal authority undermines the material realities of his power by alienating him from his family. His eldest son Alvaro is shot after several failed attempts at armed resistance against the American invasion, his second son Luis Gonzaga leaves the state with an American army captain to pursue painting (a vocation dismissed by Santiago as insufficiently manly), and his two daughters Angela and Susanita (the favored daughter) marry Americans against Santiago's wishes, as he stubbornly struggles to maintain tradition. Thus, Don Santiago offers a rigid portrayal of the hidalgo patriarch. He eventually dies alone, estranged from his family, a fistful of earth fruitlessly clenched in his palm.

As many critics have noted, the novel voices a clear critique of American colonization in South Texas and how the resulting social order left Texas Mexicans living as a conquered population. Born on January 18, 1904, in the small border town of Roma, Texas, González experienced this racist society personally. Although a member of the emerging Mexican American middle class with long-standing ties to the region, she nevertheless had firsthand knowledge of the persistent inequities of South Texas life, which included a social structure akin to the Jim Crow South.[47] In 1910, her family relocated to San Antonio so that the González children could benefit from better educational opportunities, including instruction in English. In 1918, González earned her teaching certificate and began teaching while pursuing a Bachelor's degree in Spanish, graduating from Our Lady of the Lake College in San Antonio in 1927. Teaching full-time at Saint Mary's Hall, González completed her master's degree in history at the University of Texas at Austin in 1930, a monumental achievement for a woman of color in the racist and sexist academic climate of the 1930s. Through friendships with renowned folklorist J. Frank Dobie (architect of some of the most famous legends in Texas history, such as those surrounding the Texas Rangers) and Carlos E. Castañeda (pioneering historian and librarian at UT Austin), González served as president of the Texas Folklore Society from 1930 to 1932, the first woman to achieve the position. She married Edmundo E. Mireles in 1935, and a few years later in 1939, moved with her husband to Corpus Christi where she taught high school and lived until her death in 1983.

González's professional career included numerous publications, several of which were Spanish language textbooks. As an academic, she conducted fieldwork in South Texas, which served as the basis for her master's thesis, and she later published the folk stories of South Texas Mexicans, such as "Folklore of the Texas-Mexican Vaquero" and "America Invades the Border Towns." Her research on folklore would be the source material for the collection *Dew on the Thorn*, though its publication would have to wait some fifty years. Her folklore, teaching, and historical work were the central focus of González's career, and her research on South Texas influenced her narrative fiction.

González found herself in the complicated position of being both married and a successful scholar and teacher. Women, including a significant share of married women, were increasingly a part of the U.S. workforce in the interwar period.[48] González's successes as scholar and teacher modeled a professional existence that challenged the limitations on women's labor, but she was unable to repeat that success as a writer of fiction. In the late 1930s, González began work on *Caballero*, which she described as "the only book of its kind [giving] the Mexican side of the war of 1848."[49] After beginning the novel on her own, González collaborated with Eimer to write a historical romance. Despite the authors' concerted efforts to find a publisher, the novel remained in manuscript form until the 1990s, when scholars José Limón and María Cotera discovered the manuscript in the archives of Texas A&M University at Corpus Christi.

The extent of González and Eimer's collaboration is somewhat uncertain, although González, already at work on the novel, invited Eimer to join her in 1937, perhaps to enhance the novel's appeal to publishers. Based on archival evidence, Limón speculates that González was largely responsible for the historical content (drawing on her academic work) and Eimer took a more leading role in romantic elements.[50] In the racist climate of the 1930s and early '40s, the authors' collaboration, like the novel's content, speaks of a desire to bridge racial and cultural divides and reach a broad audience beyond the local Mexican-origin community. María Cotera provides the fullest and most persuasive account of authorial cooperation, stating that the novel is "a collaborative text about collaboration, a text that self-consciously enacts the politics of its production within its pages" and sees in the novel's joint authorship and cross-racial romances a critique of Mexican patriarchal authority.[51] A politics of collaboration offers a practical approach to publication and soliciting readers, given the material, technological, and capitalist obstacles to completing their project.

Collaboration offered a model for intercultural and gendered cooperation in a world still limited by traditional masculinity. González, bilingual in Spanish and English, chose to write the text in English, a decision that suggests a desire to reach an English-speaking audience that included Mexican Americans but extended beyond them into Anglo society. The linguistic choice enabled the authors to market their novel to a broader audience, but three major publishers—Macmillan, Houghton Mifflin and Bobbs-Merrill—rejected González and Eimer's manuscript.[52] Nonetheless, their solicitation (albeit unsuccessful) of a major publisher, one with access to national literary markets, invited a national dialogue about Mexican American civic participation. Additionally, González and Eimer chose to write a historical romance, which further supports this idea. The historical romance, as Doris Sommer and Nina Silber have shown, frequently uses transracial, transcultural, or transnational unions to consolidate regional or racial divisions in the service of national unity.[53] These popular fictions—romantic, sentimental, or sensational—typically depicted the rigid Mexican patriarch oppressing his family and whose unjust reign can only be undone by an Anglo suitor. This prevalent image of Mexican American manhood became a stock plot and a dominant narrative of national contact with

Mexico. While *Caballero* utilizes many of these same plot devices, the text does not reproduce them but expands on the possibilities for Mexican American manhood. Written by a Mexican American woman in partnership with an Anglo co-author, the novel ambitiously attempts to bridge the hostile racial divide, but also to achieve personal economic success by intervening in American culture and in the leisure activities of the middle class (novel-reading). While the partnership produced a novel, it neglected to find a publisher and as such was an economic failure. Still, in an economic climate in which female labor was circumscribed not by law but by social power, the imagined terrain of manhood and economic citizenship allowed the authors to critique the limitations of both economic opportunity and racialized difference.

The Decline of Traditional Mexican American Manhood

González and Eimer's depiction of the oppressive patriarch Santiago was hardly unfamiliar. Much of the popular fiction that drew upon the U.S.-Mexican War for its content depicted the Mexican patriarch as dictatorial, uncaring, impotent, or even draconian. In fact, the tyrannical Mexican male became an almost necessary convention in order to justify U.S. imperial aims through romantic union. In her excellent account of nineteenth-century sensational literature, Shelley Streeby identifies a recurrent theme that associates "Mexico and Spain with patriarchy and coercive force, [and consequently] these narratives represent the United States, by contrast, as the land of modernity and relative freedom for women."[54] In novels such as Ned Buntline's *Magdaléna*, Joseph Holt Ingraham's *The Texan Ranger*, Augusta Evans's *Inez*, or Harry Halyard's *Chieftain of Churubusco*, the American invasion of Mexico presents an opportunity for the Mexican female to free herself from the yoke of patriarchy, usually through romantic union with an Anglo invader.[55] In this way, the international romance between Anglo men and Mexican women (the international romance typically weds a conquering male to a conquered female) displaces the violence of territorial conquest, a trope that González and Eimer recycle.

Santiago's narrative position reflects González and Eimer's reality. As immigration from rural Mexico increased, the feudal patriarchal attitudes inhibited the full economic participation of women while reinforcing their domestic labor responsibilities within the family.[56] And as changes to the traditional family structure intensified and more Chicana women entered the workforce, this further strained both the masculine role within the family and the public-private divide advocated by some Mexican Americans. Seeking to overcome both gendered restriction and economic ostracization, González and Eimer sought a national audience who would be familiar with and were the primary consumers of the romance genre. Yet *Caballero* imagines Mexican American manhood as productive male citizenship. The novel's patriarch and the presumed titular "caballero," Don Santiago is the third-generation hidalgo to preside over the Rancho La Palma de Cristo, established in 1748 under a land grant from the Spanish colonial government. While Santiago as patriarch would be immediately recognizable as a kind of stock character, González and Eimer craft his character with an interiority and emotional range that exceeds stock plots.[57] The novel begins on the eve of the American occupation of Texas in 1846 and introduces Santiago as "a bas-relief of power and strength" whose defined features "could only be chiseled by generations of noble forbears."[58] Filled with "arrogance," Don Santiago was "lord of land miles beyond what his eye could encompass, master of this *hacienda* and all those that would soon gather before him" (*Caballero* 3). From the onset, Santiago's authority was unquestioned, his national allegiance to Mexico steadfast if nostalgically granted. Yet his inflexible attachment to a waning nationalism and the masculine privileges it enables, and his inability to adapt to changing social conditions, ultimately dooms him.

Encouraged by his father, the pompous and pugnacious Alvaro, whose "lustful, possessive eyes" lay claim to both the property and women of the rancho, is brazen and impetuous, and, as a friend of a fictionalized Juan Cortina, opposes the Anglos at all costs (5). For Santiago and his son Alvaro, manhood is determined through their ability to command and by their sexual prowess. Alvaro's sense of masculine authority, as an upper-class hidalgo and descendent of the prestigious Mendoza y Soría line, is intimately associated with his ability to acquire his desires, including sexual desires. Santiago and Alvaro reproduce the tyrannical and aggressive Mexican American men prevalent in the sensational literature about the U.S.-Mexican War.

As such, Santiago's or Alvaro's demise at novel's end would hardly have been surprising. Like in Atherton's *The Californians*, the Anglo male announces the patriarch's death in symbolic conquest of Mexican women and culture. After Alvaro is shot dead and Santiago's daughter Susanita returns to the Rancho La Palma de Cristo with her American husband Robert Warrener and their newborn daughter, "anticipation kept faces bright" as the family expects, reservedly, a reconciliatory homecoming (335). But the family cannot locate Santiago, after which Warrener and a *vaquero* named Simón, fearing the worst, ride out to "the place we called *papá*'s altar," a clearing on a bluff overlooking the ranch where "Don Santiago's father's father saw Rancho La Palma de Cristo in a dream from there" (335–6). Santiago's "altar" connects Santiago's own vision of himself and his role as guardian of traditional manhood, the site for the intersection of land, history, and material representation of possessive manhood. For Santiago, the altar signifies a place where "pride could have a man's stature," where he can observe "all this that I can see, and far beyond, is mine and only mine" (32–3). From this vantage point, like his "father's father" before him, Santiago holds fast to the illusion of uninterrupted perpetual masculine authority, impervious to national conflict, vested in a solitary individual, and patrilineally inherited: the rancho would persist "after him by Alvaro, and his sons, and their sons. Let the world whirl in madness. Rancho La Palma would never change. The Mendoza line would never die" (33). With Alvaro's death, Luis Gonzaga's departure, and the marriage of both his daughters to Anglo males, Santiago can no longer deny the massive social changes that have taken place in South Texas. He dies at his altar, resolutely clinging to "a scoop of earth, brown and dry," desperately grasping for the world he once knew (337).

In this instance, however, the demise of the patriarch is critical of conquest. In the same scene, the novel's last, Warrener reflects upon the political climate that caused Santiago's death and "the men piling into the new state [who] were asserting their rights as 'Americans,' wearing the rainbow of the pioneer as if it were new and theirs alone. Already talking loudly about running all Mexicans across the Río Grande from this 'our' land" (336). Warrener's reflection, made in the same location in which began the initial colonization of the territory in 1748, casts doubt upon the legality of the American conquest of Texas and on the racialization of its Mexican-origin inhabitants. Warrener acknowledges previous claims to land rights by undermining Anglo settler claims and placing them in a longer historical framework. The possessive statement, "from this 'our' land," remains ambiguous and could refer ironically to the settlers' assertions, to Warrener's marital association with the Mendozas, or facetiously to the author's own generational but contested affiliation to Texas. The ambiguity enables *Caballero* to critique Mexican American manhood and open up space for economic citizenship.

Santiago's dying grasp of the earth, "dying in the aloneness he had made," takes on heightened significance, as he cannot continue as steward of Mexican American manhood in the new world of capitalist and commercial agribusiness (336). His antagonism to Americans and failure to accept their victory, "scarcely believ[ing] that a *gringo* would *buy* what he wanted," precludes his investment in the new capitalist economy (300, emphasis in original). Throughout, the novel dissolves existing familial obligations in favor of other forms of association which further emphasize the Texas Mexicans' associations to the land. Whereas, in reference to "our ancestors," Santiago reminds the reader that the land "was theirs by right of royal grants, ours by right of inheritance," by 1848, inheritance was no longer a viable or visible (documentable) claim to authority or ownership (50).

Santiago no longer represents Mexican American manhood and his masculine performance does not align with the practices of productive citizenship because it relies on a system of production (the debt peonage of the hacienda) rendered obsolete by national conflict. As a figure of Mexican American manhood, Santiago cannot adapt in the face of modernity, in its agricultural, economic, cultural, and political aspects. His and Alvaro's deaths pave the way for alternative masculinities that model economic citizenship. Imagining social belonging as affiliation rather than inheritance, the novel introduces a new idiom of collective belonging through which to conceive of citizenship.

Caballero's Alternative Manhoods

Labor historian David Montgomery has argued, "The citizen-producer was customarily depicted as male," and González and Eimer use this masculine association to their advantage in their depiction of Texas

Mexican society.[59] As much as he condones Alvaro's brash behavior and womanizing, Santiago is far less accepting of his second son, Luis Gonzaga, condemning what he perceives as unmanly. Yet Luis presents an important alternative. He aspires to become an artist, a professional choice that, in Santiago's eyes, is more "like a woman . . . An artist— insult to a father's manhood! A milksop, and his son!" (6). Santiago associates artistry with effeminacy, and the novel implies a homo- erotic if not queer relationship between Luis and Captain Devlin.[60] Luis challenges Santiago's harsh imperiousness and provides a poten- tial outlet for alternate modes of cultural cooperation. His decision to leave the ancestral home at Rancho La Palma de Cristo instigates a crisis in patriarchal authority, which Luis chooses, with some regret, to abandon. Cotera asserts that Luis's departure "is not a retreat to indi- vidualism or an escape from the bounds of community, but a gesture toward collaboration with a different kind of community" that defies Santiago's insistence on retaining masculine dominance in Texas Mexi- can society (223). Cotera sees in Luis's relationship with Devlin one similar to the relationship between González and Eimer—finding alli- ance neither through nation or race, but as artists, "a conceptual move that deconstructs geopolitical boundaries and generates a creative third term from the clash" (223). Luis departs with Devlin to Balti- more, New York, and ultimately Spain, maintaining only epistolary connection to his home and family. Luis and Devlin's friendship, erotic or otherwise, indicates the possibility of a transcultural partnership based on their economic alliance. In the urban centers in the eastern United States, Luis "was even earning his way," writing to his family that Devlin "puts a price on them [his paintings] which is shockingly high. That makes them of value and to be desired, [Devlin] says, and it seems he is right" (293). Through their affiliation and schooled by Devlin, Luis learns how to capitalize on his artistic talent, a skill often left out of the emerging capitalist economy. (One can't help but read González's own desire here for her "art" to provide her with a liveli- hood as well.)

Patriarchal society, like that associated with the hidalgo mode of so- cial organization that Santiago represents, depended on common ances- try and blood ties in determining social relations. In lieu of kinship, and building on Cotera's reading, the novel utilizes artistic collaboration to establish new social relations that depend on other forms of social alliance. The novel rehearses this process through the difference between "filiation," "the natural continuity between one generation and the next" (16), and "affiliation," alternatives to human relations "provided by institutions, associations, and communities whose social existence was not in fact guaranteed by biology."[61] Luis's commitment to affiliation over filiation, a useful counterpoint to and critique of Mexican patriarchy, functions as an instrument for the articulation of social change by justifying Luis's departure through his need for personal freedom and possibly safety. However, the novel issues a perplexing statement: "Luis Gonzaga had willfully turned his back on his people to take up life with the *Americanos*" (219). In choosing to leave South Texas to seek personal and professional development, Luis chooses individual fulfillment over collective participation, a politics of collaboration obtained at the cost of one's community that cannot be ignored. How does one attain individual security without harming communal interest? Seeking a more egalitarian and inclusive society, *Caballero* turns elsewhere for a manhood that is non-patriarchal and nonsexual, focused more on civic and economic participation than on dominance.

In counterpoint to the stock oppressive Mexican patriarch, Santiago's neighbor and fellow caballero Don Gabriel del Lago is the only male figure to attain a place within both Anglo society and Mexican culture. Gabriel offers the figure of Mexican American manhood best suited for social improvement, but only allied with and supportive of female agency. Throughout the novel, Gabriel serves as a transcultural mediator for the community. He is the Mendoza y Soría's most frequent visitor and the bearer of political and social news, including the original warning of the American invasion. Ever resourceful, Gabriel recognizes the long-term repercussions that will follow the American incursion and identifies the possibilities for social inclusion: relocate within the new geopolitical boundaries of Mexico, assimilate into Anglo American society, or mount an armed yet ill-fated resistance (14–15). Gabriel rejects Santiago and Alvaro's impassioned calls to violent resistance, and instead yields to Santiago's widowed sister Doña Dolores's pleas for more reasoned patience.

About midway through the narrative, friends, family, and neighbors converge on the Rancho La Palma in celebration of Santiago's saint's day.

As the festivities wear on, the older men gather together to debate current events. From among the men,

> Gabriel del Lago quickly took the lead by saying, "Even though my host [Santiago] does not agree with me, I feel I must speak what is on my mind, for it may be a long time until we again get together. We are a beaten, a conquered people, and we *rancheros* are a group apart and but a handful. It is all very high-sounding, this dying for a cause, but death is death, our families are left without protection when we are gone, our land will be for anyone to take." (217)

Against the prevailing current of thought among his peers, Gabriel bravely ventures forth a dissenting opinion. Even though his opinion is unpopular, he acknowledges the American conquest of Texas (and all northern Mexico). Gabriel concedes that they are a "conquered people," and distinguishes between the "*rancheros*" and other occupants of South Texas. He asserts that they retain a cohesive sense of communal identity, "a group apart and but a handful" even against political conquest. The rancheros' tightly knit community limits the options for social enunciation. While the men speak of and rally for armed revolt, Gabriel tempers their bellicosity with pragmatism. While dying for the Mexican state may be "high-sounding," a glorious death leaves their families "without protection," open to the intrigues of the American occupiers. The family, both literally and as a metaphor for community, ultimately pays the price, and death leaves the community open for exploitation.

Gabriel's voice of reason and coalition ventures some prefigurative components of social accord. Less an appeal to assimilation than to economic self-preservation, Gabriel tries to organize the community to combat the Anglo occupation through nonviolence:

> We have titles, and I am told they are recognized but must be recorded with the new government, which seems sensible to me and should seem to you. The war has not touched us here, and there is no blood on our hands. There are many who bear us no ill will, and if we go with courtesy and dignity, it is my belief that we will be treated so in return. (217)

Calling for the group to act "sensible," Gabriel distinguishes between active combatants and the unfortunate civil victims of military might. Unlike soldiers of the Mexican army (or by extension the revolutionaries of the Borderlands War), those at the gathering remain without "blood on our hands," which allows for the possibility of civil exchange. Gabriel invokes categories of universal citizenship, "courtesy and dignity," but links those to the practical economic matter of recording their land rights. Gabriel's proposition perhaps places undue faith in legal institutions of justice, but he is the only Mexican American man of his generation in the novel to accept the historical inevitability of the U.S. occupation and to adapt to the new social and economic opportunities. Although Gabriel refers to the U.S.-Mexican War, his comments allude to the Borderlands War of 1915. Through Gabriel, González and Eimer discourage violence as a means toward social progress. Gabriel opposes associations of Mexican Americans and violence that preclude national integration. The novel points to noncombatants as the recipients of retaliatory state-sanctioned action; death leaves families without protection, and only with "no blood on our hands" can Mexican Americans earn the rights of citizenship. As such, manhood is rewritten in service of potential intra-communal alliances.

Gabriel's appeals to nonviolent inclusion culminate with an "astonishing proposal" to marry Santiago's eldest daughter Susanita (247). At first reluctant, Santiago eventually consents to the proposal in hopes of extinguishing Susanita's love for the American Captain Warrener and preserving his lineage within Mexican American culture. Despite his initial revulsion, Santiago affirms their relationship and assuages his momentary guilt for imposing unhappiness on his daughter by stating, "The children would bind the marriage" and "his grandchildren, without alien blood" would formalize the union through kinship (250). Susanita, later accused of disgracing her family by travelling unchaperoned to save Alvaro from Anglo captors, eventually nullifies the betrothal and marries Warrener.

During Gabriel and Susanita's short-lived courtship, Gabriel's alternative masculinity is rendered puerile. "Cavorting with Susanita . . . [has Gabriel] looking like a boy in his father's best suit. Acting like a boy," Gabriel deviates from the assertive, leadership role he held among the ranchero men. His unexpected decision to marry Susanita, explained as "lovesickness," seems less about romantic union than it does about gar-nering Santiago's support for his conciliatory ideals. During the family discussion over Susanita's future, González and Eimer repeat the phrase "they would follow him [Santiago]" three times (281–2). Unable to con-vince Santiago of his political and social strategy, Gabriel relies on filial ties. Yet the process transforms him from nonconforming mediator and leader into an inchoate man, a boy parading in men's clothing (221). Gabriel's reparative venture aimed at affirming social order through marriage between pedigreed families, rather than cementing his posi-tion as leader of the group, converts him into an object of ridicule and ostracizes him. The union, doomed from the outset, does not reconcile the novel's cross-cultural tensions.

However, Gabriel demonstrates his willingness to forge affiliative bonds across cultures. He places his trust in the American economic and political system through Red McLane, an Anglo newcomer and political opportunist who seizes the American occupation as an occa-sion for personal gain through alliance with the Mexican population. McLane is known for his business savvy, with either an "extraordinary shrewdness and foresight or that peculiar magnetism to draw money which seems to be a gift"; he "has money and will always have money," a point that he uses to woo Angela (71, 211). Under English common law, married women lost their property rights, a legal status known as feme covert, while under Mexican law inherited from Spain, married women retained their property rights and were entitled to one-half of commu-nity property.[62] Gabriel solicits McLane to survey and secure his land rights, concluding, "Unless we go to Mexico and stay completely Mexi-can we must conform in part" (327). More than a declaration of an inten-tion to assimilate, Don Gabriel is complicit in a troubled protectionism that seeks to safeguard his economic and political security, acceding to the Anglo need for "straight lines, definite lines" while he "admired the efficiency" of American capitalism (324–5). Gabriel's willingness to co-operate with McLane by asserting his land rights invokes the Treaty of Guadalupe Hidalgo's guarantee of Mexican property, but his coopera-tion also reveals "how rights in property are contingent on, intertwined with, and conflated with race."[63] The constitutionally defended right to "life, liberty, and property" was systematically and legally divested from

Mexican Americans following the U.S.-Mexican War. Gabriel recalls the national promise of equality and asserts his status as property-owning citizen as the basis for economic independence and a path toward national inclusion. Rather than dismiss his decision to engage with the American legal system as merely assimilationist or an attempt "to justify for the reader the role that some of the Mexican elite would eventually play in the future oppression of the Mexican working class," Gabriel lays claims to Mexican American manhood as a participant in a national economy."[64] Through Gabriel, the novel ruminates on what might be possible if Santiago "were not the true *caballero*" and representative of Mexican American manhood (325).

In Gabriel, Mexican American manhood is neither violently revolutionary nor assimilationist nor accomodationist; rather, Gabriel demonstrates a form of public manhood that is pragmatic and internalized within the framework of a U.S. nation-state, faithful in the possibility of social inclusion on the basis of economic participation. In González and Eimer's novel, economic citizenship is only possible when supported by cross-gender collaboration. *Caballero*'s deployment of Mexican American manhood does not communicate dependence on masculine authority, but rather demonstrates the ways in which Mexican American women participated in the creation of Mexican American manhood. Gabriel's assertion of economic citizenship is reinforced by his marriage to Dolores. Gabriel models a pragmatic, integrationist position, but his role cannot be fully understood without equal attention to his wife, Santiago's sister, Dolores. The marriage between Gabriel and Dolores happens quickly in the penultimate chapter, but ties up the loose plot lines, reconciling rancho life with the increasing migration of Mexican Americans to urban spaces. Gabriel travels to San Antonio to register his property, where he reunites with Dolores, realizing "they had always loved each other and were discovering it only now" (323). Independent, impertinent, and unabashedly antagonistic to Santiago's authority, Dolores is contradictorily progressive and the guardian of social decorum, yet values individual happiness over custom.[65] "Like a spoon that keeps the broth stirred so the grease cannot rise to the top," Dolores moves freely among the rancheros, tempering the men's volatility (216).

Throughout the novel, Dolores boldly challenges her brother's authority. Conversely, Dolores serves as the custodian of social decorum. In public, she frequently acts "the proper gentlewoman, taking the parting bows and murmuring compliments of the men with an exact measure of dignity, putting her charge before her" (243). As the novel progresses, Dolores remains steadfast in this role and "her code of self-possession and assurance were the fixed attributes of the true lady, which no disaster either real or rumored could change . . . She was completely mistress of herself" (14). Her sense of decorum extends even to patriarchal manhood, and when Santiago's emotions overrun his restraint, "Dolores ran and closed the door of her brother's room, against the agonized sound of his weeping," shielding the family and servants from his emotional display (234). Dolores protects her brother's standing by closing the door, serving as guardian not only of domestic tradition, but of Mexican American manhood.

However, these moments are never offered at the expense of her own independence, as Dolores finds space within social decorum to assert her agency. Fully cognizant of social norms, she nonetheless modifies tradition to suit the situation. She is the proxy of cross-cultural contact, subtly arranging meetings between Susanita and Angela and their suitors. Her refusal to accede to Santiago's authoritarianism indirectly inspires Gabriel to action. One may "wonder if Don Gabriel would have dared to propose as he had if the old ways were still with them—would have done so now, had not Dolores lifted a barrier," but yet, "it did seem right for Dolores and Gabriel to marry, so very right" (329). Dolores explicitly states she has always resented "a man ruling me as if I were a bought slave, but here in this house there is nothing that can be done about it" (238). Dolores's bold statement chides Santiago's wife Maria Petronilla for her submissiveness, but invoking the analogy to a "bought slave" alludes to a long history of gender inequality in the home and workplace. While historically women were granted and expected to hold authority in domestic matters, as a widow living in her brother's home, Dolores depends on the family for her subsistence; according to custom, she should defer to her sister-in-law's authority as mistress of the Rancho La Palma but does so reluctantly, proudly stating that in her own home, "the orders would not come from only *one* pair of lips, I can tell you that!" (25).

In the emotional aftermath of the children's climactic departure from the hacienda, Dolores reproaches Santiago, stating, "As for *your* house, it was our father's and therefore mine also, and I refuse to be driven from it. If I go at any time, I shall return whenever it pleases me" (314). Dolores claims paternal inheritance as equally her own and contends a woman's entitlement to property rights against the (Spanish and Mexican) custom of primogeniture, which traditionally vests property rights through male succession. Like Gabriel, Dolores sees economic citizenship as essential to independence and equality. The marriage with Gabriel enables Dolores "to at last have a place where she would not be secondary" and offers an avenue for her to realize her desires (326).

Gabriel's spontaneous but sincere "proposal by proxy touched the individualism in her and exhilarated her" (324). Curiously, the marriage proposal, an alliance that until the late twentieth century legally designated women as dependents of their husband, sparks Dolores's independent spirit, her "individualism." As a widow, a feme sole (unmarried woman), living under Mexican and then Texas law, Dolores depends on Santiago as arbiter of the family estate. With her husband Anselmo's land presumably still in the possession of his family, Dolores lives without any separate property or means of sustaining herself. Despite technically having access to legal rights as a feme sole, she could not conduct herself as a free woman due to her financial dependence and the social limitations on women's access to employment.

In a time when white American manhood turned to recreation and leisure as substitute sites for the enactment and confirmation of masculine worth, the workplace increasingly became a corporatized space outside their control.[66] For Mexican Americans, subject to racial discrimination that often precluded the possibility of entering into the workplace at all let alone on equal terms as their "white" male counterparts, leisure activities held little value as a proving ground for manhood. Instead, work itself was still the discursive space in which men struggled to be men. The editor of Mexico City's *Mexican Herald*, F. R. Guernsey, even claimed that the first signs of the brewing Mexican Revolution were the result of men out of work, and cross-border labor issues impacted both sides of the border. Guernsey highlighted regions where "unemployed men, being of this frame of mind, were easily worked upon by Mexican agitators who had taken refuge in the United States," as well as "the activities of bad characters on the American side of the border."[67]

At the same time that caused "many men to abandon their faith in the marketplace as certain to confirm their manhood," the first three decades of the twentieth century saw a flurry of labor legislation emerge that, on the surface, protected the labor conditions of women.[68] In Texas, the same period also saw several legal changes to married women's property rights.[69] However, beneath those laws, the nation institutionalized separate spheres for men and women, largely by regulating the workplace and investing in motherhood as the proper realm of women's work. In both the diegetic world of the novel and in González and Eimer's historical moment, avenues through which to participate as equal members of civil and political society were strictly controlled. Even González, an accomplished, educated woman, could not find venues for publication, despite taking on an Anglo co-author. At the end of *Caballero*, Dolores mediates her assertion of economic and political independence through Gabriel. Marrying Gabriel grants her authority, albeit limited, as spouse; collaborating with Gabriel allows her to exercise economic independence. Gabriel places his financial resources at her disposal: "I have money, we could live wherever *you* wished" (324, emphasis added). Her marriage grants a degree of wealth and, in San Antonio's emerging Mexican American society, potentially enhances her social standing. Although the marriage contract subsumes personal freedom under coverture, Dolores exchanges legal independence for cultural and economic power. Furthermore, her status as a married woman is perhaps more palatable for a national Anglo audience familiar with the marriage resolution of the romance genre. In addition to its generic utility in the resolution of a romance, what appears to be an abnegation of women's rights is actually an attempt to perpetuate cultural integrity through claims to social norms and a strategy to achieve communal cooperation between Mexican American men and women. Dolores and Gabriel's marriage is romantically motivated, but their relatively advanced age prevents the likelihood of the marriage producing offspring. The nonproductive union relies on affiliative networks for the reproduction of social order and the sustainment of communal identity, and creates space for mutual development. Dolores prides herself on being "a woman a man could talk to," and conversely, she talks to and through men to achieve her goals (240). The representation of Mexican American manhood becomes a crucial tool in the cultural reworking of women's rights. The detour into Dolores's womanhood elucidates how women helped shape Mexican American manhood. González and Eimer use Mexican American manhood as a tool to imagine a cooperative Mexican American society modeled on economic citizenship and visible through their marginalized characters. Gender performance is not only determinative of economic rights, but becomes an instrument through which to appeal for economic independence and political equality.

In both *George Washington Gomez* and *Caballero*, the authors use a textual strategy of marginalization to show Mexican American manhood as a site for the aggregation of national ethnic identity through multiple claims to economic citizenship.[70] Registered in the texts' political unconscious, economic citizenship underwrites the political organization that the novels seek to achieve. Revising genre meant revising possibilities for Mexican Americans, and that revision entails economic freedom by positioning Mexican Americans as citizen earners. A strategy of marginalization identifies alternative subject positions that are repeatedly overlooked by critics of both American and Chicana/o literature. Marginalization does not occur exclusively between colonizer and subalterns, but within each community, or within the mythos of that community, hierarchical distinctions exist. When texts emerge as part of minority canons (an inevitable result of recovery work), marginalization can also refer to people or characters within minority counter-narratives that are left out of the prevailing new discourse. Reading the peripheral spaces reveals how even minority discourses gain hegemonic strength, and helps uncover the complexity of the Latina/o experience.

Economic citizenship helped resolve the inter- and intra-cultural conflict through models of social inclusion and participation that invert the presumption of Mexicans as migratory, temporary, or cheap labor, instead centering labor as illustrative of the rights of citizenship. In the novels analyzed here, writers and social organizers Paredes and González and Eimer worked to counteract these processes, to distance Mexican American from real and perceived associations with recent immigrants, in order to affirm the status of Mexican Americans in the region and the place of Mexican Americans in the national imaginary. Their efforts, alas, were unsuccessful, as they failed to find publishing houses through which to distribute this message. By the mid-century, other forms of public identity and political collaboration superscribed claims to economic citizenship.

Despite the different ends to which these authors strive, they use economic citizenship to articulate Mexican American manhood as it changed in the mid-century. Economic citizenship as a figure of Mexican American manhood demands that readers see Chicanos not as migrants, recent arrivals, or even outsiders to national culture, but rather as producers of the very market logic that Chicano Studies (with its focus on working class actors and activism) has so long critiqued. These claims to economic incorporation would fall on deaf ears, and throughout the mid-century Mexican Americans struggled to move beyond the fields in search of social possibility and to define a productive manhood, to surpass the social forces binding Mexican Americans to working class status. Decades later, during the Chicano Movement, the conditions of economic possibility were strained to a breaking point that demanded new forms of social activism.

5

Queer Citizenship

José Antonio Villarreal's Pocho *and Chicano Cultural Nationalism of the Late Nineteenth Century*

When history is moving in many directions, any conclusion
is marked by uncertainty.
—Néstor García Canclini[1]

In a 1970 article entitled "Mexico and the Mexican-American," an anonymous author deliberated on the impact Mexican immigration has on the Mexican American population. The author plainly stated, "The border represents the single greatest threat to the economic and social evolution of Mexican-Americans unless bold new measures are adopted" and "the most divisive and harmful of these issues [dividing Mexicans and Mexican Americans] is migrant labor."[2] The author pointed out how "immigrants paradoxically have provided the strongest cultural bonds to Mexico while proving the most resistant to political organization in this country" (a familiar and widespread assessment of the possibility of integrating immigrant workers), yet called on the reader to look past these differences.[3] Accompanying the article was a rough, hand-drawn illustration of a balding, cigar-smoking man wearing a tie, dollar bills spilling out of his pockets while he plays puppeteer over the Rio Grande River. Together, the article and the image portrayed a Mexican origin community victimized by manipulative immigration and labor policies.

What at first glance appears a conservative stance on immigration is actually a Chicano-era appeal to Mexican American solidarity. This essay appeared in an issue of the short-lived magazine *Con Safos*, a popular but underground publication that sought to share stories and "reflections of life in the barrio."[4] Alongside articles about Chicano culture, quizzes testing readers' knowledge of urban life (such as the "Barriology Examination"), and illustrations parodying Chicano culture

Figure 5.1. "U.S.-Mexico Puppeteer," illustration from *Con Safos* Magazine, 1970, p. 20.

(most signed with the "c/s" that was the hallmark of Chicano graffiti artists), the magazine sought to inculcate in its readers a sense of common purpose. Edited by two young Chicano writers and activists out of California State University, Arturo Flores and Ralph "Rafas" Lopez Grijalva-Urbina, ten issues were published from 1968 to 1972, lauded by some as the first independent Chicano literary magazine.[5] The magazine now has cult status in Chicano culture as a relic of an earlier, more radical age. Yet the concerns that filled its pages reflect a slow and uneasy transition between the Chicano movement and earlier events.

Where the "Mexican American Generation" writers discussed in the previous chapter sought to cast men as middle-class labor, some twenty years later, on the eve of the Chicano movement, the possibility for economic integration seemed even less achievable.[6] In the ensuing decades, and increasingly throughout the 1950s and '60s, the distinction between U.S. citizen and foreigner eroded under a more generalized sense of racial difference. Despite the West and Southwest being the primary destination for Mexican immigrants and migrants, immigration was seen as a national problem and maintained continued attention across the media. Still, immigration had a paradoxical doubling, where undocumented labor was an economic necessity but brought with it continued policing of racial and national difference. Widespread concerns over immigration provoked a racialized panic that simultaneously ascribed illegality to workers invited to participate and an essential to the U.S. workforce, and "the notion that 'wetback' labor is both proper and indispensible has become so firmly implanted in Southwestern communities that its accompanying evils are taken as a matter of course."[7] Reacting to the xenophobia associated with agricultural immigration, education pioneer George I. Sanchez stated in a 1951 interview, "From a cultural standpoint [. . .] the influx of a million or more 'wetbacks' a year transforms the Spanish-speaking people of the Southwest from an ethnic group which might be assimilated with reasonable facility into what I call a 'culturally indigestible' peninsula of Mexico."[8] Speaking from the perspective of an American citizen, Sanchez was acutely aware of the collapsed difference between Mexican immigrants and Mexican American residents and citizens, and the difficulty this posed to integrating Mexican Americans into the national public.

Here, debates about immigration, labor, and nativism intersect to inform both the aims of the Chicano movement and how its participants conceived of themselves as men. As work and immigration collided to preclude the possibility of equality, Mexican Americans struggled to counteract social marginalization and to find new ways to define themselves as Americans. This chapter considers José Antonio Villarreal's novel *Pocho* (1959)—widely regarded as the "first Chicano novel"—in the context of the Bracero Program and larger debates about immigration to show how the novel gradually encouraged masculine displays in the body, paving the way for the Chicano movement, but also responding to mid-century characterizations of Mexican Americans. The novel portrays complicated pan-ethnic and queer positions that only recently have been considered part of a Chicano political agenda, and the novel's use of sexuality, especially autoeroticism, regulates the boundaries between self and other, between Mexican American and other ethnic groups, and enables different trajectories for manhood and citizenship. In calling attention to manhood, my reading asks not how the novel looks forward into a Chicano future, but how it looks backward at the earlier periods discussed in this book. The diminishing distinction between Mexican immigrant and Mexican American citizen that emerged alongside the demand for cheap labor reduced opportunities for economic mobility, and *Pocho* instead turns elsewhere to claim citizenship, locating Mexican American manhood within ideals of American democratic individualism, though unsuccessfully. The novel appealed to a familiar American foundational narrative of American democratic individualism even as it critiqued its uneven application and the political idea's inability to include Mexican Americans, which the novel dramatized through Richard's sexual ambiguity.

Richard's engagement with older ideas about American individualism point backward into an earlier time period, but also bridge forward to the Chicano movement. Reoriented to the nineteenth century, the novel contemplates the failed promise of American citizenship and opens up a different kind of future that stresses continuity across time and social movements. Similarly, in this light, the early writings and masculinist underpinnings of the Chicano movement reproduced ideas of biology, heredity, and indigeneity as internalized manhood. The novel offers what can be called queer American individualism that refused the (fu-

ture) heteronormative basis of the Chicano movement and challenged
the xenophobia of American culture. It exposes the impossibility of a
singular Mexican American cultural history, but such instability is a desirable condition as it leaves open the complexity of Mexican American
culture, past and future. In this historical frame, there is less rigidity
between what counts as Chicano and what does not; the boundaries
between Chicano and other cultural formations (Mexican American,
white, American, or even Latina/o) appear less firm than previously
understood.

Men at Arms: *Pocho*, the Bracero Program, and Immigration Policies

When the U.S. entered World War II in 1941, the American economy
shifted toward sustaining the war effort, and the U.S. labor force became
heavily directed toward these efforts, resulting in an increasing demand
for unskilled labor to fill the gap at home. More recently, scholars
have recovered stories about Mexican American contributions to the
war effort and how returning Mexican American soldiers mobilized
around the promise of social equality implicit in their service.[9] As is
well documented, they were routinely met with disappointment, continued disenfranchisement, and increased discrimination.[10] Attempting
to explain to his East Coast readers the racial dynamics in the U.S.
Southwest, a reporter for the *New York Times* writes of the "Hitlerian
sophistry" required to portray Mexican Americans as "an inferior race.
They do not rate as 'Caucasian' under California's restrictive real estate
covenants. Help-wanted signs differentiate them from 'whites.' Recently
some local school systems (which did not discriminate between whites
and Negroes) had segregated schools for 'Mexicans'—although a large
proportion of the younger generation are U.S. citizens by birth."[11]
Another reporter describes how, "despite the efforts of civic unity and
race-relations organizations" operating in California and specifically in
Los Angeles, a city described as "a melting pot of its own with large
bodies of Mexican-Americans, Japanese-Americans, and Negroes,"
Mexican American participation in World War II did little to ease
racial discrimination, even as the courts ruled educational segregation
unconstitutional.[12]

But during this period, in order to fill the void of able-bodied workers, the Mexican and U.S. governments jointly enacted the Bracero Program (1942–1964), a broad set of policies on the importation of Mexican labor to the U.S. In the first years of the program, 168,000 *braceros* (manual laborers) were recruited to the U.S., a number that quickly mushroomed, reaching approximately 425,000 annually by 1960, and culminating in millions of Mexicans entering and exiting the United States during the program's twenty-two years.[13] The majority of these migrants and immigrants crossed legally, invited by the U.S. government and employers as a necessary facet of the U.S. economy. While the Bracero Program targeted male workers, women regularly migrated, too; during the Bracero Program, women often entered the U.S. as dependents of male workers, as stipulated in their contracts. Catherine Ramirez, Patricia Portales, Jimmy Patiño, and Maggie Rivas-Rodrigues have shown how Mexican American women negotiated their position as racialized women against competing claims to nationalism and resistance in the years during and after World War II.[14]

Yet while Mexican Americans were welcomed as agricultural labor, they were simultaneously the targets of repressive immigration policies, such as Operation Wetback, which, beginning in the summer of 1954, forcibly deported over a million Mexicans and Mexican Americans, many of whom were American citizens. One unintended consequence of what the previously quoted *New York Times* reporter described as this "atmosphere of social and economic bondage" was that Mexican Americans again found themselves indistinguishable from immigrants in the public imaginary.[15] Stable middle-class employment could no longer sustain claims to citizenship, as those labors did not reflect the changing community and public perception. Despite these concerns, Mexican American groups in the 1950s often tried to ally themselves with Mexican immigrants, yet these efforts routinely met with obstacles from within Mexican American communities and from mainstream white society.

Villarreal's *Pocho*—a term that describes the mixed national and cultural heritage of Mexican Americans—responds to the "economic manhood" of the immigrant Mexican laborers flooding the U.S., a point often lost in the novel's critical reception.[16] According to critic Raymund A. Paredes, *Pocho* is "the "first 'Chicano' novel [. . .] working with no antecedents, no one on whose work to enlarge."[17] Paredes's landmark essay exhibits a recurring tendency to view the Chicano movement as the moment of inception for Mexican American cultural production. A decade later, Ramon Saldívar would reiterate Paredes's claim but expand on the possibilities it presents. Saldívar's *Chicano Narrative* (1990) was in many ways field-formative, providing the first book-length theoretical engagement with Chicano literature. For Saldívar, *Pocho* functions as a liminal text between older residual cultural forms and the Chicano movement, a "shadowy, in-between identity that is formed by individualist ideologies of which he is only dimly aware."[18] He makes clear that no single text "in any homogenous manner [can] serve as the real or fictive 'origin' of Chicano narrative," yet along with Américo Paredes's *George Washington Gomez*, it remains one of the "originary Chicano narrative texts."[19] Perhaps because of these assessments, Villarreal's *Pocho* has come to serve as the de facto cultural beginning of the Chicano movement.[20]

Since then, critics have regularly used *Pocho* to mark the start of the movement's cultural production, seeing its publication as a proleptic event in Chicano cultural history. However, the recurring insistence on *Pocho* as an originary moment in Mexican American literature reifies the absence of Mexican Americans from earlier American cultural production by orienting cultural history into the future, to the late twentieth century and beyond. *Pocho*'s centrality rests in part in its singularity, as, until relatively recently, it was thought to be one of few novels written by Mexican Americans in the mid-twentieth century. Rather than a progenitor of the Chicano movement spontaneously generating a Chicano male protagonist, *Pocho* sits within a longer historical trajectory of citizenship, manhood, and immigration that can help reframe the Chicano movement and the divergent historical subjects it left behind. I read the novel as a queer critique of American democratic individualism accessible through sexual citizenship, which decenters the heterosexual male as the basis for Chicano manhood and destabilizes the homophobia and sexism of the movement.[21] If *Pocho* is to occupy a position as the foundational moment of the movement, then we need to recognize the gendered complexity of the foundation upon which our house is built.

Reading *Pocho* in a longer genealogy of Mexican American manhood complicates the heteronormative basis of Chicano literary history. For the protagonist's father, Juan Rubio, "it was enough that he maintain his dignity as a man, that he be true to himself, that he satisfy his body of its needs—and his body needs more than tortillas."[22] The sexual drive begins the novel, as Juan asserts himself as a formidable and dangerous man in his desire for a young woman, a prostitute and dancer, at a cantina. To assert his authority, Juan shoots and kills the woman's lover and alleged pimp, and the novel's plot is put into motion through an act of sexual aggression. The violence manifests in two ways: as an assault against the reluctant prostitute ("she rubbed the four white spots on her arm where his fingers had momentarily stopped the circulation" [*Pocho* 3]) and against the man who challenged Juan's authority (Juan "calmly shot him once more as he lay writhing on the floor" [4]). With a reputation as an associate of General Pancho Villa, Juan initially shields himself from any repercussions for these actions in the town of Juarez, but even this is insufficient. His act of sexual and physical violence compels him to immigrate, as the man whom Juan kills is Mexican American, "from the other side," a fact that demonstrates the permeability of border cultures as much as it further complicates Juan's status as progenitor of Chicano subjectivity (7). The bulk of the narrative issues from the generational schism between the ex-revolutionary immigrant Juan Rubio and his Americanized son Richard, who faces the burden of cultural integration into the U.S., acknowledging that "the transition from the culture of the old world to that of the new should never have been attempted in one generation" (135). What begins as an immigration novel about the Mexican Revolution becomes a generational account of an emerging Chicano nationalism.

Like his protagonist, Villarreal's upbringing was marked by the differences between his own life and that of the white world surrounding him. He was born in Los Angeles in 1924 to migrant farmworkers, after his parents fled the intensely violent first years of the Mexican Revolution. Like his protagonist Richard, Villarreal came of age in Santa Clara, California, before leaving his home to serve in the navy during World War II. After the war, he returned to California, earned a B.A. from the University of California–Berkeley in 1950, and worked to establish himself as a writer; however, it was not until after Anchor Books published the second edition of *Pocho* in paperback in 1971, during the Chicano movement, that he was able to support himself and his family through his writing.[23] Certainly, Villarreal has a complicated if troubled relationship to the Chicano movement, at one point repudiating the political demands of the movement and prioritizing writing as his sole objective. Frances Aparicio notes, "In a literary decision of pragmatic compromising, Villarreal silences and hides the Spanish behind the English signifiers. Rather than creating a bilingual text that would reaffirm the cultural and linguistic realities of Juan and Consuelo, Villarreal opted for the needs of the dominant readership, using English to mask the Spanish of this first generation."[24] While further archival recovery has shown Villarreal was not exceptional in his linguistic choice (as seen in many of the texts discussed herein), he explicitly stated that he was more interested in reaching a broad audience than in working toward the political goals of the Chicano movement.[25] Despite Villarreal's discomfort with the movement (even as it provided an audience for his work), the cultural work that the novel has subsequently performed for and after the movement resembles the print culture of the earlier period, in that the novel disseminated a particular form of Chicano manhood and cultural nationalism through a coming of age story.

As José Aranda notes, "*Pocho* is a stridently masculinist narrative" where "Juan Rubio's narrative of failure in the United States becomes the contradictory ground upon which Richard develops a masculine identity capable of negotiating the discriminatory contours of American citizenship."[26] Richard's father is unwaveringly devoted to a single ideological position represented by Pancho Villa, who functions for him as the symbol of political and manly virtue. Juan adheres to a strict code of masculine behavior forged in conflict and under the service of Villa, and following Villa's death, decries that "there are no honest people left [. . . .] Is honor that worthless?" (14). Juan readily faces death while serving under Villa and willingly kills in his name. When Villa asks Juan to undertake a dangerous attack, Juan unquestionably accedes, stating that "at that moment if he had asked me to turn my backside and submit to him, I would have done it without a qualm" (11). Juan uses the moment to demonstrate his absolute loyalty to Villa and his cause, but does so by equating a homosexual act as worse than the possibility of death. In contrast to the rigors of rebellion, Juan sees the formal, institutionalized military spaces of the Mexican Army as effeminate, describing his commanding officers with

Figure 5.2. Picture of Villarreal and *Pocho*'s cover from *El Excentrico*, 1960, José Antonio Villarreal Papers, 1950–2010, Santa Clara University Library.

the homophobic slurs "maricon" and "fag," a practice that leads to his eventual expulsion (8). Under Juan's martial codes of honor, one's own life ranks below homosexuality in a hierarchy of manhood.

Later, Juan condemns even the possibility of any non-heterosexual, non-patriarchal sexuality, threatening to "strangle [Richard] with my own hands" should he reveal himself as gay, as "one of 'those others'" (168). (Despite the threats of violence, Richard realizes "they [homosexuals] have their place," a meek rebuttal to his father's overarching homophobia, but one that acknowledges a spectrum of sexual orientations [168].) Juan rigidly polices sexuality, which, like the border that divides the U.S. and Mexico, underpins a conciliatory logic that "we are so near to the other side that one errant bullet could do irreparable harm to our relationship," thereby tying together violence, sexuality, and nationalism (7). Juan's masculine standard is inherently contradictory, and "indeed, the father was a paradox" (103). On the one hand, manhood is beset by an ongoing, irresolvable crisis and constantly compelled to assert male authority, as "only those who are yet completely men are in danger" (14). On the other hand, according to Juan, "if a man has been a man, he will always be a man," linking manhood to irrevocable bodily if not biological determinism (15). As a refugee from the revolution, Juan symbolically stands in for the immigrant experience depicted as a masculine trauma from which he never fully recovers. Even though the events in the narrative take place during the Great Depression, these episodes reflect as much on the Bracero Program, in its heyday during the 1950s when Villarreal was writing. It is into this embodied contradiction that the novel's chief protagonist, Richard, is born.

Chicano Sexuality's Forgotten Past

Richard, exposed to the homophobia and patriarchal inequality of his father, struggles to suture multiple national, gendered subject positions with social alliances that are organized around class. Early in the narrative, labor organization is conducted in at least four languages— "English, Spanish, Portuguese, and Italian—but as the group grew, it became increasingly difficult to maintain order" because of the escalating diversity among its participants, and this figures prominently in

Richard's negotiation of gendered cultural authority (48). The workers prepare to strike against exploitative working conditions, during which the prepubescent Richard admires the white daughter of a farm owner, Marla Jamison, for her physical characteristics (the "most beautiful thing he had ever seen") and her authoritative, manly display; Marla, "defiant," confronts and calls the men "cowards," "without even the guts to talk, without even the guts to look squarely at us" (54). Since her father "never had a son," Marla is free to cross gendered boundaries, and because "she had worked among men all her life, and knew their vernacular well," she maintains a degree of authority over the men (52, 55). Villarreal reminds the reader of the Jamison family's respect for the farm workers, identifying Mr. Jamison as a "good man" who fraternizes with the laborers, raised his daughter "to be the kind of girl who would go with him, Jack Perreira [a laborer], to the high-school senior prom," and "even got drunk in their company" (52, 55). Here, Villarreal describes a complicated relationship between Anglo and Mexican that does not subscribe to simple binaries of opposition forged through mutual if uneven labor. The workers threaten to strike and the potential loss of the pear crop infuriates Marla, who hopes to "shame them into behaving like men" (54). Shotgun-toting, multi-lingual, and authoritative Marla holds the men's attention not for her physical attractiveness but for the respect she commands from them. Marla presents an alternative figure of authority, not just outside the familial space but female. She signals Richard's first recognition of the limits to the post-revolutionary masculinity of his father, and her influence lingers until the novel's end, when Richard reflects upon "all the beautiful people he had known": the community that raised him, including Marla Jamison (187).

Richard's circle of friends mirrors the pan-ethnic makeup of the workers and, as John Alba Cutler has shown, "There is no Mexican-American Generation in the novel in the sense of a cohort of Mexican Americans who identify with one another as a community"; instead, a shared working class status unifies the group.[27] In place of common cultural identity, Richard must actively negotiate competing masculine values across ethnicity, calling attention to the ways in which none, individually, suffice. Imitating Marla's authoritative persona, Richard "aped her stance, and oddly his small figure was not farcical to the men" (53). Marla's masculine influence is licensed in part by her unmarked racial status as white, but throughout the novel, pan-ethnic solidarity is forged through sexuality, and often at the cost of female agency. Until the onset of puberty, a Portuguese American childhood friend, Zelda, served as Richard's peer group's leader, dominating with her spunk and ferocity. Yet when sexual curiosity creeps into their lives, Zelda is goaded into a sexual act as testament to her daring and courage. Richard himself is one of the driving forces, playing into her courage and desire to lead, which problematically fractures the group along gendered and sexual lines. Following the first of these encounters, "it was understood now that she did not belong in the way she had, and it was on occasions when she especially missed the old joyfulness of their camaraderie that she joined them somewhere, usually at the Rubio barn, and paid with her body for their company" (119). This scene provides an example of, as Ben Olguin observes, many "Latino-authored war narratives [which] are replete with 'male' bonding scenes involving sexual violence against women."[28] Here, the group rehearses a deplorable masculine dynamic that normalizes sexual violence.

While Zelda pays the price for incipient pan-ethnic solidarity, for Richard the scene enables their pan-ethnic bonds. Zelda agrees to have sex with all the boys in order to prove her own "manliness," but she at first refuses to sleep with the Japanese American Thomas. Richard, however, insists that Thomas be included, asking, "How do you think he was born?" (118). Richard goes further, using sexuality to extend pan-ethnic male homosocial privilege, invoking his own authority within the group to demand that Thomas be included: "If he [Thomas] doesn't do it, nobody's gonna do it." The friends are shocked by Richard's brazen command, acting "like you was the boss or something," but Zelda reluctantly accedes to the inclusionary logic of his imperative, choosing group solidarity over personal safety, since "after all, you're one of the gang" (119). For Richard and his friends, who fail to recognize the courage Zelda exhibits by submitting her body to the desires of her male peers, the sexual act is seen as a physical expression of male dominance. Moreover, these acts primarily support homoerotic bonds among the friends, lacking any intimacy between Zelda and the participants. Richard "felt extremely good" objectifying and being the object of devotion for his female companions (both Zelda and the Oklahoma-raised Protestant Mary confess their "love" for him), choosing masculine privilege and refusing their equality (141).

While Richard purports not to ascribe to the violent expressions of masculine performance, he nonetheless reproduces their violence unwittingly. Yet his understanding of manhood remains unstable. Throughout, Juan remains the most potent model of manhood—described by Richard as "not the kind of man that can be told what to do by anybody" (94). To some extent, Juan represents an extreme version of Kimmel's self-made man. For Kimmel, the self-made man's value is in his ability to manipulate capitalist culture to achieve economic success, and Juan's insistence on remaining unbound and untethered to a particular political or economic system asserts an independence exceeding even the self-made man. As a Mexican exile clinging to the nostalgic memory of a fallen revolution with dreams of eventual return, Juan never commits to the United States as anything other than a transitory residence, even as "deep within he knew he was one of the lost ones" (31). Unlike his father, Richard realizes the permanence of his residency in the U.S., and from this realization ensues intergenerational patriarchal conflict.

Invoking a rhetoric of manliness, Richard challenges his father by reminding Juan, "You taught me that I was a man. I was never a niño to you but a macho, a buck, and you talked to me like a man" (130). To garner the respect of his father, Richard must convince Juan to recognize Richard's own masculinity. He does so, and Juan professes, "You are right also, my son, in that you are a man, and it is good, because to a Mexican being *that* is the most important thing. If you are a man, your life is half lived; what follows does not really matter" (131, emphasis original).[29] Juan affirms Richard's manhood, but does so under the stipulation of national citizenship; Richard is a man inasmuch as he is Mexican. For Juan, Richard's national obligation is synonymous with family; as Ricky Rodriguez has convincingly shown, the heteronormative family possesses a powerful identificatory force in Chicano culture, and uncovers "the ways that Chicana/o cultural nationalism and notions of *la familia* continue to be codified by dominant articulations of masculinity" (21).[30] Yet Richard cannot comply, "refus[ing] to accept sexual satisfaction as the sublime effort of life" and afraid that "a man who lived such a life as his father could call this existence happiness" (129, 132).

Perhaps the most visible rift between Richard and Juan is in their perception and treatment of João Pedro Manõel Alves, known as Joe Pete. Joe Pete works as a shepherd in the Santa Clara area and leverages a profound influence over Richard. A Portuguese immigrant, he provides Richard a window to global culture and access to "poets and painters, and all about Portugal and Africa, and about nature," things that otherwise are outside the scope of his limited adolescent experience (89). This connection to the broader world is what draws Richard to Joe Pete, who reminds Richard that "no man is better than another, any more than every man is equal, simply because we are all different from each other," a point made more poignant because of Joe Pete's own sexuality (82). Joe Pete reveals to Richard that he is a closeted gay man, who "found himself strongly attracted to men," although supposedly these urges have "disappeared now" (84). Joe Pete's repressed sexuality haunts him throughout his life, and he wrestles with himself in the hope that "before long I will surely be well again," internalizing social pressure against homosexuality that pathologizes his sexual orientation (84).

Joe Pete's repressed sexuality pushes him into repeated acts of sexual displacement, or at least confusion. He reveals to Richard an episode with "a great poet" with whom he "discoursed much" that resulted in a threesome with the poet and his wife (86). Later, he is accused of raping a young girl, another disturbing act of sexual violence that complicates the novel's sexual politics but does not negate Richard's sympathetic view of him. In the novel's traditional social world, Joe Pete's actions are deemed sexual deviance, yet the novel begs the question, how much of his behavior is caused by his social alienation due to his sexual orientation? When the police come to investigate the case, young Richard finds himself explaining sexual difference to the state authorities. The police officer is unsure of how to approach the issue, but Richard bluntly states, "Was he a homosexual? No, he wasn't," teaching "a new word to the man" (89). Joe Pete's story ends with Juan's equally furious and terrified reaction about the possibility of his son's complicity in homosexual acts, threatening to kill a police officer for merely associating his son with homosexuality.

The scene foreshadows Richard's later encounter with the law, yet Joe Pete and Richard's nonsexual relationship (as far as the reader knows) blossoms into a close friendship. Thus, homosexuality connects Richard's own burgeoning sexual awakening with global or pan-ethnic alliances, and Richard's sense of developing manhood is not opposed to homosexuality, but rather dependent on it.[31] In contrast to Juan's masculinity that demands heterosexual coupling as an affirmation of a man's sexuality ("because only a Mexican woman can appreciate the fact that her husband is a man" [94]) or to reproduce the material conditions of everyday life ("if only to do the work around the house" [84]), Joe Pete offers an alternative experience that emphasizes individuality and tolerance. His ostracization because of sexual difference mirrors the social alienation of ethnic minorities in the novel, and exposes the contradictions of intolerance practiced by the Mexican American community's attachment to gender norms. As with Marla, Richard returns to Joe Pete in the novel's final page, and the "thought of his friend Joe Pete Manõel, though not forgotten, did not hurt as much" (102). Perhaps such frank treatment of non-normative sexuality seems out of place in a mid-century novel about ethnic identity, but acknowledging its presence reframes the origins of Chicano manhood. The novel is rife with sexuality in a variety of forms (heterosexual, homosexual, violent, pederasty, etc.) and goes into surprising detail about the sexual lives of its characters and specific sexual acts, yet the novel's adoption within Chicano literature omitted its sexual plurality. Conflicted by the unequal gendered distribution of social power, Richard distances himself from patriarchal forms of masculine authority and experiments with others. In the process, he begins to internalize the ideals of American democratic individualism.

The Autoerotics of Citizenship: Individualism and the Body

Although Richard is drawn to Joe Pete's cultural knowledge, he feels compelled to affirm his own heterosexuality, reminding the reader that "his father was as fanatical about masculinity as Joe Pete Manõel was about [his roots in the Portuguese] royalty" (90). Here, Villarreal equates masculinity with heterosexuality, but Richard is unconvinced by the implied syllogism, as his encounters with Joe Pete and others routinely test the boundaries of sexual orientation. Repeatedly, Richard tries to refuse socially codified forms of masculine behavior, however unsuccessfully, claiming, "He would never be ashamed again for doing something against the unwritten code of honor. Codes of honor were really stupid—it amazed him that he had just learned this—and what people thought was honorable was not important, because he was the important guy" (108). His focus on his individuality and the need to define masculinity internally leads Richard to understand his relationship with his friends through sexual acts, and conversely, sexual acts help him distinguish himself from his social group. The relationship between sexuality and the novel's portrayal of the individual self is most visible in the scenes of masturbation. In what might seem a strange inclusion in an ethnic American novel from the mid-twentieth century, Villarreal includes a long and detailed scene of masturbation by Richard and his peers. Here, masturbation as a social act offers a corporeal expression of group identity and social belonging, one that troubles neat assumptions about Chicano cohesiveness and group dynamics.

Beyond its function as self-stimulation, masturbation enables gratification without sociality or intimacy. It focuses sexuality on the individual instead of as a shared act, creating a boundary between self and other. Such emphasis on the individual comes at a cost, and relying on one's own body to assert masculinity poses a paradox because masturbation is non-reproductive and, as George Mosse tells us, has historically been regarded as not only a threat to the health of the individual but also to the health of the nation.[32] For Richard, bodily control serves to police the boundaries between himself and others, as part of an ethnic immigrant community and somehow separate from it. Richard's internal focus picks up on other forms of American manhood; as Michael Kimmel notes, "The [Great] Depression had forced many men to abandon their faith in the marketplace as certain to confirm their manhood," and white manhood came to be "redefined away from achievement in the public sphere and reconceived as the exterior manifestation of a certain inner sense of oneself" (136). In the novel, Richard tries to assert external control through the control of his body. He is not interested in publicly proving his manhood in front of friends, but rather of affirming his sexual prowess to himself through autoerotic play. His desired mastery of the body (and its pleasure) gradually imposes a heightened gender division that subsumes earlier attempts at cross-gender collaboration under his own sexual drive. Autoeroticism thus sexually represents the paradox of national citizenship: how to ally oneself with a larger group yet maintain the individuality necessary to claim citizenship.

For Richard and his friends, group masturbation provides a scene of what Eve Kosofsky Sedgwick describes as male homosocial bonding where, among his male peers, the expression of social prowess is performed through "the erotic pastime of youth."[33] Masturbation serves a dual-edged sword; Richard is at once compelled to perform the act but also distrustful of its social outcomes. Despite this, masturbation becomes central to their social organization, albeit problematically. Initially, Richard "sensed that for him there was something unnatural in the act—not morally or physically wrong but wrong in a manner he did not wholly understand" and thus he hesitates to participate with the other boys (113). Richard distrusts masturbation because he insists that "intimacy demanded that a sexual experience be shared" (113). Yet even moments of collective self-gratification lack the social intimacy. Richard's youthful experience with sexuality both distances him from and affixes him to his friends, as they discuss the sexual act and at times compete with each other to prove their manliness. With the counsel of his closest friend, the Italian American Ricky, he eventually gains the confidence to submit to his own physical urges.

The novel pays close attention to the bodily fluids masturbation produces and the associated fears it generates in Richard: "the horrible visions of a dripping, deformed creature someday crawling out of the plumbing to claim him for a father in the eyes of the world" (114). Following the climactic conclusion of the act, Richard calls out, "I'm a father, I'm a father," linking onanism with parental authority but also with the creative act, both sexual and writerly. Unable to express his fears and confusion verbally, his naïve sense of procreation, rendered in patrilineal terms, and the act's perceived potential as progenitor of some future self offer a strange juxtaposition. Despite his initial discomfort, the sexual act enables Richard to see himself as creator, if only of some misguided idea of procreation. Earlier he could dismiss the potential dangers of sexual self-indulgence, but that changes: "It had been so easy to scoff at his friends for believing the idea, but now that he was one of them, he was not so sure as he had been" (114). Through masturbation

Richard recognizes the limits imposed on his individuality; he struggles with the apparent similarity between himself, his own body and its needs, and those of his friends. He "never joined the others, and hid his secret from them," trying to maintain his individuality, until eventually one of his friends tricks him into confessing his own actions, exposing the fantasy of his own exceptionalism (117).

There is a disconnect between Richard's own desire for sexual individuality and his need for collective, emotional intimacy. These moments of individual sexuality unhinge social norms, and, in contrast to his friends, Richard is much more comfortable with verbal expressions of emotion and intimacy than with physical ones. The verbal expression of intimacy, however, ruptures the connection with Ricky; their friendship is tested when Richard verbally expresses his admiration for his friend, openly stating, "We love each other" (112). Ricky accuses Richard of being queer, replacing intimacy with homophobia, which leaves Richard infuriated, accusing him of ruining their friendship, "killing one of the nicest things we both have!" and leaving him to realize that "they could be friendly, perhaps, but they could never be friends again" (112). The novel depends on heterosexism to diffuse the homosocial and even homoerotic charge of these and other encounters, as in the case of Zelda. The strict adherence to heterosexual norms that require the suppression of emotion prohibits a continued alliance.

Following this unraveling, Ricky cautions Richard, worried that he will "go wrong [. . .] running around with all kinds of funny people," including *pachucos* and "a couple of guys that looked queer as hell" (177). Confident or perhaps unsure of his own sexuality, Richard is less threatened by the sexual orientation of others, defending both his freedom of association and the individual rights of others to live their lives as they see fit. He refuses to be judged by his associations, claiming that "if I know a guy who stole something, that doesn't make me a crook" (177). However, despite a stated desire to associate with whomever he chooses, he still cannot free himself entirely from the prevailing social attitudes that criminalize homosexuality, one of several contradictions surrounding sexuality in the novel.

Masturbation becomes a convenient expression for internalized manhood because it demonstrates a kind of sovereignty, over the self and metonymically as a political being. Indeed, masturbation allows the individual an outlet for the expression of sexual identity while maintaining control over the body and delimiting sociality. The self-gratifying act and the perceived self-sovereignty it grants produce horizontal affiliations among the boys themselves, affiliations that both underwrite and undermine their collectivity. Nonetheless, these alliances bely the supposed unity of the Chicano male subject. By emphasizing the individual and internalized expression of manhood, and exposing the contradictions inherent in it, *Pocho* struggles to define the boundary between self and other, between a Chicano male subject and other ethnic subject positions. These sexualities become a socially symbolic act, a forgotten piece of the novel's place as foundational text of the Chicano movement.

A Chicano Critique of American Democratic Individualism

Richard tries to solidify the boundaries between himself and his social group by regulating his sexual activity. By locating manhood on and in the body, *Pocho* attempts to resolve the tension between nativism and foreignness, depicting its protagonist as part of a pan-ethnic community but also as an independent actor not reducible to foreignness. Lázaro Lima has argued, "*Pocho* made Mexicanness intelligible to the majority culture by affirming—through a novel written in English, by a Mexican, about Mexicans in the United States—that Mexicans were not part of the geographic integrity of the country," and cemented an image of Mexicans in the U.S. imaginary as foreigners or immigrants, despite a century of cultural and national participation.[34] Lima's interest is in the Latino body as a site used to "disembod[y] subjects from the protocols of citizenship," yet in contrast to Lima's reading of *Pocho*'s foreignness, the invocation of queerness and sexuality in *Pocho* empowers the Chicano body as the contradictory terrain through which to critique American democratic individualism, a decidedly U.S. national concept emerging from the earlier period.[35]

Individualism is a central tenet of American political and social philosophy, a cornerstone of the mode of liberal democracy practiced in the United States seen in the discourses of individual rights and self-governance, the myth of self-reliance and capitalist achievement, or as a moral philosophy. Scholars trace American democratic individualism back to a much earlier period in the formation of the American republic, to Alexis de Tocqueville or the transcendentalist thought of Ralph Waldo Emerson or Henry David Thoreau. At its core, American democratic individualism, "as theorized or regularly lived, maintains the view or exemplifies the sentiment that people—whether all or only some— count or matter apart from their roles, functions, or place in society," according to George Kateb, in one of his more prominent statements.[36] Individualism is inseparable from democratic life and supports ideas of meritocracy where the only barriers to individual achievement— regardless of gender, race, or class status—are effort and hard work. These ideas have become central and formative components of American identity.

Throughout the novel, Richard is preoccupied with the possibilities of and limits imposed upon his individuality. Throughout, he ruminates on "the feeling that *being* was important, and he *was*—so he knew that he would never succumb to the foolish social pressures again" (108, emphasis in original). Richard repeatedly worries about "the demands of tradition, of culture, of the social structure on an individual. Not comprehending, he was again aware of the dark, mysterious force, and was resolved that he would rise above it" (95). Richard occupies a precarious position between intense attachment to and repugnance with the possibility of individuality. Although he insists on his distinctiveness, the possibility of personal uplift, the Horatio Alger–style "up by your bootstraps" mentality so closely associated with American culture, is replaced by an intensely individualistic notion of identity and cultural belonging. In his drive for individuality detached from culture, Richard pulls back from all social institutions—his friends, the church, his family (131). He reacts against even the liberal acquaintances he makes when he enrolls in community college, as "they constituted a threat to his individuality" (175). He goes so far as to reject all forms of social attachment, and it is the freedom of possibility that emerges from individuality:

> I can be a part of everything, he thought, because I am the only one capable of controlling my destiny. . . . Never—no, never—will I allow myself to become a part of a group—to become classified, to lose my individuality. . . . I will not become a follower, nor will I allow myself to become a leader, because I must be myself and accept for myself only that which I value, and not what is being valued by everyone else these days. . . . Like a

Goddamn suit of clothes they're wearing this season or Cuban heels. . . .
A style in ethics. (152–3)

Richard wants neither to be part of a larger group nor to distinguish himself within it as a leader. He asserts the importance of the individual self as the ultimate arbiter of value, a hyperbolic expression of democratic individualism detached from all social networks. Such complete attachment to the singularity of the self offers an exaggerated form of the ideal, one that butts against the ideals of the Chicano movement. Nor do the pachucos/zoot suiters offer a viable alternative, as the allusion to the ephemerality or superficiality of the suit of cloth, since even ethnic affiliations are unsatisfactory to Richard's insistence on his individuality.[37]

Richard's discomfort with collective identity echoes Ralph Waldo Emerson's dictum, "What I must do is all that concerns me, not what the people think."[38] In his canonical essay "Self-Reliance," now a touchstone for discussions of American individualism, Emerson expounds on the meanings of individualism and success, stating, "My life is for itself and not for a spectacle."[39] Emerson articulates a commitment to the individual apart from his or her social worth, and Emerson and his intellectual descendants remark on the threat posed to the individual by society.[40] Individualism is a central facet of American democratic life, but implicit in Emerson's position is a masculine privilege enabled by the invisible labor of women and people of color. In reading *Pocho* within Emersonian individualism, Richard attempts to adopt the racial and gendered privileges typically granted to the male subject Emerson imagines. Like a zoot suit, he tries on this foundational story associated with American manhood but cannot reconcile his individuality with the realities of life as a racialized Mexican American.

Political scientist Jack Turner builds upon the work of George Kateb and others, offering an exposition of American individualism that attempts to include non-majoritarian perspectives. Turner proposes that American democratic individualism has been central to the political philosophy of the United States even as he critiques individualism for the blind spots it produces about the possibility for self- or communal improvement. Turner turns to the writings of prominent African Americans thinkers such as Frederick Douglass, Ralph Ellison, and James Baldwin to identify how the "racially oppressed individual must fight for a positive sense of self in an environment designed to make him feel irreparably damaged or inhuman."[41] Turner's project is instructive of the ways that minoritarian subjects are forced to confront American individualism as the *barrier* to social advancement, since American democratic individualism frames individual failure as exclusively shortcomings of personal exertion or ability rather than the product of systemic inequality or exclusion, requiring individuals to "critically evaluat[e] inherited moralities and revis[e] them appropriately" and "experience . . . trying to achieve it in the face of systematic subjugation."

Richard's insistence on individuality is as much a cogitation on the idea of American democratic individualism as it is a dramatization of cultural mixing embodied by the figure of the *pocho*, placing him squarely within this American tradition. However, the novel's queer sexuality unsettles any commitment to individuality, posing an embodied contradiction. Despite repeated scenes of sexual acts and sexual violence, he refuses to accept sexuality as the pinnacle of social and self-fulfillment: "I am what you say [a man], not only because of what I carry between my legs but because I have put it to use. There must be more!" (131). Richard finds himself uncomfortable in both public life and private home, forced to accept his transitional status, but never fully accepting of that position, what Chris Newfield holds as "a balance between individual and community that forms *the* enduring tradition of American political sensibility [. . .] that allows its loss of both private autonomy and public sovereignty to *feel OK*."[42] Richard is variously arrogant, condescending, sexist, and often unsympathetic. Nonetheless, he presents a conflicted position, one that offers a non-nationalist claim to citizenship grounded in queerness and discomfort, and that exposes the failures of the promise of uplift while not surrendering its capabilities. Here lies Richard's potential to reanimate Chicano Studies for our current moment, yet without desiring to recover nor confirm Richard as the quintessential Chicano subject. Rather, given the central status of the novel within Chicano culture, when placed within a longer, U.S.-national Mexican American past, the novel and its protagonist enable different possible futures.

Not just foreshadowing the Chicano subject, *Pocho* offers an account of individualism in American society that recalls that of Tocqueville some two centuries earlier and discussed at the beginning of this book.

Tocqueville places his faith in the institutions of government, before whom all citizens share a universalized equality, an equality that breaks down in private lives. Tocqueville claims, "Each [American] is willing to acknowledge all his fellow-citizens as his equals, but he will only receive a very limited number of them amongst his friends or his guests [. . .] Whatever may be the general endeavor of a community to render its members equal and alike, the personal pride of individuals will always seek to rise above the line, and to form somewhere an inequality to their own advantage."[43] Toqueville describes the tension between individuality and group identification inherent in political participation, one that Richard struggles with throughout the novel. He both distances himself from his social group and refuses to partake in the institutions that promise universal equality, attempting to deny all efforts of inclusion even as he cannot escape its processes of racialization. The contradiction between supposed institutional equality and individual inequality is exposed through his encounters with the police, the institution trusted with enforcing the state's laws.

Until he enlists in the navy, Richard refuses to participate in or validate the authority of either state institutions or cohesive group identity. In a crucial episode, Richard and his friends are out searching for car parts, a theft contemplated though never enacted, when some officers accuse them of posing a racialized, sexual threat. The boys were unaware of their alleged proximity to two women, yet a police officer charges, "You think you can come here and just take a clean white girl and do what you want!" (158). Richard and his friends are profiled and arrested on suspicion of attempted rape, but are soon found innocent. Afterward, one police officer invites Richard to join the local police force, prompted by the need for a Mexican American "on the side of law and order," which Richard ardently refuses, saying, "I'm no Jesus Christ. Let 'my people' take care of themselves" (162). The novel acknowledges Mexican Americans as a growing demographic and the need to include this growing segment of the population within the apparatus of the nation-state. Since the police force historically served to enforce the subordinate status of Mexican Americans, the novel refuses the possibility of its role as an institution of social progress. Still, in rejecting the officer's proposition, Richard disclaims social bonds born out of shared cultural background. There is no sense of civic responsibility here, but rather an egotistical sense of his connection to the world. Richard even questions, "Who the hell were his people? He had always felt that all people were his people—not in that nauseating God-made-us-all-equal way, for to him that was a deception; the exact opposite was obvious" (162). At the same time that he denies cultural unity, he exposes the contradictions in a presumed universal subject, a fiction that he immediately recognizes as a "deception." His increasing isolation from both white and Mexican American cultural forms culminates in a complete dismissal of all forms of cooperative action, yet isolation is also untenable and Richard undulates between these extremes.

The reference to "my people" is bracketed, calling into question the very possibility of such a category. As political scientist Cristina Beltrán points out, a core "principle of the movement [was] the celebration of community and the critique of American individualism," which "viewed American society and culture as defined by its overemphasis on the individual at the expense of the community."[44] *Pocho* was the prototypical cultural formation for the movement, yet its young protagonist is deeply ambivalent about both the communitarian concerns of the Chicano movement and its critique of individualism. It is Richard's confrontation with the structures of power—the police, that institution of state regulation—that "gave him a new point of view about his world" and "that for the first time in his life he felt discriminated against" (162–3). Previously Richard was naively blind to racial and social differences in his life, where agents of law were not representatives of a system of exclusion but "people—in fact, neighbors. One evening had changed all that for him, and now he knew that he would never forget what had happened tonight" (163). Richard emerges from the encounter a changed person, and perhaps the most tragic consequence is the way in which this scene alienates Richard from his friends. Richard, having spent some time in an interrogation room with a police officer, becomes the object of his friends' suspicion:

> And now they [his friends] were thinking that if he had not been there, they would not have been accused by association, and therefore not beaten. They were right of course. And, in a way he had betrayed them, but they did not know this. [. . .] And he knew that from this moment things would not be the same for them again. Something had happened

to their relationship, particularly to his relationship with Ricky. More than ever he knew they could never be friends again, because somehow he represented an obstacle to the attainment of certain goals Ricky had imposed upon his life. (164)

Richard's commitment to individuality fractures even the pan-ethnic alliances he had previously built, recognizing the competing individual aims that each of them possess. Where Ricky had earlier enabled Richard's embodied fantasy of individualism, he now exposes its impossibility. The mere fact of Richard's ethnic makeup—his brownness—represents the obstacle to Ricky's own aspirations for social mobility, which Richard is no longer able to disregard.

Pocho poses a constitutive contradiction between the imagined universal subject of national identity and the embodied ethnic subject that Richard and the novel have come to represent.[45] The contradiction between Richard's ahistorical aspirations and the reality of his immediate environment demonstrates the paradox represented by the novel. This contradiction echoes the concerns found in one of the founding documents of the Chicano movement, *El Plan de Santa Barbara*, the manifesto demanding the institutionalization of Chicano Studies in California and across the U.S. nation and foundational tract of MEChA, the Movimiento Estudiantil Chicano de Aztlán [Chicana/o Student Movement of Aztlán], a group organized for the empowerment and educational achievement of its members and community.[46] The 157-page *Plan* begins with an acknowledgment that

> power must be taken, here, as elsewhere. [. . .] The key to this power is found in the application of the principles of self-determination and self-liberation. These principles are defined and practiced in the areas of control, autonomy, flexibility, and participation. Often imaginary or symbolic authority is confused with the real.[47]

The novel is at odds with one of the primary directives of the movement, that "Chicanismo simply embodies an ancient truth: that man is never closer to his true self as when he is close to his community."[48] The *Plan de Santa Barbara* goes further, equating the intellectual and political development of a man as both caused and indicated by educational attainment: "higher education must contribute to the formation of a complete man who truly values life and freedom."[49] The "complete man" as an achievable, teleological status seems a specious claim, especially under the limited characteristics held by the movement, yet the assertion of such makes evident the close connection between manhood and the movement's cultural identity.

At novel's end, Richard expects (and is expected by his family and friends) to go to college, a choice he rejects, choosing instead to enlist in the navy. His enlistment signals the contradictory position he inhabits, insisting on his own individualism while confirming the obligation presented by the state. But enlistment is also a desire for communal attachment, to labor for the common good, but one that favors national affiliation over local alliance. He dissociates from the local, pan-ethnic communities he had formed throughout his life and his life choices, particularly his enlistment, embodying "the contradictions between Americans' construction of the autonomous self and Americans' seeming insistence on group loyalty."[50] Richard leaves the novel "thinking little of the life he had left behind—only of the future" (186). This orientation to the future, to possibility imagined and achievable, shapes Richard's final reflection. The future-oriented positionality recalls Jose Esteban Muñoz's précis on the state of queer studies, where "queerness is essentially about the rejection of a here and now and an insistence on potentiality or concrete possibility for another world."[51] Richard leaves his hometown, his family, his childhood friends, posing the question, "What about me? Because he did not know, he would strive to live. He thought of this, and he remembered, and suddenly he knew that for him there would never be a coming back" (187). For Richard there is no return to a past unable to resolve the contradictions of his individualism, offering "queerness as collectivity" only for an unknown future that, as Muñoz insists, is "visible only in the horizon," but the horizon extends temporally both forward and backward.[52] This ambiguity, between past and future, between self and community, is a late twentieth-century incarnation of an earlier formulation which cleaved Mexican Americans to U.S. citizenship, simultaneously attaching and severing Mexican Americans from the nation.

Queer citizenship as cleaving enables a return to the earlier period. Thomas Paine, whom I discuss as useful interlocutor of Mexican American manhood and citizenship, concludes *Common Sense* with a call to action and a warning:

> We ought to reflect, that there are three different ways by which an independency may hereafter be effected; and that one of those three, will, one day or other, be the fate of America, viz. By the legal voice of the people in Congress; by a military power; or by a mob: It may not always happen that our soldiers are citizens, and the multitude a body of reasonable men; virtue, as I have already remarked, is not hereditary, neither is it perpetual. Should an independency be brought about by the first of those means, we have every opportunity and every encouragement before us, to form the noblest, purest constitution on the face of the earth. We have it in our power to begin the world over again.[53]

Paine prognosticates a future America in similar terms to what we see in the novel, where the military and other state institutions offer the possibility of equitable citizenship, which he lauds as a desirable outcome of a truly democratic society. Paine anticipates the ways in which racialized citizens, specifically here Mexican Americans, may reconstitute American social and political life. He reminds us that virtue is not "hereditary, neither is it perpetual," a cultural and social force constantly needing to be redone, a challenge encoded and unresolved in the novel. It is in this sense that Richard imagines a future: neither to perish in the service of a country that disavows his inclusion nor to flee his world by denying his cultural heritage, but instead offering the readers and our field the chance to "begin the world over again."

The Long History of Chicano Cultural Nationalism

Pocho's queerness enables continuity between past and present found elsewhere within the Chicano movement. One need only glance at Victor Villaseñor's novel *Macho!* (1973) to glean its own ambitions. The novel, which the original publisher Bantam Books promoted as "the first great Chicano novel" (a contestable claim), proudly declares itself a masculine triumph.[54] The exclamatory title animates the now-ubiquitous term "macho" as a marker of Chicano cultural identity and a unique if not defining feature of the Chicano movement. Emphatically and unapologetically titled, *Macho!* explains the immigrant's journey to the United States as a foundational process through which one attains the status of male privilege, as those who "return with money to burn, agrees and calls himself lucky and *muy macho*."[55] The novel about a Mexican migrant's journey was once a staple of Chicano literature, but now serves more as a historical reminder of the period's entrenched masculinism. Simplistic in structure and characterization, its short-comings easily prefigure the Chicana feminist critique of the gendered failures of the movement. Despite this, the novel highlights a shift in Mexican American manhood in the later twentieth century leading up to the Chicano movement.

Macho!, a novel about masculinity, immigration, and the Chicano movement, poses a question it can never quite answer: in what way is the movement of peoples across national borders implicated in the masculinist underpinnings of the Chicano movement? Both *Pocho* and *Macho!* offer a neat dramatization of the shift that occurred in the mid- to late twentieth century where, after a century of institutional failures and legal and social exclusion, Mexican American manhood turned inward toward an internalized mode of citizenship that involved strict regulation of the body. The Chicano movement was both a formative and transformative moment in the history of Mexican Americans in the United States. From the early 1960s through the 1980s, the activists and social organizers capitalized on widespread frustration with racialized inequality and on growing intolerance with the United States' discriminatory policies toward people of color and the Global South, as well as through alliances with other ethnic groups in the United States. Chicanos demanded that social and governmental institutions make good on the promises of an equal society, and were able to achieve material changes to the laws and structures to a degree previously, and perhaps still, unmatched. These changes are perhaps most recognizable in the protests organized by agricultural labor (led by César Chávez and Dolores Huerta, among others) but extended into every facet of life, including jury selection, access to higher education, and employment opportunities. In the academy, activists were able to establish permanent programs dedicated to the history and culture of Latino ethnic groups. The current thriving field of Latino Studies owes its existence to the gains achieved by Mexican,

Puerto Rican, Cuban, and other ethnic national activists during this period, which has increasingly moved into historical memory. In recent years there has been a resurgence in scholarship on the Chicano movement and its legacies.[56] Part of this resurgence comes from the historical distance from the civil rights era, as a new generation of scholars and activists engage with and often reassess the impact of these earlier events.[57]

Though its origin is disputed, "Chicano" was reinvigorated as nomenclature, symbol, and idea of politicized and proud Mexican American identity. The term itself functions as a political act the editors of the *Los Angeles Times* felt compelled to explain as an etymological action compared to the use of the term "black": what had once been an "insult," now "Chicano and black are political, cultural and social terms and have nothing to do with erudite dictionaries," but instead reclaim political activism and ethnic identity.[58] Ruben Salazar, the journalist slain during the National Chicano Moratorium March of August 1970, offered another explanation of the political importance of the term "Chicano." In an article published just months before his death, he wrote why "can't we [Mexican Americans] just call ourselves Americans? Chicanos are trying to explain why not. Mexican-Americans, though indigenous to the Southwest, are on the lowest rung scholastically, economically, socially, and politically. Chicanos feel cheated. They want to effect change now."[59] Salazar explained how through nomenclature, Chicanos sought to position themselves as politically active agents of change, part of but distinct from the more generalized category of American or Mexican American, "flaunt[ing] the barrio word Chicano—as an act of defiance and a badge of honor."[60] The adoption of the name was part of an active transformation of ethnic identity that sought to break with the past, a renewal of ethnic pride and a rupture from past positions. Chicanos adamantly refused assimilation and equally opposed social ostracization, calling for the nation to grant access to economic and political rights; as Salazar described, "Chicanos, then, are merely fighting to become 'Americans.' Yes, but with a Chicano outlook."[61] Asserting a "Chicano outlook" is not equivalent to rejecting American-ness, but rather acts as a call for integration, a nuanced distinction that *Pocho*'s Richard is unable to take.

Nonetheless, during the Chicano movement, citizenship, as a strategy of political engagement, meant resistance to the nation-state and its racist practices, alliance with other oppressed ethnic and third world peoples, and a demand that the U.S. nation recognize the shortcomings of its democratic promises, exposing the contradictions of its imperial projections.[62] One of the central principles around which the Chicano movement mobilized its various constituent groups was nationalism, a familiar idea of past centuries. This idea was encoded into "El Plan Espiritual de Aztlán" (1969), a document largely regarded as the foundational text of the second phase of the Chicano movement. Written by the poet Alurista (Alberto Baltazar Urista Heredia) for the occasion of the First National Chicano Liberation Youth Conference, "El Plan Espiritual" sought to formalize an agenda around which group activism could coalesce. The conference, held on March 23, 1969, in Denver, Colorado, and hosted by Rodolfo "Corky" Gonzales's (author of the now-canonical poem "I Am Joaquin") Crusade for Justice, empowered Mexican American youth under the label Chicano to advocate for the social and political rights from which they had been systematically excluded. In his description of nationalism, Corky Gonzales tries to dispel the "old stereotype of a Mexican-American asleep under his sombrero in the shade of a cactus," instead recalling the words of Cortina by reminding his audience "to accept the right of self-determination for the Chicano."[63] The document rekindled the idea of Aztlán, a mythical Aztec homeland that stretched from the U.S. Southwest through Central America, announcing "before the world, before all of North America, before all our brothers in the bronze continent we are a nation, we are a union of free pueblos, we are Aztlán," a rallying cry for the disparate Mexican American population divided by region and location as well as legal status as immigrant, resident, or citizen of the United States. Aztlán provided a claim to space that is territorial, but free from the geopolitical boundaries that map the continent. "El Plan Espiritual" thus invoked a political tradition common in Mexico but familiar in the United States as well, in which a document serves to articulate the goals and rationale of a particular group against a standing government. This particular plan marked a development in the aims of Mexican American protest, moving from the fields and exploitative labor practices that César Chávez championed in the early 1960s to a more pointed attempt to change the institutions of social reproduction, namely the system of both lower and higher education.

The movement's insistence on nationalism as a foundational organizing principle was itself a product of the legacy of nineteenth- and twentieth-century U.S. colonial expansion in the western hemisphere, as well as an attempt to ally itself with other anti-colonial movements of the Global South.[64] In contrast to traditional nationalism, the cultural nationalism contained within "El Plan Espiritual" de-emphasized territoriality as central to a national project, and favored de-territorialized alliances among people of shared cultural backgrounds organized around seven goals: unity, economy, education, institutions, self-defense, culture, and political liberation. These far-ranging organizational aspirations sought to appeal to a wide spectrum of the Mexican American population and to offer a broad strategy needed to bridge regional and class divisions. Cultural nationalism bases political unity on what Michael Hames-Garcia sees as consisting of "three components: *indigenismo*, a privileging of unity over internal difference, and a conservative ideology of the family."[65] Through the triangulation of these elements, Chicano nationalism reconnected Chicano identity to indigeneity, but also created a fairly restrictive formulation of Chicano identity that espoused *mestizo* identity and that emerged from what one Chicano activist called the "biological fusion of originally antagonistic groups."[66] Thus, "El Plan Espiritual" located masculine identity in the body, in biological claims to a pre-national existence that was hyperbolic and minimized the possibility for male-female collaboration. "The call of our blood is our power," the plan stated, issuing a demand for unity and consensus derived from the body and grounded in aggression, virility, and biological difference that preceded national status.[67] Despite *Pocho's* queerness, the biological claim to masculinity in the Chicano movement attached itself to heterosexuality. As Cherrie Moraga states, "When El Plan Espiritual was conceived a generation ago, lesbians and gay men were not envisioned as members of the 'house' [. . .] We were not counted as members of the 'bronze continent.'"[68] And as Ramon Gutierrez notes, "Chicano men initially regarded the feminist critique as an assault on their Mexican cultural past, on their power, and by implication, on their virility. If Chicanos were going to triumph in their anticapitalist, anti-colonial revolt, divisiveness could not be tolerated."[69] The centering of heterosexual masculinity within the Chicano movement was at some distance from the earlier periods, when Mexican Americans—men and women—wielded ideas of manhood for the community's good, despite not always directly benefiting from such actions.

The unified, bodily notion of Chicano nationalism was present across the movement and offered a historical if de-nationalized past. In 1975, in an address before the third meeting of the National Association for Chicana and Chicano Studies (NACCS, one of the enduring institutional contributions of the civil rights movement still active today), Peter Cirilio Salazar explained the "Social Origins of Chicano Nationalism." In his address, Salazar asserts that one of more noticeable attributes about the form of Chicano nationalism is that it "appears to be most conspicuous by its absence during the nineteenth century, [although] it is significant to view both the forces working for and against it during this period."[70] Salazar traces Chicano nationalism back to the first Spanish colonial settlements in North America, but in claiming the absence of cultural nationalism in earlier periods, he distinguishes between the current conceptualization of Chicano nationalism and earlier formulations of cultural unity. Whereas earlier understandings of Mexican American culture sought to capitalize on the democratic political discourse and more integrated social life, the Chicano movement's strategy of resistance moved away from these discourses seen as assimilationist or accommodationist.

Salazar exhibits a tendency common to the Chicano movement, discrediting many earlier attempts at the improvement of Mexican American lives that did not overtly or even antagonistically "resist" U.S. authority. This tendency ignores the ways in which national manhood offered a tactic through which earlier writers and thinkers sought to shape regional and national cultural life. Still, Salazar draws on the work of political theorists Karl Deutsch, K.K. Silvert, and especially Anthony D. Smith, stating that nationalism developed "to overcome regional and class conflicts by embracing the cohesive and shared values of liberty, equality, and fraternity," values central to Mexican American manhood throughout the long nineteenth century.[71] Salazar even points to how "the cohesive function of fraternity temporarily worked to resolve this dilemma by stressing the unifying values of a common culture and homeland," yet seeks to distance the movement from earlier nationalist projects.[72] While earlier Mexican Americans sought to minimize the distance between themselves and other forms of white manhood, the movement emphasized rupture—from the past and from the nation-state—and sharply enunciated the boundaries between Chicano and non-Chicano, man and woman.

Rupture from history enabled activists to determine the markers of inclusion and even "authenticity."[73] It provided galvanizing momentum by encouraging the actors of the movement to become agents of their own success, "forged in the common struggle against outsiders and in the attending growth of a collective sense of pride and identity among social groups, or classes, which made up the community."[74] Unlike the nationalism of the nation-state that developed out of European political theory, Salazar argues that it is more productive to analyze the "social function of Chicano nationalism," articulating cultural nationalism as an extension of cultural citizenship, as Flores and Benmayor have explained. Salazar reminds his audience that previously, "any effective nationalist appeal from Chicano cultural heroes, or social bandits, as well as any anti-social act, organized or spontaneous, which sought to express common Chicano goals, has been repressed, termed a criminal act, and stripped of nationalist meaning by Anglo police, judiciary, and mass media," linking the late twentieth century to a century earlier, but unable to see the methods through which such earlier "heroes or social bandits" utilized the tools available to them.[75] In other words, Salazar sees the past events through the legacies of history, and what lingers are "the commonly held principles of self-determination, economic development and cultural autonomy [that] have emerged as significant Chicano nationalist values."[76] The important distinctions between the Chicano movement and subsequent memory of it have, as an unintended consequence, a funneling effect that includes certain individuals and groups that coincide with a fairly strict version of Chicanismo, and excludes or obscures others. Emphasizing the need for culture as a remedy to economic disenfranchisement, "El Plan Espiritual" imagined the Chicano subject through *hermanidad* (brotherhood or fraternity), repeated in the sixth organizational goal which calls for unity based on "cultural values of life, family, and home [that] will serve as a powerful weapon to defeat the gringo dollar value system and encourage the process of love and brotherhood."[77] Here, the call to national unity is premised on hermanidad, a decidedly masculinist concept, not of the unmarked white national male citizen, but of those left out of the structures of the U.S. nation-state. "El Plan Espiritual" states, "Brotherhood unites us, and love for our brothers makes us a people whose time has come and who struggles against the foreigner 'gabacho' who exploits our riches and destroys our culture."[78] Brotherhood inverts the native-foreign distinction by centering Chicano males as original occupants of a pre-national U.S., but to do so, it relies on a normalized male subject, a fraternal alliance among those feeling victimized by racialized practices of American history, what it calls the "common denominator that all members of La Raza can agree upon."[79] There is a tautological switch here, where the path to resistance presumes a shared past that only comes into existence through the act of calling it into existence and disregarding other experiences. In moving to separate the Chicano from the U.S. nation, Chicano nationalism calls for a resistant or oppositional subject that is often at odds with the historical realities of earlier Mexican American actors. Despite its efforts at inclusivity and representation, and the countless ways in which the movement created enduring social improvement for the lives of Mexican Americans and others, it normalized a masculinist Chicano subject, as shown by the insightful and powerful critique of Chicana feminists such as Cherrie Moraga, Gloria Anzaldua, Sonia Saldívar-Hull, Norma Alarcón, and others.[80] Historically, however, Mexican American manhood functioned more elastically.

Returning to *Macho!*, in moments the novel seems to acknowledge the injustice of patriarchal difference in Mexican and Mexican American society. Roberto's sister Esperanza is shown as competent and ambitious, the first daughter in the village to have gone to school, taking charge of the family's finances in Roberto's absence. (Esperanza explicitly denounces the restrictions placed upon women, stating, "If I were a man . . . hell, I would have left this lousy place years ago! [. . .] If I were a man, I'd break all the customs every day!"[81]) Esperanza voices her dissatisfaction with the limits placed upon her, a momentary recognition of the gender inequality in Mexican and Chicano life, but the protagonist is limited by his own entrenchment in masculine privilege; he can only understand her desires through the lens of gender difference: "She was smart and quick, and [I] liked her as a person, a friend, someone to talk to. Almost like another man" (*Macho!* 37). Rather than acknowledge her abilities and support her ambition, he disregards her behavior as unbecoming, as "hopeless. She would never get a husband the way she behaved" (38). To their detriment, neither the novel nor the movement fully overcame the masculinist impulses that shaped Chicano cultural life. Instead, looking at an earlier moment, one that predates the Chicano movement, we find the possibility for a different memory of the Chicano movement and of a future left behind.

As the product of a long century of Mexican American political and cultural participation, Chicanos sought to distinguish themselves from white American men, but also, and equally important, *as* American men—not immigrants, but as citizens of the U.S. and rightfully empowered to critique the nation's shortcomings. This is not to absolve Chicano manhood of its heteronormative, oppressive masculinity. But rather than view the position of the Chicano movement in opposition to the U.S. nation, perhaps it is time to recognize those demands *as part of* the nation's ongoing quest for equal rights. To acknowledge the nation's difficult and discriminatory racial past is not to condemn the nation, but rather to hold ourselves responsible for its successes and failures as joint actors in a collective ongoing political project.

Epilogue

Notes toward the Past's Future, or the Future's Forgotten Past

As early as 1989, Mario T. Garcia identified the "need to integrate Chicano history within U.S. history. Still too closely tied to the political spirit of the Chicano movement, which stressed alienation from American life and distance from traditional American values," the narrative of American national history tended to cast Mexican Americans through the lens of either "victimization" or "resistance."[1] Since then, much progress has been made integrating Mexican Americans into all aspects of American life, yet there remains much to be done.

In 2016, Republican presidential candidate Donald Trump ran a campaign that shocked the political establishment. His campaign energized a working class electorate who felt left out of an increasingly diverse, global, and stratified country, and he issued a stark warning to immigrants in the United States. During the official announcement of his candidacy for president of the United States, Trump stated, "When Mexico sends its people, they're not sending their best. They're not sending you. They're not sending you. They're sending people that have lots of problems, and they're bringing those problems with us. They're bringing drugs. They're bringing crime. They're rapists. And some, I assume, are good people."[2] It was a polarizing move to garner political support and media attention, as Trump, ignoring the centuries-old discourse of uplift and integration into the U.S., effectively castigated all immigrants to the United States as detrimental to national character and the nation's well-being.[3] Despite the inability to provide evidence to support his claims, he would later add to his racist and xenophobic remarks, claiming that, if elected president, he would build a wall along the 2000-mile U.S. border with Mexico (which he claimed would be paid for by Mexico), deport undocumented non-citizens (an estimated nine to eleven million people), block remunerations to Latin American countries, and end *jus solis*, the right of citizenship by birth on sovereign land. Though the remarks cited here focus on Mexicans, Trump's racist views are not limited to Latinos, and he links immigration from Latin America to that from other areas of the world, particularly the Middle East, collectively alleged to pose a threat to national security.[4] Trump's proponents hailed his publicity stunts as anti-establishment, politically incorrect but "telling it like it is"; his critics (including the Mexican government) were quick to chastise Trump for distorting the truth and promoting racism and national division. Trump's protectionist stance, which led to his fellow Republican contenders following suit, resonated with a substantial and vocal part of the national electorate.

Trump's campaign capitalized on economic uncertainty and conservative reaction to the shifting demographics of the nation-state, riding a populism reminiscent of Andrew Jackson (without the military credentials) that advocated a nativist stance on the national constituency. Regardless of an individual's position on the political spectrum, Trump's comments revealed a poignant truth about race in the twenty-first century: despite claims about a post-racial society, racial tension remain a potent if latent issue in American society.[5] In a climate of political correctness (against which Trump's political opportunism has claimed authority), notions of race are now heavily intertwined with other categories of individual identification or group belonging, such as national status, sexual orientation, or religious affiliation. Perhaps the most pernicious effect of Trump's presidential bid was the national platform it provided for a directly expressed xenophobia, a political license to the critics of diversity and racial equality.

Reacting to Trump's perceived disregard for political civility, Andrea Tantaros, a female reporter speaking on a nationally broadcasted news show, claimed, "The left has culturally tried to feminize this country [. . . and Trump presents] blue collar workers' last hope to get their masculinity back."[6] Tantaros, like many in the media, saw in Trump a voice for those who believed their social power to be dwindling. Her response articulates an important if implicit facet of the conjunction of Trump's xenophobic stance on the nation and the self-perception of the working class American male. Tantaros links manhood to social issues of immigration and citizenship, thereby rendering citizenship the proxy for the fear of a diminution of political privilege; according to this view, the foremost threat to the value of citizenship is immigration.

Yet alongside the campaign vitriol that demonized immigrants and foreigners, President Trump's message delivered a narrative of America that selectively recreated the nation's past. The promises to "Make American Great Again" offered voters a return to what can only be described as a nostalgic view of a unified and homogeneous American culture. Yet even his choice of slogans failed to recognize historical reality. President Woodrow Wilson coined the phrase "America First" to define his support for keeping America neutral in the escalating global conflict that was World War I.[7] The "America First" campaign originated with the United States' involvement in foreign wars and its role in a global order, but its focus quickly shifted inward. In a speech to the patriotic women's organization Daughters of the Revolution, President Wilson stated that despite attempts to disparage the loyalty of those "fellow-citizens born in other lands," "some of the best stuff of America has come out of foreign lands, and some of the best stuff in America is in the men who are naturalized citizens of the United States."[8] Against a growing "America First" movement that opposed U.S. involvement in World War I, Wilson suggested a survey of "all foreign born citizens of the United States, for I know the vast majority of them came here because they believed in America, and their belief in America has made them better citizens than some people who were born in America."[9] Wilson was reacting to a national debate about the place of immigrants in American society and the potential threats posed by global forces such as World War I, but it's a debate that rages on, that is familiar, and that can generate contemporary political zeal. Still, what distinguishes Wilson's position for neutrality from Trump's 2016 campaign rhetoric is the distinction between foreign aggression and internal foreignness that collapsed these differences into an emerging xenophobia.

Responding to Wilson's "América Primero" platform, the influential newspaper *La Prensa* published a biting critique of such isolationist and potentially nativist positions. The newspaper states, "El más elemental de los deberes de cualquiera nacion digna de respeto y de llevar el nombre de civilizada, es el de protoger a sus propios ciudadanos contra el asesinato y violencia. [. . .] El gobierno de los Estados Unidos, ha faltado al cumplimiento de este deber, de la manera más pública y notoria"

[The most basic duties of any dignified and respected nation that merits the name civilized, is to protect its citizens against murder and violence [. . .] The U.S. government has failed to fulfill this duty in a most public and notorious way].[10] The article provides a pressing reminder of the obligations a nation has to its citizens, but more tellingly speaks to the long-standing engagement of Mexican Americans in the U.S. nation.

Describing Asian Americans, Lisa Lowe reminds that "'legal' and 'illegal,' 'citizen' and 'noncitizen,' and 'U.S.-born' and 'permanent resident' are contemporary modes through which the liberal state discriminates, surveys, and produces immigrant identities."[11] For Lowe, immigration is the terrain on which universal rights and capitalist interest collide, where marking bodies as "illegal," undocumented, or citizen enables the nation-state to resolve often-conflicting positions. Mexican Americans cannot be reduced to any one of these modes, but instead need to be better integrated into our shared cultural history. Although they are no more recent arrivals than the European immigrants of the nineteenth century, Mexican Americans have a different story about the immigration experience. This book puts Mexican American manhood in dialogue with earlier formulations of American manhood and within a U.S. national culture that documents shared democratic values and political participation. American democracy may be just an ideal, and it is certainly flawed and often unjust, but now, more than ever, we need to recommit to the promise of a liberal, secular, multiracial democratic government.

Stories matter. The stories we tell about ourselves matter. How history gets told, what we imagine history to look like, and who has the power to tell that story all have direct and material effects on people's lives, especially in times of reactionary backlash, nativism, and xenophobia. Locating Mexican American manhood as part of the process of U.S. national development and expansion—alternatingly supportive and critical—demonstrates how we are part of U.S. national history. Mexican American history *is* U.S. national history.

ACKNOWLEDGMENTS

Countless individuals and organizations have encouraged me throughout the many years I worked on this project, in ways that I suspect I am yet to realize. I am indebted to all of you for your influence, inspiration, and guidance. These words expressing my gratitude are slight, but the feeling behind them runs deep.

To begin, I would like to thank the many institutions and organizations that have supported the research and writing of this work. This project was partially supported by Indiana University's New Frontiers in the Arts & Humanities Program and the College Arts and Humanities Institute, whose financial contributions allowed me time and resources to complete the archival research. I would also like to thank IU's Office of the Vice Provost for Faculty & Academic Affairs for providing financial support. To the staff at the University of Texas Benson Latin American Collection and the Dolph Briscoe Center for American History, the University of Houston's Recovering the U.S. Hispanic Literary Heritage Project, the IU Wells and Lilly Libraries, Yale University's Beinecke Library, Western Carolina University's Hunter Library, Santa Clara University Library, and UCLA's Chicano Studies Research Center, my sincere thanks for your help accessing the archives that are the skeleton of this book. I would also like to thank the organizers and participants in the Newberry Seminar in Borderlands and Latino Studies, whose workshop helped revise my first chapter. A special thanks to the wonderful people at Arte Público Press and the Recovery Project, Gabriela Baeza Ventura, Carolina Villarroel, and the entire staff for repeatedly making space for me to use their incredible collections, and to its director Nicolás Kanellos, who has been a source of knowledge throughout my career.

I am grateful for the many friends and teachers who shaped my thinking. This project has its roots in my graduate school days at the University of Texas, where much of what I learned took place both in and out of the classroom. Thank you to Phil Barrish, Kirby Brown, Cary Cordova, James Cox, Frank Guridy, Kathryn Hamilton Warren, José Limón, John Mckiernan-Gonzalez, Gretchen Murphy, Deb Paredez, Domino Perez, Caroline Wigginton, and at the University of Chicago, Ken Warren. John Morán González has been a tireless supporter and I am thankful for his encouragement as advisor, mentor, and now friend.

Friends and colleagues near and far have read drafts, pointed me to new sources, and, directly or indirectly, shaped the manuscript; I am fortunate to have benefited from their insight. My thanks to all my colleagues in English at IUB, whose friendship and conversation provided an invaluable intellectual community, especially Scot Barnett, Purnima Bose, Ed Comentale, Jonathan Elmer, Jen Fleissner, Ross Gay, Rae Greiner, Paul Gutjahr, Vivian Halloran, Christoph Irmscher, Scott Herring, Patty Ingham, Ivan Kreilkamp, Stephanie Li, Adrian Matejka, Jesse Molesworth, Monique Morgan, Walton Muyumba, Rebekah Sheldon, Katie Silvester, Nikki Skillman, and Shane Vogel, who helped me inhabit the profession. IU's community extends well beyond the English Department, and I am equally grateful for the support of Deb Cohn, Andres Guzman, Karen M. Inouye, Jonathan Risner, Olimpia Rosenthal, Micol Seigel, and Stephanie Smith, as well as Sarah Neelon, Jessica Millward, and Tobias Wofford. I greatly benefited from regular exchanges with Laura Foster and Victor Quintanilla. I am indebted to my colleagues in IU's Latino Studies Program, which provided a second home on campus. For their vision and camaraderie, I am grateful to Anke Birkenmaier, Arlene Diaz, Bernard Fraga, Sylvia Martinez, Mintzi Martinez-Rivera, Micaela Richter, and especially John Nieto-Philips, who mentored me since I arrived at IU. To all my students who forced me to better explain, thank you, especially those in my fall 2016 graduate seminar, who helped refine my thinking on many of the texts discussed herein. My thanks to Cynthia Martinez, Jed Kuhn, Willy Palomo, Gionni Ponce, and Nathan Schmidt.

Though spread across the country, my colleagues in the field of Latino Studies have provided invaluable friendship and feedback over the last several years. My sincerest gratitude to Jesse Alemán, José Aranda, Raul Coronado, John Alba Cutler, Kirsten Silva Gruesz, Laura Halperin, Jennifer Harford Vargas, Olga Herrera, Carmen Lamas, Rodrigo Lazo, Marissa Lopez, Yolanda Padilla, Elda Maria Roman, Ralph Rodriguez,

Ricky Rodriguez, Kristy Ulibarri, Maria Windell, Bill Orchard, one of my greatest teachers, and Mark Goldberg, my oldest friend with whom I unknowingly began this work decades ago.

I would also like to thank the anonymous readers at NYU Press, whose attentive reading reshaped and greatly improved the manuscript; Sheri Englund, a piercing reader; and the talented staff at NYUP, including Alisha Nadkarni and Eric Zinner, who believed in and shepherded the project.

To my family, who have supported me throughout and taught me the meaning of community—how to make it, how to sustain it, and why it matters—thank you. As a first generation American, much of my childhood was spent trying to reconcile my parents' stories of home with my own sense of place. These experiences shaped my understanding of the world in ways still unfolding. I am indebted to my abuelos, Alberto y Ana, David y Dina, whose life journeys across the globe imparted countless lessons. Un abrazo para mi Bobe, for always bringing comfort. A giant thank you to the Kunianskys and to my extended family, by kin or closeness, in Houston, Atlanta, Bloomington, and Mexico. To Jess, my sister, friend, and confidante, thank you for always being there. My parents arrived in the U.S. shortly before I was born, and dedicated their lives to improving ours. I can never express the gratitude I feel for your unwavering love and support; with much love, this book is dedicated to you.

Helena and Jacob, whose smiles and laughter each day renew my faith in the world, bring me joy and purpose, and coming home to you is the highlight of each day. Finally, this endeavor would have been impossible without Rachel, who challenges, motivates, and sustains me, you are my partner and best friend in all things; I say, insufficiently but with unyielding love, thank you. You three are my world. To all my family, your presence is in each of these pages.

NOTES

INTRODUCTION

1 Many scholars, among them Gerald Poyo, Angela Castañeda, and Ramon Gutierrez, have demonstrated that the long history of the peoples we now call Latina/os
predates the U.S.-Mexican War. Early Latina/os were the product of colonization
between Europeans (especially Spain) and indigenous peoples inhabiting what
is now the United States. The U.S.-Mexican War is an artificial temporal marker,
but it is nonetheless a useful bookend for thinking through the cultural history of
Mexican American manhood, in part because it emphasizes national conflict.

2 Much has been written and debated about the treaty and its effects, and its
granting of citizenship is a point to which I return throughout the book. For a
discussion of the treaty and its articles, see Griswold del Castillo, *The Treaty of
Guadalupe Hidalgo*.

3 What little information the novel provides about the Native Americans among
whom Lola was raised suggests they were in southern Arizona, near the juncture
of the Gila and Colorado rivers, where there are twenty-one federally recognized
tribes (Ruiz de Burton, *Who Would Have Thought It?*, 34). It is possible that the
novel refers to any of these, but it also likely that Ruiz de Burton was using "Indians" as a generic plot device rather than as a specific tribal reference.

4 Ruiz de Burton, *Who Would Have Thought It?*, 63.

5 Ruiz de Burton, *Who Would Have Thought It?*, 214.

6 Julian denies the charges against him, but insists on the primacy of the institutions of justice: "If I had said all that, sir, I think I would still have the right to a
trial and defense" (*Who Would Have Thought It?* 215). While the novel critiques
the exclusionary practices through which capitalism overrides democratic values,
at the same time it paints an ambiguous picture of the potential for democracy
when biases overrule universal principles.

7 For a discussion of Ruiz de Burton and whiteness, see Alemán, "Thank God,
Lolita Is Away from Those Horrid Savages"; and González, "The Whiteness of the
Blush." For Ruiz de Burton, race, and the hemisphere, see Murphy, *Hemispheric
Imaginings*, especially chapter three.

8 Two of Ruiz de Burton's novels were recovered by Rosaura Sánchez and Beatrice
Pita, published by Arte Público's Recovering the U.S. Hispanic Literary Heritage
Project. The massive efforts coordinated by the recovery project were fundamen-
tal to the revived study of Latino cultural history, and the work done by scholars

associated with it and similar projects are central to this book. Ruiz de Burton's novels have since taken on near-canonical status, perhaps in part due to how American culture privileges the novel form.

9 "Manifest destiny" was often used as shorthand for U.S. territorial expansion after journalist John O'Sullivan coined the term in 1845 in the *Democratic Review*. It was no coincidence that O'Sullivan also coined the phrase the "Mexican Question" in the essay "Annexation," published just one month later in the same magazine. The two ideas are intertwined, though the latter has since come to be associated with immigration and not with conquest. See Rivera, *The Emergence of Mexican America*.

10 There are important distinctions between Mexican Americans and the broader category Latino, which I discuss later. Given the country's demographics and history, I examine Mexican Americans as paradigmatic of the broader movement of Latinos in the public imaginary.

11 For a discussion of immigration and nativism, see Curran, *Xenophobia and Immigration*; Perea, *Immigrants Out!*; Benn Michaels, *Our America*.

12 Higham, *Strangers in the Land*, 3.

13 The Know Nothing Party was formed in 1844, just before the U.S.-Mexican War, but was most active politically after the war, in the 1850s.

14 *El Clamor Público*, August 14, 1855, 34. For a brief history of the newspaper, see Kanellos, *Hispanic Periodicals in the United States*.

15 "Keep Out the Aliens," *Albuquerque Morning Journal*, April 15, 1922, 8. Coincidentally (or perhaps not), this piece ran adjacent to a statement claiming that the YMCA is "a man-factory where boys are turned into useful citizens."

16 *Kansas City Star*, January 3, 1922, 20. The Border Patrol began as part of a national restriction on immigration, attached to the Immigration Act of 1924.

17 "Mexicans Watching Quota Move Here," *New York Times*, March 5, 1928, 8. The *Times* reported the counterargument calling for a quota: "The Mexican immigrant is detrimental to the country, that he is Socialistic if not Communistic, and that he robs an American working man of a job." While some claims are less impactful today, such as the unsubstantiated claim that "low living standards of the Mexicans made them undesirable," the former could be ripped from contemporary newspapers.

18 For a discussion of U.S. national fears about incorporating Mexicans after the U.S.-Mexican War, see Weber, *Foreigners in Their Native Land*. For the nativist response in the early twentieth century, see Reisler, *By the Sweat of their Brow*.

19 See, for instance, Ignatiev, *How the Irish Became White*; Brodkin, *How Jews Became White Folks*; Roediger, *Working Toward Whiteness* and *Wages of Whiteness*.

20 Ngai, *Impossible Subjects*, 8.

21 For discussions of the Bracero Program, see Overmyer-Velásquez, *Beyond the Border*; Cohen, *Braceros*; Calavita, *Inside the State*.

22 The notion of Latinos as a "sleeping giant" in U.S. politics is frequently deployed by the media, yet some scholars have taken issue with the characterization. For a

critique of the Latino political bloc, see Beltrán, *Trouble With Unity*. For a discussion of anti-immigration politics (an "anti-migrant hegemony"), see Gonzales, *Reform Without Justice*.

23 Gonzales, *I Am Joaquin*, 91. Gonzales's work helped catalyze civil protest, but his notion of Chicano identity was decidedly masculinist, "bold with machismo" (64) and grounded in a "struggle for my sons" (82).

24 Chavez, *The Latino Threat*.

25 Scott, *Extravagant Abjection*, 95.

26 Nelson, *National Manhood*.

27 Ibid, 6, 27.

28 Sedgwick, "Gosh, Boy George," 12.

29 Kimmel, *Manhood in American*; Rotundo, *American Manhood*; Putney, *Muscular Christianity*; Kaplan, *Anarchy of Empire in the Making of U.S. Culture*. Kimmel's work has been particularly influential in masculinity studies, and I return to his text throughout.

30 Harper, *Are We Not Men?*.

31 Larsen, *Passing*, 17.

32 hooks, *We Real Cool*, xii.

33 Wallace, *Constructing the Black Masculine*, 5–6.

34 Kimmel, *Manhood in America*, 129.

35 Kaplan, *Anarchy of Empire*, 99.

36 For a Chicana critique of the movement, see Anzaldua, *Borderlands/La Frontera*; Moraga and Anzaldua, *This Bridge Called My Back*; Saldívar-Hull, *Feminism on the Border*; Trujillo, *Living Chicana Theory*; Kaplan, Alarcón, and Moallem, *Between Woman and Nation*; Castillo, *Massacre of the Dreamers*.

37 Queer-of-color critique marked a powerful shift in our understanding of intersectionality and brought attention to the ways that sex and gender are implicated in constructions of race, class, and ethnicity. See Ferguson, *Aberrations in Black*; Muñoz, *Disidentifications*; Holland, *Erotic Life of Racism*; Hames-Garcia, *Identity Complex*.

38 There has been a great deal of excellent scholarship on the legal exclusion of Latinos, especially regarding land claims following the Treaty of Guadalupe Hidalgo. See, for instance, Sánchez, *Telling Identities*; Gómez, *Manifest Destinies*; Orozco, *No Mexicans, Women or Dogs Allowed*; Olivas, *Colored Men and Hombres Aqui*; Garcia, *White But Not Equal*.

39 I invoke the term "aspirational citizenship" with some reservations. Some, like Jayal's use of it for India, suggest a desire for a just and equal society. My skepticism comes from the potential pitfalls of "aspirational" as it has been deployed by neoliberal policy. For a discussion of aspirational citizenship, see Bosniak, *Citizen and the Alien*, and Raco, "Neoliberal Urban Policy."

40 For a general overview of global citizenship in contemporary political thought, see Carter, *The Political Theory of Global Citizenship*.

41 Carter, *The Political Theory of Global Citizenship*, 6.

42 Tocqueville, *Democracy in America*, 193.

43 Ibid, 194.

44 Tocqueville, *Democracy in America*, 192–23. Despite his condescending tone and his omission of the intervening presence of the United States in the history of Mexico, Tocqueville was in some way prescient, as Mexico would revise its constitution several times over the next century to manage the various regional and national interests. See Tocqueville, *Democracy in America*, 357–70.

45 Throughout the 1920s, the San Antonio newspaper *La Prensa* (see chapter three) routinely provided quotations by Tocqueville, in Spanish, as nuggets of wisdom to inspire their readers. See, for instance, November 23, 1916; July 16, 1918; December 5, 1920; or July 17, 1921.

46 In tracking the development of Mexican citizenship, Lomnitz sees a gradual move from liberal equality where "ideal" citizenship offers the chance for national unity to, at the turn of the century, an emphasis on order and economic development as the key to national strength.

47 Lomnitz, "Modes of Citizenship in Mexico," 292.

48 For a discussion of Mexican citizenship in the nineteenth century, see Lomnitz, "Modes of Citizenship in Mexico." The essay was translated for a Mexican readership as "La construcción de la cuidadanía en México" in *Metapolítica*. For a discussion of Mexican citizenship and the public sphere, see Aguirre, "Cuidadania ante el espacio publico." For the role of republicanism and Spanish influence in the founding of the Mexican state, see Chust and Frasquet, "Orígenes federales del republicanismo en México, 1810–1824."

49 Quoted in Kimball, *Jefferson: The Road to Glory*, 107.

50 See Sollors, *Multilingual America*.

51 Gruesz, "Alien Speech, Incorporated," 26.

52 Marshall, "Reflections," 5.

53 Ferguson, *Aberrations in Black*, 3.

54 Ritter, "Jury Service and Women's Citizenship," 483.

55 At least until 1920 at the federal level, only men could vote, and whether or not an individual fit the eligibility requirements was often cast as a question of manhood. Until 1870, men of color were excluded from voting, and following the passage of the Fifteenth Amendment, suffrage was legally extended to non-white men. Cultural constructions of manhood helped articulate or restrict men's eligibility for the privileges of citizenship. For instance, the threat of black sexuality was used to rationalize extralegal restrictions of African American voting rights, as seen in texts like Charles Chesnutt's *Marrow of Tradition* (New York: Houghton Mifflin, 1901). For a discussion of black masculinity, see Stokes, *Color of Sex*; Richardson, *Black Masculinity and the U.S. South*; Hodes, *White Women, Black Men*; Wiegman, *American Anatomies*.

56 Coronado, *A World Not to Come*, 138.

57 See Coronado's discussion of Catholic political thought, 229–38. His discussion of how the broadsheet formally mimics hierarchies of authority is particularly illuminating.

58 Bosniak, "Citizenship Denationalized," 450.

59 In his essay "Citizenship and Social Class," Marshall divides citizenship into civil, political, and social categories, a loose structure that has subsequently been expanded upon and critiqued. Marshall's analysis of "social citizenship" has been particularly influential in its focus on social equality and the government's role in providing access to comparable standards of living (Marshall, "Citizenship and Social Class").

60 Flores and Benmayor, *Latino Cultural Citizenship*.

61 See Mookherjee, "Affective Citizenship"; Berlant, *Queen of America Goes to Washington*. Kessler-Harris explores how work was essential to asserting the privileges of citizenship, and how work was then constricted by gender in *In Pursuit of Equity*.

62 See Luis-Brown, *Waves of Decolonization*; Edwards and Gaonkar, *Globalizing American Studies*; Balibar, *We the People of Europe?*; Dower and Williams, *Global Citizenship*.

63 For a discussion of "legal realism" in American law, whereby judges at the appellate level reflect their own social views of the world as much as the legal statutes, see Leiter, *Naturalizing Jurisprudence*.

64 Fox, "Difficult Transition," 152. Fox defines "autonomy" as the ability of a state or its members to develop independent goals and to organize to that purpose. In contrast, a state's "capacity" is its ability to get its constituent members to follow the stated goals. See also Fox, *Politics of Food*.

65 Thinking of gender in this way is something akin to Mikhail Bakhtin's notion of the chronotope, for whom the chronotope represents the interdependence of space and time and how those categories are present in and represented by language. See Bakhtin, *Speech Genres and Other Late Essays*, especially his essay on the Bildungsroman, pp. 10–59.

66 For a critique of the "resistance paradigm," see Aranda, "Contradictory Impulses"; Luis Mendoza, *Historia*; Rodriguez, "Chicano Studies and the Need Not to Know."

67 This is its first known usage as listed in the *Oxford English Dictionary*, and its emergence likely a contraction of Latin American (itself a French term dating to the mid-nineteenth century).

68 Lopez, *Chicano Nations*, 6–7.

69 See U.S. Census data for 2016, summarized at "FFF: Hispanic Heritage Month 2016," www.census.gov/.

70 In *A Thousand Plateaus*, Gilles Deleuze and Felix Guattari provide a poststructuralist model for imagining social critique through a concept of "assemblage." The text suggests that a book or archive organized rhizomatically (their metaphor for the assemblage) can resist the structures of domination (intellectual or institutional) that dictate social bonds, instead extending outward, horizontally, and in multiple simultaneous directions. Their text is particularly useful for imagining a political theory in which challenges to the nation come from non-state actors.

CHAPTER 1. OUTLAW CITIZENSHIP

1 U.S. Congress, House, *Difficulties on the Southwestern Frontier* (hereafter referred to as *DSF*), 80. Cortina issued two proclamations in late 1859, one dated September 30, and the other quoted above, and would continue to issue proclamations periodically during his active military and political career over the subsequent three decades. An original copy of the 1859 proclamations can be found in the National Archives. All citations of the English version of Cortina's proclamations are from *DSF*. Several proclamations are also reproduced in Thompson, *Juan Cortina and the Texas-Mexico Frontier, 1859–1877*.

2 Numerous studies have examined the bandit as a process of racialization following the U.S.-Mexican War. Elliott Young, Benjamin Johnson, Susan Lee Johnson, Maria A. Windell, and others have explained the way real or fictional bandits have played a role in shaping historical development across a wide stance of geographical and temporal locations. See Young, *Catarino Garza's Revolution on the Texas-Mexican Border*; B. Johnson, *Revolution in Texas*; S. Johnson, *Roaring Camp*; Windell, "Sanctify our Suffering World with Tears."

3 According to the *Oxford English Dictionary*, cleave can mean "to pierce and penetrate, to separate or sever by dividing or splitting," but also "to stick fast or adhere, to attach or remain steadfast."

4 Many historians contend that armed resistance culminated with the "Plan de San Diego" and the Borderlands War of Texas in 1915, after which violence no longer seemed a reasonable alternative, although the model could be extended to the Brown Berets of the Chicano movement.

5 In her excellent work on popular cultures, Shelley Streeby demonstrates the ubiquity of Mexican American as bandit and how it shaped national perceptions of Mexican Americans by working to "redefine and restrict a white national identity [and] by identifying a community of people of Mexican origin and other Spanish-speakers with a 'foreign' criminality" that demarcate the limits of legality and illegality, the national and alien (*American Sensations*, 256).

6 Johannsen, *To the Halls of the Montezumas*, 176.

7 For Mexican Americans and banditry, see Denning, *Mechanic Accents*; Johannsen, *To the Halls of the Montezumas*, especially pp. 186–203; and Streeby, *American Sensations*.

8 Johannsen, *To the Halls of the Montezumas*, 291.

9 According to Eric Hobsbawm's classic definition, social bandits emerge as precursors to organized political change. For Hobsbawm, the social bandit's main concern "is the defence or restoration of the traditional order of things" before he was wronged, but for many Mexican Americans, the traditional order of things often meant unequal social and political status (*Primitive Rebels*, 26).

10 Juan Alonzo describes the "productive ambivalence" of the bandit stereotype, Jaime Javier Rodriguez discusses how the bandit represses Mexican Americans from history, and Robert McKee Irwin locates the bandit figure within the

transnational U.S.-Mexico borderlands. Others such as William A. Nericcio and Charles Ramirez-Berg have tracked the bandit figure across more mainstream popular culture, including television and film. Maria Windell finds that "transamerican sentimental diplomacy" serves as a counterpoint to the violence enacted by many *Murieta*'s male characters.

11 Paredes, *With His Pistol*, 124–5.

12 Many texts of the Chicano movement, such as Rodolfo Gonzales's *I Am Joaquin*, Oscar Zeta Acosta's work, Luis Valdez's "Bandido," and even, to some extent, Sandra Cisneros's portrayal in "Eyes of Zapata," champion the bandit as anti-authoritarian and anti-national.

13 Cutler, "Disappeared Men," 584.

14 Warner, *Letters of the Republic*, 35.

15 The constant and continuing revision of the Murieta story testifies to its long-standing cultural relevance. Among the more significant retellings, Robert Hyenne translated the story into French, Carlos Mora published a Spanish translation (1867), and Frederick MacCrellish published an authorized second edition, *History of Joaquin Murieta, the King of California Outlaws, Whose Band Ravaged the State in the Early Fifties* (1871). Subsequent authors expanded the Joaquin lore, including Horace Bell's *Reminiscences of a Ranger* (1881) that recounts Joaquin's "first escapade"; Gertrude Atherton's *Los Cerritos* (1890), describing the life of Joaquin's alleged illegitimate daughter, Carmelita; Hubert Howe Bancroft's histories of California, which included an amalgamated version; Walter Noble Burns's *Robin Hood of El Dorado: The Saga of Joaquin Murrieta, Outlaw of California's Age of Gold* (1932), a novelized biography; and more loosely, many attribute to Joaquin the origin of the character of Zorro. In 1904, the famous Mexican publisher Ireneo Paz (grandfather of Nobel Laureate Octavio Paz) published another Spanish translation in Mexico City. Perhaps most famously, however, is Rodolfo "Corky" Gonzales's epic poem "I Am Joaquin" (1967), which helped galvanize the Chicano movement.

16 For instance, Louis Owens sees in Ridge's novel a displacement of Ridge's desire for intratribal revenge, and James Cox states how Murieta "initiat[ed] in the Native novel tradition a critique of the way that texts function as tools of domination" (Owens, *Other Destinies*, and Cox, *Muting White Noise*, 26).

17 See Arteaga, *Chicano Poetics*, and Pérez-Torres, *Movements in Chicano Poetry*. Luis Leal chronicles its widespread dissemination. Jesse Alemán cogently argues for the way Ridge's life and novel offer violent allegories of assimilation that reveal its inherent contradictions, connecting the author and character through a symbolic disassociation between head and body, between individual and the community.

18 Ridge, *Life and Adventures of Joaquin Murieta*, 74–75.

19 Ibid, 8, 15, 79, and 157. Joseph Henry Jackson states in the introduction, "Nor is it surprising that such outlaws were aided covertly by sympathetic countrymen," referring to Mexican Americans as external to the United States (xvi).

20 Ridge, *Life and Adventures of Joaquin Murieta*, 148.

21 Ibid, 145.

22 Ibid, 78.

23 Rifkin, "For the Wrongs of Our Poor Bleeding Country," 28–29.

24 See Griswold del Castillo, *Treaty of Guadalupe Hidalgo*, and David Potter, *Impending Crisis*.

25 The most thorough account of Cortina's life and exploits is Jerry D. Thompson's *Cortina: Defending the Mexican Name in Texas*.

26 See Emerald, *Cortina, the Scourge*; Gonzalez and Raleigh, *Caballero*; Paredes, *George Washington Gomez*.

27 *DSF*, 12.

28 Ibid, 20.

29 Ibid, 22.

30 Ibid, 31.

31 Ibid, 33.

32 Acuña, *Occupied America*, 46. For Cortina as bandit, see also Rosenbaum, *Mexicano Resistance in the Southwest*.

33 *DSF*, 74.

34 The only extant copy of Cortina's Proclamations in Spanish are at Yale's Beineke Library (Figure 1.1). A note attached to the Spanish version of the September Proclamation in the Yale archive claims a later Proclamation is on file at the Milwaukee Public Library, but I have been unable to locate this document.

35 "Proclamation," November 23, 1859. Quoted in *DSF*, 79.

36 Cortina's actions were transmitted across the nation, in newspapers in Texas, New Orleans, Baltimore, New Mexico, South Carolina, and New York, among others. During the occupation of Brownsville, the *New York Times* stated, "Public attention is at this moment diverted from the outbreak at Harper's Ferry to one of another sort" (November 11, 1859). Yet unlike Harper's Ferry, which Cortina's actions anticipated by about three weeks, and which remains in historical memory as a justified yet doomed revolt conducted in the name of freedom and justice, Cortina's actions are labeled seditionist and secessionist.

37 *DSF*, 21, 40.

38 Ibid, 39, 21.

39 "Later from Brownsville. Another Fight—Cortina Victorious!! Full Particulars," *Southern Intelligencer*, 2.

40 Greenberg, *Manifest Manhood*, 11.

41 *DSF*, 42, emphasis added.

42 *DSF*, 43.

43 For a discussion of southern manhood, see Friend and Glover, *Southern Manhood*; Friend, *Southern Masculinity*; and to some degree, Silber, *Romance of Reunion*.

44 *DSF*, 80.

45 Elsewhere he talks of "secret conclaves" and "shadowy councils," both of which would resonate with male homosocial secret societies then prevalent. See Carnes, *Secret Ritual and Manhood in Victorian America*.

46 *DSF*, 70.

47 *DSF*, 71.

48 *DSF*, 72.

49 The text of the Plan de Ayutla is widely available, including on the website of the Museum of the Constitution at the National Autonomous University of Mexico City (UNAM, http://www.museodelasconstituciones.unam.mx). Unless otherwise noted, all translations from the Spanish are my own.

50 *DSF*, 72, and from "'Proclama' del Ciudadano Nepomuceno Cortinas," September 30, 1859, Yale Collection of Western Americana, Beinecke Rare Book and Manuscript Library, Yale University (Figure 1.1).

51 Paine, *The Writings of Thomas Paine*, 56.

52 Larkin, *Inventing an American Public*, 270.

53 Foner, *Tom Paine and Revolutionary America*, 56.

54 Cortina, "'Proclama.'"

55 *DSF*, 75.

56 Ibid, 70.

57 Ibid, 71.

58 Based upon his interpretation of this work, Manuel Martín-Rodríguez observes that the recovery of a "plethora" of Latina/o "narratives, memoirs, personal letters, testimonials, journalistic pieces, and poems [. . .] while enriching our knowledge of the Chicana/o literary past, further complicate the task of reconstructing its history" (*Recovering Chicano/a Literary Histories*, 797). Martin-Rodriguez points to how "the diverse and contradictory tensions that have shaped" Chicana/o literatures are often omitted from Chicana/o literary histories that critically organize them (804).

59 Lopéz et al., *Una Breve Reseña*.

60 Kauffmann, translator, *Vicente Silva and his Forty Bandits*.

61 Cabeza de Baca, *We Fed Them Cactus*, 96.

62 Erlinda Gonzales-Berry notes that Cabeza de Baca advocated for the admission of Spanish speakers to national citizenship (*The Contested Homeland*, 171).

63 Meléndez, *So All is Not Lost*, 79.

64 *Sol de Mayo*, May 7, 1891, 1.

65 Ibid.

66 Meléndez, *So All is Not Lost*, 66.

67 For a discussion of race and New Mexican statehood, especially its relation to manhood, see Rivera, *The Emergence of Mexican America*; Noel, "I am an American"; and Mora, *Border Dilemmas*.

68 For a discussion of how romance novels linked heterosexual union and national unity in Latin America, see Sommer, *Foundational Fictions*.

69 Wasserman, *Everyday Life and Politics in Nineteenth Century Mexico*, 69.

70 Glantz, "Huerfanos y bandidos," 143.

71 Frazer, *Bandit Nation*, 12–13.

72 Dabove, *Nightmares of the Lettered City*, 6–7.

73 M. Cabeza de Baca, *Historia de Vicente Silva*, 46. Hereafter cited in this chapter parenthetically in the text.

74 Chaves's dying statement, as reported by Cabeza de Baca, recalls Tiburcio Vasquez's published deathbed piece (1875) cautioning the Mexican American population of California to adhere to the law and civility.

75 Garza's memoir, entitled "La lógica de los hechos" ["The Logic of the Action"], is housed in the Benson Latin American collection at the University of Texas at Austin. The manuscript has never been published in the United States, and was only published in Mexico as part of the 2010 centennial celebration of the Mexican Revolution (1910) and the bicentennial of Mexican independence (1810). Quotations throughout the rest of this section are from pages 22–35 of the manuscript.

76 Garza would later write of the mutual co-dependence between these neighboring towns, defining regional unity that crossed the national border: "Brownsville ni Matmoros son poblaciones que puedan vivir de por si solas, pues ambas se necesitan (comercialmente hablando), y sin el auxilio de una o otra, la clase proletaria se perjudica altamente" [Brownsville and Matamoros are places that cannot exist independently, but rely on each other (commercially speaking), and without the help of one and the other, the working class would be severely impaired] ("La lógica de los hechos," 29).

77 In a strange and literal coincidence of literary violence, Garza wrote that an assassination attempt against his partner Léon A. Obregón was thwarted by a bundle of newspapers he carried under his coat, which stopped a bullet meant to end his literary attack on Mexican American inequality (33).

78 In his superbly researched biography, Elliott Young shows how Garza and his followers were "motivated by their desire to maintain their freedom and autonomy as border people" (*Catarino Garza's Revolution*, 7). Young's emphasis on regional identity is well supported in Garza's accounts, yet Garza often explains his work in its implications specifically for a U.S.-based, Mexican-origin population. The transnational and regional connections were vital to the sustenance of the area's populations, but the nation-state would ultimately function as the primary guarantor of political enfranchisement.

79 For a discussion of voting and the political machines in South Texas in the early twentieth century, see Montejano, *Anglos and Mexicans*. These practices are fictionalized in Paredes, *George Washington Gomez*.

80 Garza, "La Lógica de los hechos."

81 Castillo and Camarillo, *Furia y Muerte*, 1.

82 Ibid, 2.

83 Ibid, 3.

84 Ibid, 9.

85 Kazanjian, *Colonizing Trick*.

CHAPTER 2. FANTASY CITIZENSHIP

1 Cervantes, *Emplumada*, 43.

2 Carrillo, *Cuentos Californianos*, 38.

3 Ibid, 42.

4 Throughout the essay, I use Carey McWilliams's term "fantasy heritage" in reference to the legends and cultural practices surrounding Old Spanish Californios, the mission past, and boosterism (locations and events such as parades and "fiesta days" festivals) that emerged as a result of the imaginative recreation of historical California. See McWilliams, *North From Mexico*.

5 William David Estrada discusses how the Spanish past influenced a variety of social relations and public spaces, particularly in the Los Angeles central city plaza. See Estrada, *The Los Angeles Plaza*.

6 While I deploy the term "multilingual," this book generally focuses on the bilingual Spanish and English Mexican American culture. Bilingualism does not adequately describe the linguistic complexity of Mexican American and Latina/o life and in part represents my own linguistic limitations. In keeping with Werner Sollors's imperative to reimagine American literature through a multiplicity of languages that better represent its cultures, I use the term "multilingual." See Sollors, *Multilingual America*.

7 See Starr, *California: A History*, especially chapter five, and Orsi, *Sunset Limited*.

8 Throughout the 1880s, Bancroft chronicled the history of California and the western U.S., collecting documents and narratives from both the English- and Spanish-speaking population. See Lopez, "Political Economy of Early Chicano Historiography," and Robinson, *Mexico and the Hispanic Southwest*.

9 See Gillman, "Otra Vez Caliba/Encore Caliban." For a discussion of the novel in the context of Latin America and the Mexican borderlands, see Irwin, "*Ramona* and Postnationalist American Studies." In relation to novels of domesticity, see González, "Warp of Whiteness."

10 The novel was published in multiple editions well into the twentieth century and still remains in print. Along with tourist sites claiming to be the real-life locations of fictional events, *Ramona* also spawned numerous consumer products such as perfume and beer, and businesses renamed themselves in reference to the novel. Since 1923, the novel has been staged at the annual Ramona Bowl in Hemet, California, and has been made into at least four films, including a 1910 version by D.W. Griffith and a 1928 version starring Mexican superstar Dolores del Rio. See DeLyser, *Ramona Memories*.

11 DeLyser, "Ramona Memories," 894.

12 Ibid, 893.

13 Kropp, *California Vieja*, 13. Kropp notes how fantasy heritage paradoxically and "simultaneously celebrat[ed] the Spanish past and denigrated the Mexican present [. . .] a central method Americans have used to express race and nation" (7).

14 *Ramona* was one of relatively few works of American literature to be published in translation in Mexico. See Englekirk, *Bibliografía*, 48.

15 See Fiske, *Charles F. Lummis*, and Thompson, *American Character*.

16 Turner, "Significance of the Frontier in American History," 1893.

17 Neurasthenia was thought to be the result of excessive mental activity, domestication, or "civilization," but was a widespread and influential cultural phenomenon during this period. See Lutz, *American Nervousness, 1903*.

18 Bederman, *Manliness and Civilization*, 91.

19 Lummis, *The Spanish Pioneers*, 11–12. In curious parallel, Lummis dedicates *The Spanish Pioneers* to Elizabeth Bacon Custer, wife of General George Custer, who was largely responsible for disseminating the propagandistic legend of Custer's Last Stand as heroic at the Battle of Little Big Horn during the Sioux War of 1876–77. The dedication reads, "To one of such women as make heroes and keep chivalry alive in our less single-hearted days"; the seemingly paradoxical domestic imperative of praising a woman for the maintenance of male chivalry and creating heroes bears noting.

20 Lummis, *The Spanish Pioneers*, 11–12.

21 For a discussion of the Spanish "black legend" as colonial other, see DeGuzmán, *Spain's Long Shadow*.

22 Pitt, *Decline of the Californios*, 284–94.

23 McWilliams, *North from Mexico*, 53.

24 Tuck, *Not with the Fist*, 15. Analyzing mestizaje in the population around Descanso, California, Tuck sees this social phenomenon among both Anglo and Mexican communities. She ultimately concludes that the colonization of the Mexican was a product of his "passive and apathetic" nature (100).

25 Chávez, *The U.S. War with Mexico*, 122.

26 Gómez, *Manifest Destinies*, 43–44.

27 Kettner, *Development of American Citizenship*, 264.

28 Where the Civil Rights Acts of 1866, 1870 (Enforcement Act), and 1875 "recognize the equality of all men before the law, and hold that it is the duty of government in its dealings with the people to mete out equal and exact justice to all, of whatever nativity, race, color, or persuasion, religious or political" (echoing the Fourteenth, Fifteenth, and Sixteenth Amendments), the Supreme Court's Slaughter-House decision (1873) made the individual states the guarantors of civil rights. Justice Marshall, who authored the majority opinion, stated, "There is a citizenship of the United States and a citizenship of a State, which are distinct from each other, and which depend upon different characteristics or circumstances in the individual" (Labbé and Lurie, *The Slaughterhouse Cases*, 215).

29 Ross, *Justice of Shattered Dreams*, 200.

30 See "Records of the Constitutional Convention of 1849," sos.ca.gov/archives/collections/constitutions/.

31 Willis and Stockton, *Debates and Proceedings*, 1006. Mr. Caples concluded that women should not be entitled to vote since "they lack the physical power, the

physical courage, the endurance—not to say it would interfere with and defeat the great end of creation, the reproduction of our species," giving voice to a notion of republican motherhood (1006).

32   Ibid, 1007.

33   Ibid, 1006.

34   Ibid, 1010.

35   "Constitution of the State of California," as published in California Statutes of 1880 (Sacramento: J. D. Young, Superintendant of State Printing, 1880), Article II, Section I, xxiv.

36   Ibid, 656.

37   Leider, *California's Daughter*, 4, 6.

38   Starr, *Americans and the California Dream*, 352.

39   McClure, *Gertrude Atherton*, 131, 34.

40   Leider, *California's Daughter*, 108.

41   Most of the short stories discussed here are found in Atherton, *Splendid Idle Forties*, and are hereafter cited parenthetically in the text.

42   Atherton, *The Californians*, 88. Hereafter cited parenthetically in the text.

43   It seems reasonable to surmise that the character Polk is perhaps named after President Polk, who held office during the U.S.-Mexican War. Polk's arrival and rise to power in California becomes a thinly veiled metaphor for the nation's aspirations in and conquest of the state.

44   Various scholars have discussed at length the trope of marriage resolution in nation formation and imperial conquest. For a discussion of the family in early American fiction, see Samuels, *Romances of the Republic*; for marriage resolution in Latin American novels, see Sommer, *Foundational Fictions*; and for post–Civil War national reunification through marriage, see Silber, *Romance of Reunion*.

45   Goldman, *Continental Divides*, 48.

46   Foote, *Regional Fictions*, 97.

47   *Bohemian Club*.

48   Sturken, *Tangled Memories*, 2–3.

49   Montes, *Cuatro años en Méjico*, 233.

50   Agüeros, *El Tiempo, Diario Catolico*, February 28, 1886.

51   Ibid, 2.

52   It remains unclear whether Carrillo's exile was coerced or self-imposed. His movements and ability to work were limited by the porfiriato, though immediately following his arrest Carrillo publicly asserted that his departure from his home country was voluntary. See Agüeros, *El Tiempo, Diario Catolico*, February 28, 1886. However, Carrillo left Mexico City promptly upon his release, suggesting that his "voluntary" departure was either a gesture of defiance or forced. Furthermore, in an interview shortly before his death, Carrillo discusses his expulsion, and claims to have been forced aboard the steamship, penniless and distraught (Cué, "El Autor de las Memorias de Lerdo," 5). At minimum, the inconsistent accounts suggest the conflicted relationship Carrillo had with Mexico.

53 Cué, "El Autor de las Memorias de Lerdo," 5.

54 Carrillo's novel is thought to be a fictionalized account of the life of Marquis Jorge Carmona. When originally published, the cover mistakenly read *Memorias de San Basilio*, perhaps intended to create the impression that the text was a biography of a saint. Curiously, Hector R. Olea published a purported biography of Jorge Carmona in 1951, titled *Andanzas del marquees de San Basilio*. Oleas mentions Carrillo as the original source for the work, but it is unclear whether Olea was misguided or if he intended the novel as a strange retelling of Carrillo's original tale.

55 Gomez-Quiñones, "Piedras Contra la Luna," 521. See also Sanchez, *Becoming Mexican American*, 111.

56 Gómez-Quiñones, "Piedras Contra la Luna," 517.

57 Aranda, "Returning California to the People," 15.

58 Lomeli, "Cuento Costumbrista," 212–4.

59 Ibid, 214.

60 For a discussion of the Immigration Act of 1924 and its relation to Mexico, see Sheridan, "Contested Citizenship."

61 Benhabib, *Another Cosmopolitanism*, 48.

62 See Luis Leal's introduction to Paz, *Life and Adventures*.

63 Carrillo, *Cuentos Californianos*, 38. Hereafter cited parenthetically in the text.

64 Leal, *Aztlán Y Mexico*.

65 Kanellos, "Recovering and Re-Constructing," 441.

66 Chabrán and Chabrán, "The Spanish-Language and Latino Press."

67 Kanellos, "Cronistas and Satire," 20.

68 Chabrán and Chabrán state that the story "Los primeros gambusinos" was published in Tuscon, Arizona, in 1924, but I have been unable to locate any extant copies. The search is ongoing, but I have found other interviews and reports attributed to Carrillo in various U.S. newspapers between 1886 and 1926.

69 See Anaya, Lomeli, and Lamadrid, *Aztlán: Essays on the Chicano Homeland*.

70 For a discussion of cosmopolitanism, see Benhabib, *Another Cosmopolitanism*, and Appiah, *Cosmopolitanism*.

71 In the story "El Sacrilegio," which is also framed through a found object, the dying priest regrets his vows and casts doubt on the value of the Spanish mission, inquiring, "Para que sirve un monje? Pues ni para hacer un monje" [What purpose does a priest serve? Alas, not even to create another monk] (*Cuentos Californianos* 18). Through the narrative layering of ghosts, history, and survivors, the rhetorical question superimposes historical legacy on reproduction and sexuality.

72 Brogan, *Cultural Haunting*, 2, 6. See also Gordon, *Ghostly Matters*.

73 "Panocha" functions as a double entendre here. In Spanish, "panocha" translates as an ear of corn or a candy made from flour and piloncillo. However, the word is also slang for female genitalia, the latter connotation suggesting how the story operated differently for different readers.

74 Around the turn of the century, Golden Gate Park housed a menagerie, including a bear named Monarch—this specificity further contributes to Carrillo's geographic embedment.

75 Lomas, *Translating Empire*, 85.

76 Luis-Brown, *Waves of Decolonization*, 55.

77 Fregoso, *Mexicana Encounters*, 104–5.

CHAPTER 3. EXPATRIATE CITIZENSHIP

1 Niggli, *Step Down, Elder Brother*, 322.

2 The film features famous Hollywood celebrities, including Alfonso Bedoya, whose work in *The Treasure of the Sierra Madre* (1948, "We don't need no stinking badges!") offered an enduring meme.

3 Crowther, "The Screen In Review," 37.

4 For example, the Immigration Act of 1917 provided special waivers for Mexican laborers, and while the Immigration Act of 1924 ignored migrants from the western hemisphere, it simultaneously saw the establishment of the Border Patrol on May 28, 1924. This would change radically during the Great Depression, with the forced deportation and repatriation of hundreds of thousands of Mexicans, many of whom were U.S. citizens. Later, the Bracero Movement allowed Mexican workers free access into the U.S. during World War II.

5 All references are to the first edition. This edition credits the author with the Anglicized "ph," Josephina.

6 For a discussion of México de afuera as it inflects other social formations, see Escobar, *Race, Police, and the Making of a Political Identity*; Monroy, *Rebirth*; Baeza Ventura, Gabriela. *La imagen de la mujer*.

7 Although focused on nationalism, I am indebted to the transnational methodologies of such exemplary work as Gruesz, *Ambassadors of Culture,* and Brickhouse, *Transamerican Literary Relations.*

8 Historian Gilbert G. Gonzalez finds that México de afuera's main objective was "to extend official Mexican domestic policy into the emigrant community" (*Mexican Consuls*, 1). In the 1920s and 30s, "the Mexican government endeavored to [. . .] incorporate México de afuera into a political ideology and social relations consonant with the interests of the ruling upper classes in Mexico," but the "Mexican state, especially in its policies toward the expatriate community, [also] operated within the parameters of an empire administered by its northern neighbor" (9–10). As such, Mexican Americans were directly connected to the state apparatus of the Mexican government as well as Mexico's national culture but always refracted through their experience in the U.S.

9 This is the inverse of what Brian Edwards and Dilip Parameshwar Gaonkar identify as "the *cosmopolitan strand* of American studies, [which] rejects the metaphoric unity of American experience, and in its place metonymically focuses on the differential placement of America abroad" (*Globalizing American Studies*, 15).

10 The "cosmopolitan" is but one strand of a diverse set of critical approaches (including the hemispheric studies, diaspora studies, or border studies) that can collectively be called "transnational." See, for instance, Grewal, *Transnational America*; Levander and Levine, *Hemispheric American Studies*; Saldívar, *Border Matters*; Pease, *The New American Exceptionalism*; Fluck, Pease, and Rowe, *Re-framing the Transnational Turn*.

11 See also Hoganson, *Fighting for American Manhood*.

12 Kimmel, *Manhood in America*, 62. For a discussion of Mexican immigration and the Cristero War of the 1920–30s, see Young, *Mexican Exodus*. For immigrants as future citizens, see Motomura, *Americans in Waiting*, and Daniels, *Not Like Us*.

13 Kanellos, "Recovering and Re-Constructing."

14 Bruce-Novoa, "*La Prensa* and the Chicano Community," 150–56, 151.

15 Kanellos provides an indispensible survey of these newspapers in *Hispanic Periodicals in the United States*.

16 One of the exiles, Ignacio E. Lozano, became the owner of two highly influential newspapers, San Antonio's *La Prensa* and Los Angeles's *La Opinion*. Lozano moved to the U.S. from Marin, Nuevo Mexico, a town just outside Monterrey.

17 Kanellos, *Hispanic Immigrant Literature*, 8.

18 For critical treatments of the novel of revolution, see Dessau, *La novela de la revolucion Mexicana*; Franco, *An Introduction to Spanish-American Literature*; Monsiváis, "Notas sobre la cultura mexicana"; Rutherford, "The Novel of the Mexican Revolution."

19 Venegas, *The Adventures of Don Chipote*, 28.

20 Ibid.

21 Analogous to this is how cultures adapt to changes in nationality through the various social models of assimilation, acculturation, integration, syncretism, or transculturation, each describing distinct modes of interaction between individuals and cultural practices.

22 As stated per Section 101(a)(22) of the Immigration and Nationality Act, available on the U.S. Department of State's website, "Renunciation of U.S. Nationality by Persons Claiming a Right of Residence in the United States," travel.state.gov/.

23 For the legal status of dual nationality, see the Department of State's website, "U.S. Citizenship Laws & Policy," travel.state.gov/.

24 Pérez, *El Coyote, The Rebel*.

25 Ibid, 154. Hereafter cited parenthetically in the text.

26 Kanellos and Martell, *Hispanic Periodicals in the United States,* 100–101.

27 Limón, "El Primer Congreso Mexicanista," 86.

28 Reprinted in Limón, "El Primer Congreso Mexicanista," 107. Selections of the various speeches given by the attendees of the event can be found in *Primer Congreso Mexicanista*.

29 "Esfuerzo Supremo," *La Cronica*, September 3, 1910, 3. All quotations in the following two paragraphs come from this soure.

30 For a discussion of Hughes as Justice, see Freund, "Charles Evans Hughes as Chief Justice."

31 See Henretta, "Charles Evans Hughes."

32 "Discurso de Mr. Hughes," *Revista Mexicana*, 6–8.

33 Ibid, 6.

34 Ibid, 7.

35 Until the implementation of the Good Neighbor Policy circa 1934, the U.S. frequently intervened militarily in Latin America: Mexico, 1914 (Veracruz) and 1916–17 searching for Pancho Villa (New Mexico); Dominican Republic, 1916–24; Haiti, 1915–34; Panama, 1903–79; Nicaragua, 1912–33; and variously in Cuba and Honduras.

36 "Discurso de Mr. Hughes," *Revista Mexicana*, 8.

37 Democratic Party Platforms, "Democratic Party Platform of 1912," www.presidency.ucsb.edu/.

38 Later that year, the Immigration Act of 1917 (also known as the Asiatic Barred Zone Act) defined categories of immigrants as well as regions that were deemed undesirable.

39 Constitution of 1917, Article 11. The text of the original Constitution was published in the *Diario Oficial: Organo del Gobierno Provisional de la República Mexicana*, published February 5, 1917, www.diputados.gob.mx/.

40 Critic Donna M. Kabalen de Bichara insightfully points out that "according to Article 30 of the Mexican Constitution of 1857, Niggli would not have qualified for Mexican citizenship precisely because her parents were Scandinavian American and not Mexican. However, with the revision of Article 30 in the Mexican Constitution of 1917 [which allows for birthright citizenship], Niggli did indeed acquire a legal claim to Mexican citizenship" (*Josephina Niggli as a Regional Voice*, 107).

41 "It's Up to You Now, Mr. Voter," *Colfax County Stockman*, 2.

42 "La Tragedia Mexicana," *El Eco del Valle*, August 12, 1911, 1.

43 "Civismo y Educacion," *El Eco del Valle*, February 24, 1912, 1.

44 Turner, "A Crime Upon the Children of Our Land," 4.

45 For an excellent discussion of anarchy in Mexico, see Streeby, *Radical Sensations*.

46 "An Open Letter to the President of the United States of America," *La Prensa*, July 25, 1919, 1.

47 Ibid.

48 Regrettably, the second half of the piece continues on a separate page, which is no longer extant in the archive and lost to history.

49 García Naranjo, "Hermoso Fragmento," 5.

50 Ibid.

51 García Naranjo, "La Resurreccion de la Patria," 2.

52 Ibid.

53 For the Mexican influence in U.S. culture, see Delpar, *Enormous Vogue of Things Mexican*.

54 For a discussion of American modernism and expatriates, see Monk, *Writing the Lost Generation.*

55 This is the title of John Kenneth Turner's famous exposé of the Díaz regime, published in 1910. A documentary made in 1913 borrowed the title, *A Trip Through Barbarous Mexico.* I use it as a kind of shorthand for portrayal of Mexico as barbaric or "uncivilized."

56 See Anzaldua, *Borderlands/La Frontera*; Suzanne Bost, *Mulattas and Mestizas*, pp. 52–4; Martínez, *Josefina Niggli*; Rebolledo, *Women Singing in the Snow.*

57 For a discussion of Niggli as "folk dramatist," see Orchard and Padilla's introduction to *The Plays of Josefina Niggli.*

58 Orchard and Padilla, "Lost in Adaptation," 107.

59 Poore, "Books of the Times," 17.

60 Martínez, *Josefina Niggli*, 139.

61 Mora-Torres, *The Making of the Mexican Border*, 9.

62 This, too, has its novelistic counterpart. The señora Miranda (Veronica's mother, Domingo's potential mother-in-law) was "a thin, nervous woman who represented Guatemala on the Pan American Round Table" (*Step Down, Elder Brother*, 77). The Pan American Round Table (PART) "is not an ordinary women's club, not an institution nor a system. It does not affiliate and is not to be referred to as a "club". It has no fund raising affairs, solicits no outside contributions. It operates on dues collected from—and the generosity of—all its members. It is non-political, non-sectarian, and non-federated, and is designed to interpret itself in acts tending to draw more closely the social and cultural bonds of the Americas. The whole purpose of the PART is to acquaint the members with the language, geography, history, literature, arts, culture and customs of the republics of the Western Hemisphere, for through knowledge, understanding is gained—and understanding leads to friendship." This was one of several pan-American groups that rose to prominence during the period of the Good Neighbor ("Brief History," www.partt.org).

63 Lutenski, *Locating the Modern Mexican*, 25–6.

64 Niggli, *Step Down, Elder Brother*, 106, 108. Hereafter cited parenthetically in the text.

65 The current patriarch, Uncle Agapito, a calculating businessman and banker, serves as a symbol of finance and commerce, a champion of Americanization and representative of the "North American" influence.

66 Huerta led a counter-revolutionary coup against then-president Francisco Madero, brutally assuming power during an intensely bloody period known as "la decena tragica." After being forced from office a year later, he was arrested in 1917 by the United States after meeting with German spies during World War I.

67 Lomnitz, "Final Reflections," 335.

68 Bárcenas is only able to return after a case of mistaken identity, in which a newspaper reports the death of his son, who shared his name, as Bárcenas's own (*Step Down, Elder Brother* 364).

69 Pratt, "Arts of the Contact Zone," 34.

70 Ibid, 37.

CHAPTER 4. ECONOMIC CITIZENSHIP

1 Kimmel, *Manhood in America*, 70.

2 "Deportation Talk Revived," *New York Times*, February 16, 1936, E11.

3 The most comprehensive account of Mexican repatration during the Great Depression is Balderrama and Rodríguez, *Decade of Betrayal*. See also Hoffman, *Unwanted Mexican Americans*.

4 Gutiérrez, *Walls and Mirrors*, 59. For a detailed analysis of LULAC and the distinctions between Mexican Americans and Mexican immigrants, see Gutiérrez, especially chapter three.

5 Ibid, 59.

6 Kimmel, *Manhood in America*, 136.

7 Schmidt Camacho, *Migrant Imaginaries*, 96; Schedler, *Border Modernism*, 115, respectively. In this sense, social collaboration as the hallmark of Mexican American manhood marks the connection to the late twentieth century *movimiento* by emphasizing social organization under a shared cultural vision.

8 Ibid, 65.

9 Kessler-Harris, *In Pursuit of Equity*, 63.

10 Ibid, 12.

11 For an excellent analysis of the development of Mexican American "bicultural" assimilationist identity, see González, *Border Renaissance*, especially chapter three.

12 José Limón has shown that "the violence of that unsuccessful and bloody insurrection led Mexican Americans, especially their leaders, to seek other routes to social equality (*Américo Paredes*, 4). For a discussion of the Plan de San Diego, the Borderlands War, and the seditionist movement, see Harris and Sadler, "The Plan of San Diego"; Johnson, *Revolution in Texas*; and González, *Border Renaissance*.

13 Cutler, *Ends of Assimilation*, 20.

14 Otey Scruggs has shown that leading up to the Bracero Program, "Mexican-Americans also objected to proposals to bring labor in from Mexico. Restrictions on the employment of aliens in war industries meant that many Mexicans long resident in the United States who had failed to become citizens would be forced to remain in the field" ("Evolution of the Mexican Farm Labor Agreement," 142).

15 *Weekly Labor Herald*, December 19, 1941, 4. This report came out months before the start of the Bracero Program, which allowed hundreds of thousands of Mexican laborers to enter the country as season labor. Officially, the Bracero Program almost exclusively contracted and admitted men (the language in the agreement between ambassadors called for the "Mexican Worker and *his* family"), though women would often accompany them as both laborers and in other roles ("Migratory Workers").

16 Kimmel, *Manhood in America*, 73.

17 Montejano, *Anglos and Mexicans*, 9.

18 Weber, *From South Texas to the Nation*, 5–6. For Mexican Americans as migrant labor, see Cohen, *Braceros*; Castañeda, *Ex Mex*. For female labor in the Chicano movement, see Sánchez, "The Chicana Labor Force."

19 Foley, *The White Scourge*, 5. For Mexican American race and labor, see Garcia, *A World of Its Own*.

20 See Zamora, *Claiming Rights and Righting Wrongs*.

21 For an analysis of how gender-defined roles operate at the familial and state levels in a comparative context, see Sainsbury, *Gender, Equality and Welfare States*.

22 For a general account of how gender intersects with Mexican American history and race, see Ruiz, "Morena/o, Blanca/o, y Café con Leche." For a discussion of gender and shifting social roles between Anglos and "Hispanics," see Deutsch, *No Separate Refuge*.

23 For an overview of scholarship on woman's suffrage as a movement, see Clapp, "The Woman Suffrage Movement." For a discussion of feminism and conservative ideology in mid-century women's rights, see Benowitz, *Challenge and Change*; Benowitz, *Days of Discontent*.

24 For discussions of the novels as examples of these genres, see, respectively, Limón, "Mexicans"; Saldívar, *Borderlands of Culture*. The romance frequently functions as an institutional reconciliation between ethnic or racial groups under the banner of a new nation; see Streeby, *American Sensations*. For romance in domestic or sentimental fiction, see Baym, *Woman's Fiction*. For a discussion of the family and national politics in romances, see Samuels, *Romances of the Republic*. For national consolidation and romance novels in Latin America, see Sommer, *Foundational Fictions*. As a genre, the bildungsroman attempts to reconcile the contradictory nature of the individual as a subject within the nation and in the face of modernity. See Bakhtin, "Bildungsroman and its Significance"; Moretti, *Way of the World*; Doub, *Journeys of Formation*.

25 Literary scholars critique genre's usefulness because of its impurity or "contamination" by other genres, but still rely on generic labels to classify texts. See Derrida, "Law of Genre."

26 Paredes, *George Washington Gomez*, 16. Hereafter cited parenthetically in the text.

27 Saldívar, *Chicano Narrative*, 166, 186.

28 This phrase recurs repeatedly and becomes a guiding expression throughout.

29 Novels such as James Weldon Johnson's *Autobiography of an Ex-Colored Man*, Abraham Cahan's *The Rise of David Levinsky*, D'Arcy McKnickle's *The Surrounded*, Jacob Riis's autobiographical *Making of an American*, and to a lesser degree *The Education of Henry Adams* and Mark Twain's *The Adventures of Huckleberry Finn* all chronicle their respective protagonists' search for a position as a racial subject or seeking to understand U.S. social order, though each takes radically disparate approaches and meets with divergent ends.

30 Limón, *Mexican Ballads, Chicano Poems*, 24.

31 Soto, *Reading Chican@ Like a Queer*, 97. Soto's invocation of a potentially queer subjectivity in Chica@ literature is a powerful reminder of the need not to naturalize certain performative acts of gender while at the same time recognizing their power within the field.

32 Paredes, *With His Pistol*, 124.

33 Sorensen, "Anti-Corrido of *George Washington Gomez*," 112.

34 For discussion of the corrido, see Limón, *Mexican Ballads, Chicano Poems*; Libretti, "'We can Starve Too.'"

35 Sheridan, "Contested Citizenship," 7–8.

36 For a discussion of the relationship between whiteness and labor, see Roediger, *Wages of Whiteness*; Foley, *The White Scourge*; Zamora, *World of the Mexican Worker in Texas*.

37 Sheridan, "Contested Citizenship," 13.

38 Mendoza, *Historia*, 155.

39 Limón, *Américo Paredes*, 35.

40 Critical treatments of Feliciano are polarized between Limón's "radical hope" and Sorensen's view of Feliciano as assimilated, enforcing the neo-imperial order he once resisted. The tension could perhaps be resolved along what Scott Lyons has elsewhere called the modernizing impulse of nationalism, the assent to social reality even as it signals a break from the traditional ways of life. Alternatively, Feliciano holds potential as a queer figure and, as adopted father, initiator of nonnormative family structure, but that discussion must be deferred to another place.

41 The novel references how they learn of the Depression through "the Spanish-language papers here and in San Antonio. They will have to print something about it in English here, sooner or later," stressing the importance of the Spanish-language newspapers as a source of information and as a unifying cultural force within and among Mexican American communities (*George Washington Gomez* 191).

42 Guálinto's "listening to" Juan exemplifies the type of communal responsibility that produces positive, productive, and potentially transformative action in the participants. This kind of listening stands in contradistinction to that which returns George G. Gomez to the valley. When Guálinto/George returns as an agent of the U.S. army, he is "listening for" the nation, undermining the community's efforts at social organization (my thanks to Lydia French for bringing this to my attention).

43 Saldívar, *Borderlands of Culture*, 177.

44 As agricultural technologies increased the productivity and value of land in South Texas, the increasing number of new Anglo settlers displaced the Mexican American ranching industry and disrupted the previously existing racial order. One outcome of these social changes was that ethnic Mexicans were forced to become laborers on lands they had previously owned. See Montejano, *Anglos and Mexicans*, chapter 9.

45 Self-reliance was a common masculine trait associated with American manhood, but as Kimmel has argued, by the early twentieth century would have been seen

nostalgically and obsolete, leaving American manhood in crisis (*Manhood in America*).

46 For a discussion of the intersection of citizenship and feminism as "republican motherhood," see Evans, *Born for Liberty*; Kerber, *Women of the Republic*.

47 González wrote a brief, unpublished autobiography collected in González, *Dew on the Thorn*, published by the Recovering the U.S. Hispanic Literary Heritage Project.

48 For a discussion of female employment during the period, see Wandersee, "The Economics of Middle-Income Family Life."

49 This quote is from González's personal correspondence to John Joseph Gorrell, quoted in the introduction to the 1996 publication of *Caballero* (González and Raleigh, xix).

50 Limón's introduction to González and Raleigh, *Caballero*, xxi. Based on correspondence between González and Eimer, Maria Cotera places the novel's origin between 1936 and 1938, formalized in 1939 with a profit-sharing contract. See *Native Speakers*, 255n1.

51 Cotera, *Native Speakers*, 224. For a discussion of the Caballero in the context of Texas history and educational reform, see González, *Border Renaissance*.

52 See Limón's introduction to González and Raleigh, *Caballero*. The Macmillan and Houghton-Mifflin (now Houghton Mifflin Harcourt) publishing houses remain two of the largest book publishers in the United States, and each operates several distinct presses and distributors. Bobbs-Merrill, based in Indiana, was a leading "trade and specialties publishing house of national stature" from 1838 to 1959, when it was purchased by the Howard Sams Company (O'Bar, *Origin and History of the Bobbs-Merrill Company*, 4).

53 See Sommer, *Foundational Fictions*; Silber, *Romance of Reunion*.

54 Streeby, *American Sensations*, 130.

55 Perhaps coincidentally, one of Susanita's friends is also named Inez and is disowned by the community for marrying an Anglo soldier.

56 See González, "Chicanas and Mexican Immigrant Families."

57 Mary Chapman and Glenn Hendler argue that, from the mid-nineteenth century forward, emotion was predominantly reserved for women, inscribed within a domestic ideology, and American men were expected to control and subvert their emotions. See Chapman and Hendler, *Sentimental Men*.

58 González and Raleigh, *Caballero*, 3. Hereafter cited parenthetically in the text.

59 Montgomery, *Citizen Worker*, 7.

60 Several critics have examined the queer possibilities in Luis and Devlion's relationship, including Cotera, T. Jackie Cuevas, and Lawrence La Fountain-Stokes.

61 Said, *The World, the Text, and the Critic*, 17. Said traces the move from filiation to affiliation as a specific characteristic, if not a problem, of modernity that leads to the establishment of cultural systems that rely on "transpersonal forms" of obligation as opposed to natural (blood) ties (19–20).

62 See Ruiz, *From Out of the Shadows*, especially chapter one.

63 Harris, "Whiteness as Property," 1714. For a discussion of the Treaty of Guadalupe Hidalgo's relationship to citizenship, see Kazanjian and Saldaña-Portillo, "Wavering on the Horizon of Social Being." In a California context, see Sanchez and Pita's introduction to *The Squatter and the Don*.

64 Garza-Falcon, *Gente Decente*, 121.

65 Dolores herself performs an anti-authoritarian manhood, but one that must be mediated through Gabriel to be socially viable. It seems that González seeks to create Mexican American masculinity influenced by both men and women.

66 See Kimmel, *Manhood in America*; Putney, *Muscular Christianity*.

67 Reprinted in the *New York Times*, July 1, 1908, 4.

68 Kimmel, *Manhood in America*, 136.

69 In 1911, married women in Texas were granted rights equal to unwed women, including the right to enter into contracts irrespective of their husbands. Legislation in 1913 and later 1921 modified laws regarding separate property, including granting women control of their separate income. It was only following the 1967 Civil Rights Act that women were granted equal rights as men. See Lazarou, *Concealed Under Petticoats*.

70 I use the term economic citizenship and not self-reliance to differentiate between the earlier Anglo American view of manhood as self-made prosperity and the Mexican American view that economic rights can be used as a means to oppose racialization and seek political rights.

CHAPTER 5. QUEER CITIZENSHIP

1 García Canclini, *Hybrid Cultures*, 266.

2 Editorial, *Con Safos*, 18.

3 Ibid.

4 In 1995, partially funded by the California Arts Council, former contributors and new writers revived *Con Safos* as a writers' workshop. See Quintantilla, "A Cultural Victory."

5 Borowsky Junge, *Voices from the Barrio*.

6 Mario Garcia coined the phrase "Mexican American Generation" to describe Mexican American leadership between 1930 and 1960 in *Mexican Americans*.

7 Hill, "Southwest Winks at 'Wetback' Jobs," *New York Times*, March 28, 1951, 31.

8 Hill, "Peons in the West Lowering Culture," *New York Times*, March 27, 1951, 31.

9 For the Mexican American role and subsequent effects of participation in World War II, see Griswold de Castillo, *World War II and Mexican American Civil Rights*; Escobedo, *From Coveralls to Zoot Suits*. For an oral history of migrant experience, see Loza, *Defiant Braceros*.

10 For a discussion of soldiering and masculinity, see Olguin, "Interrogating the Soldado Razo"; Rosales, *Soldados Razos at War*. For contemporary attitudes on minorities, see, for example, Davies, "Racial Intolerance is feared spreading on the Coast," *New York Times*, April 20, 1947, E6.

11 Hill, "Our Mexican Minority: American Me," October 24, 1948, BR6.

12 Davies, "Pacific States," *New York Times*, April 20, 1947, E6.

13 See Massey, Durand, and Malone, *Beyond Smoke and Mirrors*.

14 Ramirez, *The Woman in the Zoot Suit*; Portales, "Tejanas on the Home Front"; Patiño, "All I Want is that He Be Punished"; Rivas-Rodriguez, *Mexican Americans and World War II*.

15 Hill, "Our Mexican Minority," BR6.

16 In a letter to literary agent Harry Jacobsen, Villarreal defines "*pocho*" simply as "the name for a native of California born of Mexican parents," though the term has far wider use and meaning (Villareal, "Early Correspondence about *Pocho*, December 22, 1956").

17 Paredes, "Evolution of Chicano Literature," 93–5. Paredes was among the first to champion Chicano literature as a distinguishable subset of American literature, and, for all the important expansions and critiques since its publication some four decades ago, the essay still provides a useful catalog of Chicano writing. He comments that novel is "notable for its evocation of an ingenuous expectation: that a young man of obvious Mexican heritage coming of age in California would be treated strictly as an individual without regard for his ethnicity" (95).

18 Saldívar, *Chicano Narrative*, 66.

19 Ibid, 47, 75.

20 Saldívar elaborates on the oppositional identity Richard develops, where the novel "dispel[s] any notions one might have to grant the finality of Richard's presumed independence from either his Mexican or American value system or the privileging of liberal-democratic notions of rugged individualism," a duality central to my discussion of manhood (*Chicano Narrative*, 66).

21 One of the most piercing and beautiful critiques is Moraga, *Last Generation*.

22 Villarreal, *Pocho*, 135. Hereafter cited parenthetically in the text.

23 Vallejos, "Jose Antonio Villarreal."

24 Aparicio, "On Sub-Versive Signifiers," 797–8.

25 In an interview, Villarreal doesn't "deny" that the novel is a part of the movement, but does not consider himself involved in it. See the interview, conducted as part of the Mexican American Experience Program: "Pocho: The Novel, The Author, And Their Times."

26 Aranda, *When We Arrive*, 158–9.

27 Cutler, *Ends of Assimilation*, 29.

28 Olguin, "Interrogating the Soldado Razo," 198.

29 Interestingly, in this scene as in several others, Juan Rubio openly cries or struggles to withhold his tears. How is Juan's overabundance of emotion compatible with his views on Mexican masculinity? In reference to early American manhood, Evan Carton suggests that some authors "understand feeling to occasion a kind of self-alienation, to undo personal sovereignty" ("What Feels an American?," 29). Juan's excessive emotion rarely supplants his commitment to a particular masculine performance, except in relation to Richard.

30 Rodríguez, *Next of Kin*.

31 Juan Bruce-Novoa astutely identifies this connection, where "the privileged topic of machismo/homosexuality [serves] as a catalyst for communication between the male protagonists and for qualitative change in Juan Rubio. Yet, it must be admitted that in this context homosexuality is still an opposite pole to manhood" ("Homosexuality and the Chicano Novel," 70). Here, Bruce-Novoa also reproduces the claim of *Pocho* as the "first contemporary Chicano novel" (69).

32 Mosse, *Nationalism and Sexuality*.

33 Villarreal, *Pocho*, 113. See also Sedgwick, *Between Men*.

34 Lima, *The Latino Body*, 59. Both the "Mexican Question" and "Manifest Destiny" rationalized U.S. expansion throughout the nineteenth century.

35 Ibid, 5.

36 Kateb, "Democratic Individualism and its Critics," 276. Also see Kateb, *Emerson and Self-Reliance*.

37 Many scholars concentrate on the pachuco as a form of cultural resistance. For instance, James Smethurst finds in "*Pocho*, the pachuco is basically a figure of cultural degeneration" ("The Figure of the Vato Loco," 119). Elsewhere, Arturo Madrid explains the figures' fluidity, "which alienated them not only from Anglo America but from their parents as well" ("In Search of the Authentic Pachuco," 31, 37). Recently, Chicano scholars have argued for the importance of the Zoot Suit to Chicano subjectivity. Chon Noriega has called the zoot suit "a working-class and largely nonwhite fashion predicated on exaggerated *masculine* display" ("Fashion Crimes," 5). Catherine S. Ramirez notes that in post–World War II, during "a moment of heightened jingoism, xenophobia, and concern over shifting gender roles," the suit enabled "the gendering of Chicano resistance and style and Chicano resistance as style" ("Saying 'Nothing,'" 2–3). The zoot suit reifies manhood in the suit itself, but Richard only dabbles in zoot life and his encounters end with violence.

38 Emerson, "Self-Reliance," 33.

39 Ibid.

40 As early as 1932, in the midst of the Great Depression (depicted in the novel and described earlier), critics lamented the "passing of American individualism in the machine age" (Adamic, "The Passing of American Individualism," 423).

41 Turner, *Awakening to Race*, 9.

42 Newfield, *The Emerson Effect*, 4, emphasis in original.

43 Tocqueville, *Democracy in America*, 700.

44 Beltrán, *Trouble With Unity*, 33–35.

45 David Kazanjian identifies numerous "flashpoints" in history that expose the contradictions between the universal subject and racial specificity in various projects of nation formation and imperialism (*The Colonizing Trick*).

46 *El Plan de Santa Barbara*.

47 Ibid, 13.

48 Ibid, 9.

49 Ibid, 10.

50 Fischer, "Paradoxes of American Individualism," 367.

51 Muñoz, *Cruising Utopia*, 1.

52 Ibid, 11.

53 Paine, *Common Sense*, 45.

54 Saldívar, *Dialectics of Our America*, 110.

55 Villaseñor, *Macho!*, 39.

56 For example, Bebout, *Mythohistorical Interventions*; Montejano, *Quixote's Soldiers*; Gómez-Quiñonez and Vásquez, *Making Aztlán*.

57 See, for instance, Garcia, *The Chicano Movement*; Garcia, *The Chicano Generation*.

58 Sepulveda, "The Use of 'Chicano,'" *Los Angeles Times*, Jan 5, 1970, A6.

59 Salazar, "Who is a Chicano?," *Los Angeles Times*, Feb 6, 1970, B7. Salazar was the first Mexican American reporter for the *Los Angeles Times* to cover the Chicano movement, and was killed by a police tear gas projectile during the protests.

60 Ibid, B7.

61 Ibid.

62 The landmark collection *Cultures of United States Imperialism* (Pease and Kaplan) turned academic attention to the "exceptionalist" practices by which the U.S. simultaneously acted to expand a global empire and denied that it was doing so.

63 As reported by May, "Emergence of Militancy Seen for Chicanos," *Los Angeles Times*, Aug 25, 1969, A24.

64 The term "Global South" emerges from the hemispheric differences in the economic, political, and social development of countries, an alternative to the term "third-world." For a discussion of Global South as a concept, see Levander and Mignolo, "Introduction: The Global South and World Dis/Order," 1–11. For its use in Latino Studies, see Saldívar, *Trans-Americanity*.

65 Hames-Garcia, "How to Tell a Mestizo," 104.

66 Salazar, "The Social Origins," 205.

67 "El Plan Espiritual de Aztlán."

68 Moraga, *Last Generation*, 232.

69 Gutierrez, "Community, Patriarchy, Individualism," 49.

70 Salazar, "The Social Origins," 201.

71 Ibid, 202.

72 Ibid.

73 For a discussion of the problematic nature of "authenticity," see Cutler, "Disappeared Men."

74 Salazar, "The Social Origins," 201.

75 Ibid, 205.

76 Ibid.

77 "El Plan Espiritual de Aztlán."

78 Ibid.

79 Ibid.

80 Among the many contributions, see Moraga and Anzaldua, *This Bridge Called My Back*; Saldívar-Hull, *Feminism on the Border*; Alarcón, "The Theoretical Subject(s) of *This Bridge Called My Back*. I also draw on Kimberlé Crenshaw's theorization of the term "intersectional" in Critical Race Theory; see Crenshaw, "Mapping the Margins." For intersectionality's influence, see also Delgado and Stefancic, *Critical Race Theory*.

81 Villaseñor, *Macho!*, 38. Hereafter cited parenthetically in the text.

EPILOGUE

1 García, *Mexican Americans, 294.*

2 Washington Post Staff, "Full Text: Donald Trump Announces a Presidential Bid," *Washington Post*, June 16, 2015, www.washingtonpost.com.

3 Lee, "Donald Trump's False Comments," *Washington Post,* July 8, 2015, www.washingtonpost.com.

4 In the midst of a refugee crisis in Europe and as a response to domestic terrorism, he sought to ban entry to Muslims temporarily, playing on the nation's security fears. See Partlow, "For Mexicans, Trump's bid is getting scarier," *The Washington Post*, August 18, 2015, www.washingtonpost.com.

5 On "post-racial America," see Carbado and Gulati, *Acting White*; Bonilla-Silva, *Racism Without Racists*; and Li, *Signifying without Specifying*.

6 Tantaros was responding to a discussion on the Fox Business News show "Varney and Company," December 22, 2015, youtu.be/yOmeVXWKO4Q.

7 For a discussion of the similarities between Wilson's "America First" and Trump's "Make America Great Again," see Rauchway, "How 'America First' got Its Nationalistic Edge," *Atlantic Magazine*, May 6, 2016, www.theatlantic.com.

8 Quoted in "America First!," *Philadelphia Inquirer*, October 17, 1915, 12.

9 Ibid.

10 *La Prensa*, December 28, 1915, 3.

11 Lowe, *Immigrant Acts*, 19.

BIBLIOGRAPHY

ARCHIVAL MATERIAL/PRIMARY AND UNPUBLISHED SOURCES

Agüeros, V., ed. *El Tiempo, Diario Catolico.* February 28, 1886.

Albuquerque Morning Journal. "Keep Out the Aliens." April 15, 1922.

Bohemian Club: Certificate of Incorporation, Constitution, by-Laws and Rules, Officers, Committees, and Members. San Francisco: H. S. Crocker Company, 1904.

"Brief History of the Pan American Round Table Organizations." Pan American Round Table Organizations. http://partt.org/history.html.

Cabeza de Baca, Manuel. *Historia de Vicente Silva, sus Cuarenta Bandidos, sus Crimenes y Retribuciones.* Las Vegas: Voz del Pueblo, 1896.

Carrillo, Adolfo R. *Cuentos Californianos.* San Francisco: Cowan and Cowan, ~1922.

Colfax County Stockman (Springer, NM). "It's Up to You Now, Mr. Voter." September 3, 1910.

"Constitución Política de los Estados Unidos Mexicanos de 1917." *Diario Oficial: Organo del Gobierno Provisional de la Republica Mexicana*, February 5, 1917. www.diputados.gob.mx/.

Cortina, Juan Nepomuceno. "'Proclama' del Ciudadano Nepomuceno Cortinas." September 30, 1859.

Crowther, Bosley. "The Screen in Review: 'Sombrero' Skims Into Loew's State and a Resolute Cast Is Obscured by the Shade." *New York Times.* April 23, 1953.

Cué, Fernández. "El Autor de las Memorias de Lerdo." *Excelsior.* March 11, 1926.

Davies, Lawrence E. "Pacific States." *New York Times.* April 20, 1947.

———. "Racial Intolerance is feared spreading on the Coast." *New York Times.* April 20, 1947.

Democratic Party Platforms. "Democratic Party Platform of 1912." June 25, 1912. *The American Presidency Project*, created by Gerhard Peters and John T. Woolley. www.presidency.ucsb.edu.

Editorial. Con Safos: Reflections of Life in the Barrio, vol. 6. Edited by Arturo Flores. 1970.

El Clamor Público. August 14, 1855.

El Eco del Valle (Las Cruces, NM). "Civismo y Educacion." February 24, 1912.

———. "La Tragedia Mexicana." August 12, 1911.

El Plan de Santa Barbara: A Chicano Plan for Higher Education, Analysis and Positions by the Chicano Coordinating Council on Higher Education. Oakland: La Causa Publications, 1969.

"El Plan Espiritual de Aztlán." National Chicano Youth Liberation Conference. March 1969.

El Sol de Mayo (Las Vegas, NM). May 7, 1891. Eugenio Romero and Manuel Cabeza de Baca, eds.

Fort Worth Star-Telegram. December 1, 1918.

García Naranjo, Nemesio. "Hermoso Fragmento De Un Discurso Los Colores de la Bandera Mexicana, Segun el Lic. Nemesio Garcia Naranjo." *El Tusconese* (Tuscon). October 4, 1921.

———. "La Resurreccion de la Patria." *La Prensa* (San Antonio) September 16, 1921.

Garza, Catarino. "*La lógica de los hechos, o sean observaciones sobre las circunstancias de los mexicanos en Texas desde el año 1877 hasta 1889.*" Unpublished manuscript, University of Texas Benson Latin American Collection, 1890.

Hill, Gladwin. "Our Mexican Minority: American Me." *New York Times*. October 24, 1948.

———. "Peons in the West Lowering Culture." *New York Times*. March 27, 1951.

———. "Southwest Winks at 'Wetback' Jobs." *New York Times*. March 28, 1951.

Kansas City Star 42, no. 108. January 3, 1922.

La Cronica (Laredo). "Esfuerzo Supremo." September 3, 1910.

La Prensa (Los Angeles). "An Open Letter to the President of the United States of America." July 25, 1919.

La Prensa (San Antonio). December 28, 1915.

Lee, Michelle Ye Hee. "Donald Trump's False Comments Connecting Mexican Immigrants and Crime." *Washington Post*. July 8, 2015. Accessed January 13, 2016. www.washingtonpost.com.

López, José Timoteo, Edgardo Nuñez Gamarra, and Roberto Lara Vialapando. *Una Breve Reseña de la literatura hispana de Nuevo México y Colorado*. Chihuahua: Talleres Linotipográficos de El Alacrán, 1959.

May, Lawrence. "Emergence of Militancy Seen for Chicanos." *Los Angeles Times*, August 25, 1969.

Messersmith, G. S., and Ezequiel Padilla. "Migratory Workers, exchange of notes at México April 26, 1943," and as amended, between the American Embassy at Mexico City and the Mexican Ministry for Foreign Affairs," 57 Statute 1152, Executive Agreement Series 351.

Montes, Ramon Elices. *Cuatro años en Méjico: memorias íntimas de un periodista español*. Madrid: Impressa de la viuda de J. M. Perez, 1885.

New York Times. "Deportation Talk Revived." February 16, 1936.

———. "Mexicans Watching Quota Move Here." March 5, 1928.

———. July 1, 1908.

Niggli, Josephina. *Step Down, Elder Brother*. New York: Rinehart and Company, 1947.

Partlow, Joshua. "For Mexicans, Trump's Bid is Getting Scarier." *Washington Post*. August 18, 2015. Accessed January 13, 2016. www.washingtonpost.com.

Philadelphia Inquirer. "America First!" October 17, 1915.

———. "Four Year Immigrant Ban Approved by House Committee." January 29, 1919.

"Pocho: The Novel, The Author, And Their Times." Program #1981–07, especially 6:20–15:20. Available on *Onda Latina*. www.laits.utexas.edu/onda_latina.

Poore, Charles. "Books of the Times." *New York Times*. January 31, 1948.

"Primer Congreso Mexicanista, Verificado en Laredo, Texas, EEUU de A. Los Dias 14 al 22 de Septiembre de 1911." *Discursos y Conferencias Por la Raza y Para la Raza*. Tipografia de N. ldar, 1912.

Rauchway, Eric. "How 'America First' Got its Nationalistic Edge." *Atlantic Magazine*. May 6, 2016. www.theatlantic.com.

"Records of the Constitutional Convention of 1849." California State Archives. http://www.sos.ca.gov/archives/collections/constitutions/.

"Renunciation of U.S. Nationality by Persons Claiming a Right of Residence in the United States." U.S. Department of State. travel.state.gov/.

Revista Mexicana (San Antonio). "Discurso de Mr. Hughes." August 6, 1916.

Salazar, Peter Cirilo. "The Social Origins of Chicano Nationalism, Class and Community in the Making of Aztlán: 1800–1920." In *NACCS Annual Conference Proceedings*. 1975. scholarworks.sjsu.edu/naccs.

Salazar, Ruben. "Who is a Chicano? And What is it the Chicanos Want?" *Los Angeles Times*. February 6, 1970.

"Later from Brownsville. Another Fight—Cortina Victorious!! Full Particulars." Reproduced from the Brownsville *American Flag Extra*, October 27, 1859. *Southern Intelligencer* (Austin). November 9, 1859.

Sepulveda, Thomas. "The Use of 'Chicano.'" *Los Angeles Times*. January 5, 1970.

Turner, John Kenneth. "A Crime Upon the Children of Our Land." *Regeneracion* (Los Angeles). September 24, 1910.

"U.S. Citizenship Laws & Policy." U.S. Department of State. travel.state.gov/.

U.S. Census Bureau. "Profile America Facts for Features, CB16-FF.16." October 12, 2016.

U.S. Congress, House. *Difficulties on the Southwestern Frontier*. 36th Congress, 1st Session, 1860, H. Exec. Doc. 52, 70–82.

Villarreal, José Antonio. "Early Correspondence about *Pocho*, December 22, 1956." Jose Antonio Villarreal Papers, Santa Clara University Library Archives and Special Collections.

Washington Post Staff. "Full Text: Donald Trump Announces a Presidential Bid." *Washington Post*. June 16, 2015. Accessed January 13, 2016. www.washingtonpost.com.

Weekly Labor Herald. Corpus Christi: December 19, 1941.

Willis, W. B., and P. K. Stockton. *Debates and Proceedings of the Constitutional Convention*. Sacramento: State Printing Office, J.D. Young, 1881.

PUBLISHED BOOKS AND ARTICLES

Acuña, Rodolfo. *Occupied America: The Chicano's Struggle Toward Liberation*. San Francisco: Canfield Press, 1972.

Adamic, Louis. "The Passing of American Individualism." *American Scholar* 1, no. 4 (October 1932): 423.

Aguirre, Pablo Armando González Ulloa. "Cuidadania ante el espacio público." *CONfines* 11, no. 21 (January–May 2015): 87–106.

Alarcón, Norma. "The Theoretical Subject(s) of *This Bridge Called My Back* and Anglo-American Feminism." In *Criticism in the Borderlands: Studies in Chicano Literature, Culture, and Ideology*, edited by Hector Calderón and José David Saldívar. Durham: Duke University Press, 1991.

Alemán, Jesse. "'Thank God, Lolita Is Away from Those Horrid Savages': The Politics of Whiteness in *Who Would Have Thought It?*" In *Maria Amparo Ruiz de Burton: Critical and Pedagogical Perspectives*, edited by Amelia María de la Luz Montes and Anne Elizabeth Goldman. Lincoln: University of Nebraska Press, 2004.

Anaya, Rodolfo, Francisco E. Lomeli, and Enrique R. Lamadrid. *Aztlán: Essays on the Chicano Homeland*. Albuquerque: University of New Mexico Press, 1989.

Anzaldua, Gloria. *Borderlands/La Frontera: The New Mestiza*. San Francisco: Aunt Lute Books, 1987.

Aparicio, Frances R. "On Sub-Versive Signifiers: U.S. Latina/o Writers Tropicalize English." *American Literature* 66, no. 4 (1994): 795–801.

Appiah, Kwame Anthony. *Cosmopolitanism: Ethics in a World of Strangers*. New York: W. W. Norton, 2006.

Aranda, José. "Contradictory Impulses: Maria Amparo Ruiz de Burton, Resistance Theory, and the Politics of Chicano/a Studies." *American Literature* 70, no. 3 (1998): 551–79.

———. "Returning California to the People: Vigiliantism in *The Squatter and the Don*." In *Maria Amparo Ruiz de Burton: Critical and Pedagogical Perspectives*, edited by Amelia María de la Luz Montes and Anne Elizabeth Goldman. Lincoln: University of Nebraska Press, 2004.

———. *When We Arrive: A New Literary History of Mexican America*. Tucson: University of Arizona Press, 2003.

Arteaga, Alfred. *Chicano Poetics: Heterotexts and Hybridities*. New York: Cambridge University Press, 1997.

Atherton, Gertrude. *The Californians*. New York: J. Lane, 1898.

———. *Splendid Idle Forties*. New York: MacMillan, 1902.

Baeza Ventura, Gabriela. *La imagen de la mujer en la crónica del "México de afuera."* Juarez: Universidad Autónoma de Ciudad Juárez, 2006.

Bakhtin, Mikhail. "Bildungsroman and its Significance in the History of Realism (Toward a Historical Typology of the Novel)." In *Speech Genres and Other Late Essays*, edited by Caryl Emerson and Michael Holquist, translated by Vern W. McGee. Austin: University of Texas Press, 1986.

Balderrama, Francisco E., and Raymond Rodríguez. *Decade of Betrayal: Mexican Repatriation in the 1930s*. Albuquerque: University of New Mexico Press, 2006.

Balibar, Etienne. *We the People of Europe?: Reflections on Transnational Citizenship*. Princeton: Princeton University Press, 2003.

Baym, Nina. *Woman's Fiction: A Guide to Novels by and about Women in America, 1820–70*. Ithaca: Cornell University Press, 1978.

Bebout, Lee. *Mythohistorical Interventions: The Chicano Movement and Its Legacies.* Minneapolis: University of Minnesota Press, 2011.

Bederman, Gail. *Manliness and Civilization: A Cultural History of Gender and Race in the United States, 1880–1917.* Chicago: University of Chicago Press, 1995.

Beltrán, Cristina. *Trouble With Unity: Latino Politics and the Creation of Identity.* New York: Oxford University Press, 2010.

Benhabib, Seyla. *Another Cosmopolitanism.* New York: Oxford University Press, 2006.

Benn Michaels, Walter. *Our America: Nativism, Modernism, and Pluralism.* Durham: Duke University Press, 1995.

Benowitz, June Melby. *Challenge and Change: Right-Wing Women, Grassroots Activism, and the Baby Boom Generation.* Gainesville: University Press of Florida, 2015.

———. *Days of Discontent: American Women and Right-Wing Politics, 1933–1945.* DeKalb: Northern Illinois University Press, 2002.

Berlant, Lauren. *Queen of America Goes to Washington: Essays on Sex and Citizenship.* Durham: Duke University Press, 1997.

Bonilla-Silva, Eduardo. *Racism Without Racists: Color-Blind Racism and the Persistence of Racial Inequality in America.* Lanham: Rowman and Littlefield, 2014.

Borowsky Junge, Maxine. *Voices from the Barrio: "Con Safos: Reflections of Life in the Barrio."* CreateSpace Independent Publishing, 2016.

Bosniak, Linda. *Citizen and the Alien: Dilemmas of Contemporary Membership.* Princeton: Princeton University Press, 2006.

———. "Citizenship Denationalized." *Indiana Journal of Global Legal Studies* 7, no. 2 (Spring 2000): 447–509.

Bost, Suzanne. *Mulattas and Mestizas: Representing Mixed Identities in the Americas, 1850–2000.* Athens: University of Georgia Press, 2003.

Brickhouse, Ana. *Transamerican Literary Relations and the Nineteenth-Century Public Sphere.* Cambridge: Cambridge University Press, 2004.

Brodkin, Karen. *How Jews Became White Folks and What That Says about Race in America.* New Brunswick: Rutgers University Press, 1998.

Brogan, Kathleen. *Cultural Haunting: Ghosts and Ethnicity in Recent American Literature.* Charlottesville: University Press of Virginia, 1998.

Bruce-Novoa, Juan. "Homosexuality and the Chicano Novel." *Confluencia* 2, no. 1 (Fall 1986): 69–77.

———. "*La Prensa* and the Chicano Community." *Americas Review* 17, no. 3–4 (1989): 150–56.

Cabeza de Baca, Fabiola. *We Fed Them Cactus.* Albuquerque: University of New Mexico Press, 1994.

Calavita, Kitty. *Inside the State: The Bracero Program, Immigration, and the I.N.S.* New York: Routledge, 1992.

Carbado, Devon W., and Mitu Gulati. *Acting White: Rethinking Race in "Post-Racial" America.* New York: Oxford University Press, 2013.

Carnes, Mark. *Secret Ritual and Manhood in Victorian America.* New Haven: Yale University Press, 1991.

Carter, April. *The Political Theory of Global Citizenship*. New York: Routledge, 2001.

Carton, Evan. "What Feels an American?: Evident Selves and Alien Emotions in the New Man's World." In *Boys Don't Cry*, edited by Milette Shamir and Jennifer Travis. New York: Columbia University Press, 2002.

Castañeda, Jorge G. *Ex Mex: From Migrants to Immigrants*. New York: New Press, 2007.

Castillo, Ana. *Massacre of the Dreamers: Essays on Xicanismo*. New York: Plume, 1994.

Castillo, Pedro, and Albert Camarillo. *Furia y Muerte: Los Bandidos Chicanos*. Los Angeles: Aztlán Publications (Chicano Studies Center), 1973.

Cervantes, Lorna Dee. *Emplumada*. Pittsburgh: University of Pittsburgh Press, 1981.

Chabrán, Rafael, and Richard Chabrán. "The Spanish-Language and Latino Press of the United States: Newspapers and Periodicals." In *Handbook of Hispanic Cultures in the United States: Literature and Art*, edited by Francisco Lomelí. Houston: Arte Público Press, 1993.

Chapman, Mary, and Glenn Hendler, eds. *Sentimental Men: Masculinity and the Politics of Affect in American Culture*. Berkeley: University of California Press, 1999.

Chávez, Ernesto. *The U.S. War with Mexico: A Brief History with Documents*. Boston: Bedford/St. Martin's, 2008.

Chavez, Leo. *The Latino Threat: Constructing Immigrants, Citizens, and the Nation*. Stanford: Stanford University Press, 2008.

Chust, Manuel, and Ivana Frasquet. "Orígenes federales del republicanismo en México, 1810–1824." *Mexican Studies/Estudios Mexicanos* 24, no. 2 (Summer 2008): 363–98.

Cisneros, Sandra. "Eyes of Zapata." In *Woman Hollering Creek*, 85–113. New York: Vintage Books, 1991.

Clapp, Elizabeth J. "The Woman Suffrage Movement, 1848–1920." In *The Practice of U.S. Women's History: Narratives, Intersections, and Dialogues*, edited by Vicki L. Ruiz, S. Jay Kleinberg, and Eileen Boris. New Brunswick: Rutgers University Press, 2007.

Cohen, Deborah. *Braceros: Migrant Citizens and Transnational Subjects in the Postwar United States and Mexico*. Chapel Hill: University of North Carolina Press, 2011.

Coronado, Raul. *A World Not to Come: A History of Latino Writing and Print Culture*. Cambridge: Harvard University Press, 2013.

Cotera, María. *Native Speakers: Ella Deloria, Zora Neale Hurston, Jovita González, and the Poetics of Culture*. Austin: University of Texas Press, 2008.

Cox, James H. *Muting White Noise: Native American and European American Novel Traditions*. Norman: University of Oklahoma Press, 2006.

Crenshaw, Kimberlé. "Mapping the Margins: Intersectionality, Identity Politics, and Violence against Women of Color." *Stanford Law Review* 43, no. 6 (July 1991): 1241–99.

Curran, Thomas J. *Xenophobia and Immigration, 1820–1930*. Boston: Twayne Publishers, 1975.

Cutler, John Alba. "Disappeared Men: Chicana/o Authenticity and the American War in Viet Nam." *American Literature* 81, no. 3 (September 2009): 583–611.

———. *Ends of Assimilation: The Formation of Chicano Literature.* New York: Oxford University Press, 2015.

Dabove, Juan Pablo. *Nightmares of the Lettered City: Banditry and Literature in Latin America, 1816–1929.* Pittsburgh: University of Pittsburgh Press, 2007.

Daniels, Roger. *Not Like Us: Immigrants and Minorities in America, 1890–1924.* Chicago: Ivan R. Dee, 1997.

DeGuzmán, Maria. *Spain's Long Shadow: The Black Legend, Off-Whiteness, and Anglo-American Empire.* Minneapolis: University of Minnesota Press, 2005.

Deleuze, Gilles, and Felix Guattari. *A Thousand Plateaus: Capitalism and Schizophrenia.* Translated by Brian Massumi. Minneapolis: University of Minnesota Press, 1987.

Delgado, Richard, and Jean Stefancic, eds. *Critical Race Theory: The Cutting Edge.* Philadelphia: Temple University Press, 2000.

Delpar, Helen. *Enormous Vogue of Things Mexican: Cultural Relations between the United States and Mexico, 1920–1935.* Tuscaloosa: University of Alabama Press, 1995.

DeLyser, Dydia. "Ramona Memories: Fiction, Tourist Practices, and Placing the Past in Southern California." *Annals of the Association of American Geographers* 93, no. 4 (December 2003): 886–908.

———. *Ramona Memories: Tourism and the Shaping of Southern California.* Minneapolis: University of Minnesota Press, 2005.

Denning, Michael. *Mechanic Accents: Dime Novels and Working Class Culture in America.* New York: Verso, 1998.

Derrida, Jacques. "Law of Genre." *Critical Inquiry* 7, no. 1 (Autumn 1980): 55–81.

Dessau, Adalbert. *La novela de la revolucion Mexicana.* Translated by Juan José Utrilla. Mexico City: Fondo de Cultura Económica, 1986.

Deutsch, Sarah. *No Separate Refuge: Culture, Class, and Gender on an Anglo-Hispanic Frontier in the American Southwest, 1880–1940.* New York: Oxford University Press, 1987.

Doub, Yolanda A. *Journeys of Formation: The Spanish American Bildungsroman.* New York: Peter Lang Publishing, 2010.

Dower, Nigel, and John Williams, eds. *Global Citizenship: A Critical Introduction.* New York: Routledge, 2002.

Edwards, Brian T., and Dilip Parameshwar Gaonkar, eds. *Globalizing American Studies.* Chicago: University of Chicago Press, 2010. See esp introduction.

Emerald, John. *Cortina, the Scourge; or, The Lost Diamond.* New York: Beadle and Adams, 1872.

Emerson, Ralph Waldo. "Self-Reliance." In *Emerson: Essays, First and Second Series.* New York: Vintage Books, 1990.

Englekirk, John E. *Bibliografía de obras norteamericanas en traducción eespañola.* Mexico City: Revista Americana, 1944.

Escobar, Edward J. *Race, Police, and the Making of a Political Identity: Mexican Americans and the Los Angeles Police Department, 1900–1945.* Berkeley: University of California Press, 1999.

Escobedo, Elizabeth R. *From Coveralls to Zoot Suits: The Lives of Mexican American Women on the World War II Home Front*. Chapel Hill: University of North Carolina Press, 2013.

Estrada, William David. *The Los Angeles Plaza, Sacred and Contested Space*. Austin: University of Texas Press, 2008.

Evans, Sara M. *Born for Liberty: A History of Women in America*. New York: Free Press, 1989.

Ferguson, Roderick. *Aberrations in Black: Toward a Queer of Color Critique*. Minneapolis: University of Minnesota Press, 2003.

Fischer, Claude S. "Paradoxes of American Individualism." *Sociological Forum* 23, no. 2 (June 2008): 363–72.

Fiske, Turbesé Lummis. *Charles F. Lummis: The Man and his West*. Norman: University of Oklahoma Press, 1975.

Flores, William V., and Rina Benmayor. *Latino Cultural Citizenship: Claiming Identity, Space, and Rights*. Boston: Beacon Press, 1998.

Fluck, Winfried, Donald Pease, and John Carlos Rowe, eds. *Re-framing the Transnational Turn in American Studies*. Lebanon: Dartmouth College Press, 2011.

Foley, Neil. *The White Scourge: Mexicans, Blacks, and Poor Whites in Texas Cotton Culture*. Berkeley: University of California Press, 1997.

Foner, Eric. *Tom Paine and Revolutionary America*. New York: Oxford University Press, 1976.

Foote, Stephanie. *Regional Fictions: Culture and Identity in Nineteenth-Century American Literature*. Madison: University of Wisconsin Press, 2001.

Fox, Jonathan. "Difficult Transition from Clientelism to Citizenship: Lessons from Mexico." *World Politics* 46, no. 2 (Jan 1994): 151–84.

———. *Politics of Food in Mexico: State Power and Social Mobilization*. La Jolla: Center for U.S.-Mexican Studies, 1993.

Franco, Jean. *An Introduction to Spanish-American Literature*. New York: Cambridge University Press, 1994.

Frazer, Chris. *Bandit Nation: A History of Outlaws and Cultural Struggle in Mexico, 1810–1920*. Lincoln: University of Nebraska Press, 2006.

Fregoso, Rosa-Linda. *Mexicana Encounters: The Making of Social Identities on the Borderlands*. Berkeley: University of California Press, 2003.

Freund, Paul. "Charles Evans Hughes as Chief Justice." *Harvard Law Review* 81, no. 1 (November 1967): 4–40.

Friend, Craig Thompson, ed. *Southern Masculinity: Perspectives on Manhood in the South Since Reconstruction*. Athens: University of Georgia Press, 2009.

Friend, Craig Thompson, and Lori Glover, eds. *Southern Manhood: Perspectives on Masculinity in the Old South*. Athens: University of Georgia Press, 2004.

Garcia, Ignacio M. *White But Not Equal: Mexican Americans, Jury Discrimination, and the Supreme Court*. Tucson: University of Arizona Press, 2008.

Garcia, Mario T. *The Chicano Generation: Testimonios of the Movement*. Berkeley: University of California Press, 2015.

———, ed. *The Chicano Movement: Perspectives from the Twenty-First Century*. New York: Routledge, 2014.

———. *Mexican Americans: Leadership, Ideology, and Identity, 1930–1960*. New Haven: Yale University Press, 1989.

Garcia, Matt. *A World of Its Own: Race, Labor, and Citrus in the Making of Greater Los Angeles, 1900–1970*. Chapel Hill: University of North Carolina Press, 2001.

García Canclini, Nestor. *Hybrid Cultures: Strategies for Entering and Leaving Modernity*. Minneapolis: University of Minnesota Press, 2005.

Garza-Falcon, Leticia. *Gente Decente: A Borderlands Response to the Rhetoric of Dominance*. Austin: University of Texas Press, 1998.

Gillman, Susan. "Otra Vez Caliba/Encore Caliban: Adapation, Translation, Americas Studies." *American Literary History* 20, no. 1-2 (Spring/Summer 2008): 187–209.

Glantz, Margo. "Huerfanos y bandidos: Los Bandidos de Río Frío." *Historia Mexicana* 44, no. 1 (July–September 1994): 141–65.

Goldman, Anne E. *Continental Divides: Revisioning American Literature*. New York: Palgrave Macmillan, 2000.

Gómez, Laura E. *Manifest Destinies: The Making of the Mexican American Race*. New York: New York University Press, 2008.

Gómez-Quiñones, Juan. "Piedras Contra la Luna, México en Aztlán y Aztlán en México: Chicano Mexican Relations and the Mexican Consulates, 1900–1920." In *Contemporary Mexico: Papers of the Fourth International Congress of Mexican History*, edited by James W. Wilkie, Michael C. Meyer, and Edna Monzon de Wilkie. Berkeley: University of California Press, 1976.

Gómez-Quiñones, Juan, and Irene Vásquez. *Making Aztlán: Ideology and Culture of the Chicana and Chicano Movement*. Albuquerque: University of New Mexico Press, 2014.

Gonzales, Alfonso. *Reform Without Justice: Latino Migrant Politics and the Homeland Security State*. New York: Oxford University Press, 2013.

Gonzales, Rodolfo. *I Am Joaquin/Yo Soy Joaquin: An Epic Poem*. New York: Bantam Books, 1972.

Gonzales-Berry, Erlinda. *The Contested Homeland: A Chicano History of New Mexico*. Albuquerque: University of New Mexico Press, 2000.

Gonzalez, Gilbert G. *Mexican Consuls and Labor Organizing: Imperial Politics in the American Southwest*. Austin: University of Texas Press, 1999.

González, John Morán. *Border Renaissance: The Texas Centennial and the Emergence of Mexican American Literature*. Austin: University of Texas Press, 2009.

———. "Warp of Whiteness: Domesticity and Empire in Helen Hunt Jackson's *Ramona*." *American Literary History* 16, no. 3 (Autumn 2004): 437–65.

———. "The Whiteness of the Blush: The Cultural Politics of Racial Formation in *The Squatter and the Don*." In *Maria Amparo Ruiz de Burton: Critical and Pedagogical Perspectives*, edited by Amelia María de la Luz Montes and Anne Elizabeth Goldman. Lincoln: University of Nebraska Press, 2004.

González, Jovita. *Dew on the Thorn*. Houston: Arte Público Press, 1997.

González, Jovita, and Eve Raleigh. *Caballero*. College Station: Texas A&M University Press, 1996.

González, Rosalinda M. "Chicanas and Mexican Immigrant Families 1920–40: Women's Subordination and Family Exploitation." In *Decades of Discontent: The Women's Movement, 1920–1940*, edited by Lois Scharf and Joan M. Jensen. Westport: Greenwood Press, 1983.

Gordon, Avery F. *Ghostly Matters: Haunting and the Sociological Imagination*. Minneapolis: University of Minnesota Press, 1997.

Greenberg, Amy. *Manifest Manhood and the Antebellum American Empire*. New York: Cambridge University Press, 2005.

Grewal, Inderpal. *Transnational America: Feminisms, Diasporas, Neoliberalisms*. Durham: Duke University Press, 2005.

Griswold del Castillo, Richard. *The Treaty of Guadalupe Hidalgo: A Legacy of Conflict*. Norman: University of Oklahoma Press, 1990.

———. *World War II and Mexican American Civil Rights*. Austin: University of Texas Press, 2008.

Gruesz, Kirsten Silva. "Alien Speech, Incorporated: On the Cultural History of Spanish in the US." *American Literary History* 25, no. 1 (Spring 2013): 18–32.

———. *Ambassadors of Culture: The Transamerican Origins of Latino Writing*. Princeton: Princeton University Press, 2001.

Gutiérrez, David G. *Walls and Mirrors: Mexican Americans, Mexican Immigrants, and the Politics of Ethnicity*. Berkeley: University of California Press, 1995.

Gutierrez, Ramon A. "Community, Patriarchy, Individualism: The Politics of Chicano History and the Dream of Equality." *American Quarterly* 45, no. 1 (March 1993): 44–72.

Hames-Garcia, Michael. "How to Tell a Mestizo from an Enchirito®: Colonialism and National Culture in the Borderlands." *Diacritics* 30, no. 4 (Winter 2000): 102–22.

———. *Identity Complex: Making the Case for Multiplicity*. Minneapolis: University of Minnesota Press, 2011.

Harper, Phillip Brian. *Are We Not Men?: Masculine Anxiety and the Problem of African-American Identity*. New York: Oxford University Press, 1996.

Harris, Charles H., and Louis R. Sadler. "The Plan of San Diego and the Mexico–United States Crisis of 1916: A Reexamination." *Hispanic American Historical Review* 58, no. 3 (August 1978): 381–408.

Harris, Cheryl I. "Whiteness as Property." In *Critical Race Theory: Essays on the Social Construction of and Reproduction of "Race."* Edited by E. Nathaniel Gates. New York: Garland Publishing, 1997.

Henretta, James A. "Charles Evans Hughes and the Strange Death of Liberal America." *Law and History Review* 24, no. 1 (Spring 2006): 115–71.

Higham, John. *Strangers in the Land: Patterns of American Nativism, 1860–1925*. New Brunswick: Rutgers University Press, 1983.

Hobsbawm, Eric. *Primitive Rebels: Studies in Archaic Forms of Social Movement in the 19th and 20th Centuries*. New York: W. W. Norton, 1959.

Hodes, Martha. *White Women, Black Men: Illicit Sex in the Nineteenth-Century South.* New Haven: Yale University Press, 1997.

Hoffman, Abraham. *Unwanted Mexican Americans in the Great Depression: Repatriation Pressures, 1929–1939.* Tucson: University of Arizona Press, 1974.

Hoganson, Kristin L. *Fighting for American Manhood: How Gender Politics Provoked the Spanish-American and Philippine-American Wars.* New Haven: Yale University Press, 1998.

Holland, Sharon P. *Erotic Life of Racism.* Durham: Duke University Press, 2012.

hooks, bell. *We Real Cool: Black Men and Masculinity.* New York: Routledge, 2004.

Ignatiev, Noel. *How the Irish Became White.* New York: Routledge, 1995.

Irwin, Robert McKee. "*Ramona* and Postnationalist American Studies: On 'Our America' and the Mexican Borderlands." *American Quarterly* 55, no. 4 (December 2003): 539–67.

Jayal, Naraja Gopal. *Citizenship and its Discontents: An Indian History.* Cambridge: Harvard University Press, 2013.

Johannsen, Robert. *To the Halls of the Montezumas: The Mexican War in the American Imagination.* New York: Oxford University Press, 1985.

Johnson, Benjamin. *Revolution in Texas: How a Forgotten Rebellion and its Bloody Suppression Turned Mexicans into Americans.* New Haven: Yale University Press, 2003.

Johnson, Susan Lee. *Roaring Camp: The Social World of the California Gold Rush.* New York: W.W. Norton, 2000.

Kabalen de Bichara, Donna M. "Josephina Niggli as a Regional Voice: A Reexamination of *Mexican Village* and *Step Down Elder Brother.*" In *Recovering the U.S. Hispanic Literary Heritage,* Vol. 6, edited by Anonia I. Castañeda and A. Gabriel Meléndez. Houston: Arte Público Press, 2006.

Kanellos, Nicolás. "Cronistas and Satire in Early Twentieth Century Hispanic Newspapers." *MELUS* 23, no. 1 (Spring 1998): 3–25.

———. *Hispanic Immigrant Literature: El Sueño del Retorno.* Austin: University of Texas Press, 2011.

———. "Recovering and Re-Constructing Early Twentieth-Century Hispanic Immigrant Print Culture in the U.S." *American Literary History* 19, no. 2 (Summer 2007): 438-55.

Kanellos, Nicolás, and Helvetia Martell. *Hispanic Periodicals in the United States, Origins to 1960: A Brief History and Comprehensive Bibliography.* Houston: Arte Público Press, 2000.

Kaplan, Amy. *Anarchy of Empire in the Making of U.S. Culture.* Cambridge: Harvard University Press, 2005.

Kaplan, Caren, Norma Alarcón, and Minoo Moallem, eds. *Between Woman and Nation: Nationalisms, Transnational Feminisms and the State.* Durham: Duke University Press, 1999.

Kateb, George. "Democratic Individualism and its Critics." *Annual Review Political Science* 6 (2003): 275–305.

———. *Emerson and Self-Reliance.* Lanham: Rowman and Littlefied, 2002.

Kauffmann, Lane, trans. *Vicente Silva and his Forty Bandits*. Washington: E. McLean Press, 1947.

Kazanjian, David. *The Colonizing Trick: National Culture and Imperial Citizenship in Early America*. Minneapolis: University of Minnesota Press, 2003.

Kazanjian, David, and María Josefina Saldaña-Portillo. "Wavering on the Horizon of Social Being: The Treaty of Guadalupe-Hidalgo and the Legacy of Racial Character in Américo Paredes's *George Washington Gomez*." *Radical History Review* 89 (Spring 2004): 135–64.

Kerber, Linda K. *Women of the Republic: Intellect and Ideology in Revolutionary America*. Chapel Hill: University of North Carolina Press, 1980.

Kessler-Harris, Alice. *In Pursuit of Equity: Women, Men, and the Quest for Economic Citizenship in 20th-Century America*. New York: Oxford University Press, 2001.

Kettner, James H. *Development of American Citizenship, 1608–1870*. Chapel Hill: University of North Carolina Press, 1978.

Kimball, Marie. *Jefferson: The Road to Glory, 1743 to 1776*. New York: Coward-McCann, 1943.

Kimmel, Michael. *Manhood in America: A Cultural History*. New York: Oxford University Press, 2006.

Kropp, Phoebe S. *California Vieja: Culture and Memory in a Modern American Place*. Berkeley: University of California Press, 2006.

Labbé, Ronald M., and Jonathan Lurie. *The Slaughterhouse Cases: Regulation, Reconstruction, and the Fourteenth Amendment*. Lawrence: University Press of Kansas, 2003.

La Fountain-Stokes, Lawrence. "Queering Latina/o Literature." In *Cambridge Companion to Latina/o American Literature*, edited by John Morán Gonzalez. New York: Cambridge University Press, 2016.

Larkin, Edward. "Inventing an American Public: Thomas Paine, the 'Pennsylvania Magazine,' and American Revolutionary Political Discourse." *Early American Literature* 33, no. 3 (1998): 250–76.

Larsen, Nella. *Passing*. New York: Penguin Classics, 2004.

Lazarou, Kathleen Elizabeth. *Concealed Under Petticoats: Married Women's Property and the Law of Texas, 1840–1913*. New York: Garland, 1986.

Leal, Luis. *Aztlan Y Mexico: Perfiles Literarios E Historicos*. Binghamton: Bilingual Press, 1985.

———. Introduction to *Life and Adventures of the Celebrated Bandit Joaquín Murrieta*, by Ireneo Paz. Houston: Arte Público Press, 1999.

Leider, Emily Wortis. *California's Daughter: Gertrude Atherton and Her Times*. Stanford: Stanford University Press, 1991.

Leiter, Brian. *Naturalizing Jurisprudence: Essays on American Legal Realism and Naturalism in Legal Philosophy*. Oxford: Oxford University Press, 2007.

Levander, Caroline F., and Robert S. Levine, *Hemispheric American Studies*. New Brunswick: Rutgers University press, 2008.

Levander, Caroline F., and Walter Mignolo. "Introduction: The Global South and World Dis/Order." *Global South* 5, no. 1 (Spring 2011): 1–11.

Li, Stephanie. *Signifying without Specifying: Racial Discourse in the Age of Obama*. New Brunswick: Rutgers University Press, 2012.

Libretti, Tim. "'We Can Starve Too': Américo Paredes's *George Washington Gomez* and the Proletarian Corrido." In *Recovering the U.S. Hispanic Literary Heritage*, vol. 2, edited by Erlinda Gonzalez-Berry and Chuck Tatum. Houston: Arte Público Press, 1996.

Lima, Lázaro. *The Latino Body: Crisis Identities in American Literary and Cultural Memory*. New York: New York University Press, 2007.

Limón, José. *Américo Paredes: Culture and Critique*. Austin: University of Texas, 2012.

———. "El Primer Congreso Mexicanista de 1911: A Precursor to Contemporary Chicanismo." *Aztlan Journal* 5, no. 1-2 (Spring 1974): 85–117.

———. *Mexican Ballads, Chicano Poems: History and Influence in Mexican-American Social Poetry*. Berkeley: University of California Press, 1992.

———. "*Mexicans*, Foundational Fictions, and the United States: Caballero, a Late Border Romance." *Modern Language Quarterly* 57, no. 2 (June 1996): 341–53.

Lomas, Laura. *Translating Empire: José Martí, Migrant Latino Subjects and American Modernities*. Durham: Duke University Press, 2008.

Lomelí, Francisco. "Cuento Costumbrista Mexicano Ma Alla De Las Fronteras: Julio G. Arce Y Adolfo R. Carrillo." In *Cuento Mexicano: Homenaje a Luis Leal*, edited by Sara Poot Herrera. Mexico City: Coordinacion de Difusion Cultural Direccion de Literature, UNAM, 1996.

Lomnitz, Claudio. "Final Reflections." In *The Eagle and the Virgin: Nation and Cultural Revolution in Mexico, 1920–1940*, edited by Mary Kay Vaughan and Stephen E. Lewis. Durham: Duke University Press, 2006.

———. "La construcción de la cuidadanía en México." *Metapolítica* 4 no. 15 (2000): 128–49.

———. "Modes of Citizenship in Mexico." *Public Culture* 11, no. 1 (1999): 269–93.

Lopez, Marissa K. *Chicano Nations: The Hemispheric Origins of Mexican American Literature*. New York: New York University Press, 2011.

———. "Political Economy of Early Chicano Historiography: The Case of Hubert H. Bancroft and Mariano G. Vallejo." *American Literary History* 19, no. 4 (Winter 2007): 874–904.

Lowe, Lisa. *Immigrant Acts: On Asian American Cultural Politics*. Durham: Duke University Press, 1996.

Loza, Mireya. *Defiant Braceros: How Migrant Workers Fought for Racial, Sexual, and Political Freedom*. Chapel Hill: University of North Carolina Press, 2016.

Luis-Brown, David. *Waves of Decolonization: Discourses of Race and Hemispheric Citizenship in Cuba, Mexico and the United States*. Durham: Duke University Press, 2008.

Lummis, Charles F. *The Spanish Pioneers*. Chicago: A.C. McClurg and Company, 1914.

Lutenski, Emily. "Locating the Modern Mexican in Josefina Niggli's *Step Down, Elder Brother.*" *Western American Literature* 45, no. 1 (Spring 2010): 4–29.

Lutz, Tom. *American Nervousness, 1903: An Anecdotal History*. Ithaca: Cornell University Press, 1991.

Madrid, Arturo. "In Search of the Authentic Pachuco: An Interpretive Essay." In *Velvet Barrios: Popular Culture and Chicana/o Sexualities*, edited by Alicia Gaspar de Alba. New York: Palgrave Macmillan, 2003.

Marshall, T. H. "Citizenship and Social Class." Reprinted in *Inequality and Society: Social Science Perspectives on Social Stratification*, edited by Jeff Manza and Michael Sauder. New York: W. W. Norton, 2009.

———. "Reflections on the Bicentennial of the United States Constitution." *Harvard Law Review* 101, no. 1 (November 1987): 1–5.

Martínez, Elizabeth Coonrod. *Josefina Niggli: Mexican American Writer, A Critical Biography*. Albuquerque: University of New Mexico Press, 2007.

Martín-Rodríguez, Manuel M. "Recovering Chicano/a Literary Histories: Historiography Beyond Borders." *PMLA* 120, no. 3 (May 2005): 796–805.

Massey, Dougas S., Jorge Durand, and Nolan J. Malone. *Beyond Smoke and Mirrors: Mexican Immigration in an Era of Economic Integration*. New York: Russell Sage Foundation, 2002.

McClure, Charlotte S. *Gertrude Atherton*. Boston: Twayne Publishers, 1979.

McWilliams, Cary. *North from Mexico: The Spanish-Speaking People of the United States*. Philadelphia: J. P. Lippincott Company, 1949.

Meléndez, A. Gabriel. *So All is Not Lost: The Poetics of Print in Nuevomexicano Communities, 1836–1958*. Albuquerque: University of New Mexico Press, 1997.

Mendoza, Luis. *Historia: The Literary Making of Chicana and Chicano History*. College Station: Texas A&M University Press, 2001.

Monk, Craig. *Writing the Lost Generation: Expatriate Autobiography and American Modernism*. Iowa City: University of Iowa Press, 2008.

Monroy, Douglas. *Rebirth: Mexican Los Angeles from the Great Migration to the Great Depression*. Berkeley: University of California Press, 1999.

Monsiváis, Carlos. "Notas sobre la cultura mexicana en el siglo XX." In *Historia General de México*, edited by Daniel Cosillo Villegas, 957–1075. Mexico City: El Colegio de México, 2007.

Montejano, David. *Anglos and Mexicans in the Making of Texas, 1836–1986*. Austin: University of Texas Press, 1987.

———. *Quixote's Soldiers: A Local History of the Chicano Movement, 1966–1981*. Austin: University of Texas Press, 2010.

Montgomery, David. *Citizen Worker: The Experience of Workers in the United States with Democracy and the Free Market During the Nineteenth Century*. New York: Cambridge University Press, 1993.

Mookherjee, Monica. "Affective Citizenship: Feminism, Postcolonialism and the Politics of Recognition." *Critical Review of International Social and Political Philosophy* 8, no. 1 (2005).

Mora, Anthony. *Border Dilemmas: Racial and National Uncertainties in New Mexico, 1848–1912*. Durham: Duke University Press, 2011.

Moraga, Cherríe. *Last Generation*. Boston: South End Press, 1993.

Moraga, Cherrie, and Gloria Anzaldua, eds. *This Bridge Called My Back: Writings by Radical Women of Color*. New York: Kitchen Table, Women of Color Press, 1983.

Mora-Torres, Juan. *The Making of the Mexican Border: The State, Capitalism, and Society in Nuevo León, 1848–1910*. Austin: University of Texas, 2001.

Moretti, Franco. *Way of the World: The Bildungsroman in European Cultures*. New York: Verso, 1987.

Mosse, George L. *Nationalism and Sexuality: Respectability and Abnormal Sexuality in Modern Europe*. New York: Howard Fertig, 1985.

Motomura, Hiroshi. *Americans in Waiting: The Lost Story of Immigration and Citizenship in the United States*. New York: Oxford University Press, 2006.

Muñoz, José Esteban. *Cruising Utopia: The Then and There of Queer Futurity*. New York: New York University Press, 2009.

———. *Disidentifications: Queers of Color and the Performance of Politics*. Minneapolis: University of Minnesota Press, 1999.

Murphy, Gretchen. *Hemispheric Imaginings: The Monroe Doctrine and Narratives of U.S. Empire*. Durham: Duke University Press, 2005.

Nelson, Dana. *National Manhood: Capitalist Citizenship and the Imagined Fraternity of White Men*. Durham: Duke University Press, 1998.

Newfield, Christopher. *The Emerson Effect: Individualism and Submission in America*. Chicago: University of Chicago Press, 1996.

Ngai, Mae M. *Impossible Subjects: Illegal Aliens and the Making of Modern America*. Princeton: Princeton University Press, 2004.

Noel, Linda C. "'I am an American': Anglos, Mexicans, *Nativos*, and the National Debate over Arizona and New Mexico Statehood." *Pacific Historical Review* 80, no. 3 (August 2011): 430–67.

Noriega, Chon. "Fashion Crimes." *Aztlán* 26, no. 1 (2001): 5.

O'Bar, Jack. *Origin and History of the Bobbs-Merrill Company*. Champaign: University of Illinois Press, 1985.

Olguin, Ben. "Interrogating the Soldado Razo: Masculinity, Soldiering, and Ideology in Mexican American World War II Memoir and Theater." In *Latina/os and World War II: Mobility, Agency, and Ideology*, edited by Maggie Rivas-Rodriguez and Ben Olguin. Austin: University of Texas Press, 2014.

Olivas, Michael. *Colored Men and Hombres Aqui: Hernandez v Texas and the Emergence of Mexican American Lawyering*. Houston: Arte Público Press, 2006.

Orchard, William, and Yolanda Padilla. Introduction to *The Plays of Josefina Niggli*. Madison: University of Wisconsin Press, 2007.

———. "Lost in Adaptation: Chicana History, The Cold War, and The Case of Josephina Niggli." *Women's Studies Quarterly* 33, no. 3/4 (Fall–Winter 2005): 90–113.

Orozco, Cynthia. *No Mexicans, Women or Dogs Allowed: The Rise of the Mexican American Civil Rights Movement*. Austin: University of Texas Press, 2009.

Orsi, Richard J. *Sunset Limited: The Southern Pacific Railroad and the Development of the American West, 1850–1930*. Berkeley: University of California Press, 2007.

Overmyer-Velásquez, Mark, ed. *Beyond the Border: The History of Mexican-U.S. Migration*. New York: Oxford University Press, 2011.

Owens, Louis. *Other Destinies: Understanding the American Indian Novel*. Norman: University of Oklahoma Press, 1992.

Paine, Thomas. *The Writings of Thomas Paine, vol. I, 1774–1779*. New York: G. P. Putnam's Sons, 1906.

Paredes, Américo. *George Washington Gomez*. Houston: Arte Público Press, 1990.

——. *With His Pistol in His Hand: A Border Ballad and Its Hero*. Austin: University of Texas Press, 1958.

Paredes, Raymund. "Evolution of Chicano Literature." *MELUS* 5, no. 2 (Summer 1978): 71–110.

Patiño, Jimmy. "All I Want is that He Be Punished: Border Patrol Violence, Women's Voices, and Chicano Activism in Early 1970s San Diego." In *The Chicano Movement*, edited by Mario T. Garcia. New York: Routledge, 2014.

Pease, Donald E. *The New American Exceptionalism*. Minneapolis: University of Minnesota Press, 2009.

Pease, Donald E., and Amy Kaplan, eds. *Cultures of United States Imperialism*. Durham: Duke University Press, 1993.

Perea, Juan F. ed. *Immigrants Out!: The New Nativism and the Anti-Immigrant Impulse in the United States*. New York: New York University Press, 1997.

Pérez, Luis. *El Coyote, The Rebel*. Houston: Arte Público Press, 2000. See esp. introduction.

Pérez-Torres, Rafael. *Movements in Chicano Poetry: Against Myths, Against Margins*. New York: Cambridge University Press, 1995.

Pitt, Leonard. *Decline of the Californios: A Social History of the Spanish-Speaking Californians, 1846–1890*. Berkeley: University of California Press, 1999.

Portales, Patricia. "Tejanas on the Home Front: Women, Bombs, and the (Re)Gendering of War in Mexican American World War II Literature." In *Latina/os and World War II: Mobility, Agency, and Ideology*, edited by Maggie Rivas-Rodriguez and Ben Olguin. Austin: University of Texas Press, 2014.

Potter, David. *Impending Crisis: America Before the Civil War, 1848–61*. New York: Harper Perennial, 2011.

Pratt, Mary Louise. "Arts of the Contact Zone." *Profession* (1991): 33–40.

Putney, Clifford. *Muscular Christianity: Manhood and Sports in Protestant America, 1880–1920*. Cambridge: Harvard University Press, 2001.

Quintanilla, Michael. "A Cultural Victory: Con Safos, a Writers Group, Has Restored the Voices of Those Once Told their Stories Were 'Too Ethnic.'" *Los Angeles Times*, June 26, 1995.

Raco, Mike. "Neoliberal Urban Policy, Aspirational Citizenship and the Uses of Cultural Distinction." In *Contradictions of Neoliberal Planning: Cities Policies, and Politics*, edited by Tuna Tasan-Kok and Guy Baeten. Dordrecht: Springer Netherlands, 2012.

Ramírez, Catherine S. "Saying 'Nothing': Pachucas and the Languages of Resistance." *Frontiers* 27, no. 3 (2006): 2–3.

———. *The Woman in the Zoot Suit: Gender, Nationalism, and the Cultural Politics of Memory*. Durham: Duke University Press, 2009.

Rebolledo, Tey Diana. *Women Singing in the Snow: A Cultural Analysis of Chicana Literature*. Tucson: University of Arizona Press, 1995.

Reisler, Mark. *By the Sweat of their Brow*. Berkeley: University of California Press, 1979.

Richardson, Riché. *Black Masculinity and the U.S. South: From Uncle Tom to Gangsta*. Athens: University of Georgia Press, 2007.

Ridge, John Rollin (Yellow Bird). *Life and Adventures of Joaquin Murieta*. Norman: University of Oklahoma, 1955.

Rifkin, Mark. "For the Wrongs of Our Poor Bleeding Country: Sensation, Class, and Empire in Ridge's Joaquin Murieta." *Arizona Quarterly* 65, no. 2 (2009): 28–9.

Ritter, Gretchen. "Jury Service and Women's Citizenship before and after the Nineteenth Amendment." *Law and History Review* 20, no. 3 (Autumn 2002): 479–515.

Rivas-Rodriguez, Maggie, ed. *Mexican Americans and World War II*. Austin: University of Texas, 2005.

Rivera, John-Michael. *The Emergence of Mexican America: Recovering Stories of Mexican Peoplehood in U.S. Culture*. New York: New York University Press, 2006.

Robinson, Cecil. *Mexico and the Hispanic Southwest in American Literature*. Tucson: University of Arizona Press, 1977.

Rodríguez, Jaime Javier. *The Literatures of the U.S.-Mexican War: Narrative, Time, and Identity*. Austin: University of Texas Press, 2010.

Rodriguez, Ralph E. "Chicano Studies and the Need Not to Know." *American Literary History* 22, no. 1 (Spring 2010): 180–90.

Rodríguez, Richard T. *Next of Kin: The Family in Chicana/o Cultural Politics*. Durham: Duke University Press, 2009.

Roediger, David. *Wages of Whiteness: Race and the Making of the American Working Class*. New York: Verso, 1999.

———. *Working Toward Whiteness: How America's Immigrants Became White*. New York: Basic Books, 2005.

Rosales, Steven. *Soldados Razos at War: Chicano Politics, Identity and Masculinity in the U.S. Military from World War II to Vietnam*. Tucson: University of Arizona Press, 2017.

Rosenbaum, Robert J. *Mexicano Resistance in the Southwest*. Dallas: Southern Methodist University Press, 1981.

Ross, Michael A. *Justice of Shattered Dreams: Samuel Freeman Miller and the Supreme Court during the Civil War Era*. Baton Rouge: Louisiana State University Press, 2003.

Rotundo, E. Anthony. *American Manhood: Transformations in Masculinity from the Revolution to the Modern Era*. New York: Basic Books, 1993.

Ruiz, Vicki. *From Out of the Shadows: Mexican Women in Twentieth Century America*. New York: Oxford University Press, 2008.

———. "Morena/o, Blanca/o, y Café con Leche: Racial Constructions in Chicana His-toriography." In *The Practice of U.S. Women's History: Narratives, Intersections, and Dialogues*. New Brunswick: Rutgers University Press, 2007.

Ruiz de Burton, Maria Amparo. *Who Would Have Thought It?* Houston: Arte Público Press, 1995.

Rutherford, John. "The Novel of the Mexican Revolution." In *The Cambridge History of Latin American Literature: The Twentieth Century*, edited by Roberto González Echevarría and Enrique Pupo-Walker, 213–225. Cambridge: Cambridge University Press, 1996.

Said, Edward. *The World, the Text, and the Critic*. Cambridge: Harvard University Press, 1984.

Sainsbury, Diane. *Gender, Equality and Welfare States*. Cambridge: Press Syndicate of the University of Cambridge, 1996.

Saldívar, José David. *Border Matters: Remapping American Cultural Studies*. Berkeley: University of California Press, 1997.

———. *Dialectics of Our America: Genealogy, Cultural Critique, and Literary History*. Durham: Duke University Press, 1991.

———. *Trans-Americanity: Subaltern Modernity, Global Coloniality, and the Cultures of Greater Mexico*. Durham: Duke University Press, 2012.

Saldívar, Ramon. *Borderlands of Culture: Américo Paredes and the Transnational Imagi-nary*. Durham: Duke University Press, 2006.

———. *Chicano Narrative: The Dialectics of Difference*. Madison: University of Wiscon-sin Press, 1990.

Saldívar-Hull, Sonia. *Feminism on the Border: Chicana Gender Politics and Literature*. Berkeley: University of California Press, 2000.

Samuels, Shirley. *Romances of the Republic: Women, the Family, and Violence in the Literature of the Early American Nation*. New York: Oxford University Press, 1996.

Sanchez, George J. *Becoming Mexican American: Ethnicity, Culture, and Identity in Chicano Los Angeles, 1900–1945*. New York: Oxford University Press, 1995.

Sánchez, Rosaura. "The Chicana Labor Force." In *Essays on la Mujer*. Los Angeles: University of California Chicano Studies Center, 1977.

———. *Telling Identities: The California Testimonios*. Minneapolis: University of Min-nesota Press, 1995.

Sanchez, Rosaura, and Beatrice Pita. Introduction to *The Squatter and the Don*. Hous-ton: Arte Público Press, 1997.

Schedler, Christopher. *Border Modernism: Intercultural Readings in American Literary Modernism*. New York: Routledge, 2002.

Schmidt Camacho, Alicia R. *Migrant Imaginaries: Latino Cultural Politics in the U.S.-Mexico Borderlands*. New York: New York University Press, 2008.

Scott, Darieck. *Extravagant Abjection: Blackness, Power, and Sexuality in the African American Literary Imagination*. New York: New York University Press, 2010.

Scruggs, Otey M. "Evolution of the Mexican Farm Labor Agreement of 1942." *Agricul-tural History* 34, no. 3 (July 1960): 140–49.

Sedgwick, Eve Kosofsky. *Between Men: English Literature and Male Homosocial Desire.* New York: Columbia University Press, 1985.

———. "Gosh, Boy George, You Must Be Awfully Secure in Your Masculinity!" In *Constructing Masculinity*, edited by Maurice Berger, Brian Wallis, and Simon Watson. New York: Routledge, 1995.

Sheridan, Clare. "Contested Citizenship: National Identity and the Mexican Immigration Debates of the 1920s." *Journal of American Ethnic History* 21 no. 3 (2002): 3–35.

Silber, Nina. *Romance of Reunion: Northerners and the South, 1865–1900.* Chapel Hill: University of North Carolina Press, 1997.

Smethurst, James. "The Figure of the Vato Loco and the Representation of Ethnicity in the Narratives of Oscar Z. Acosta." *MELUS* 20, no. 2 (Summer 1995): 119–32.

Sollors, Werner, ed. *Multilingual America: Transnationalism, Ethnicity, and the Languages of American Literature.* New York: New York University Press, 1998.

Sommer, Doris. *Foundational Fictions: The National Romances of Latin America.* Berkeley: University of California Press, 1991.

Sorensen, Leif. "Anti-Corrido of *George Washington Gomez*: A Narrative of Emergent Subject Formation." *American Literature* 80, no. 1 (2008): 111–40.

Soto, Sandra K. *Reading Chican@ Like a Queer: The De-Mastery of Desire.* Austin: University of Texas Press, 2010.

Starr, Kevin. *Americans and the California Dream, 1850–1915.* New York: Oxford University Press, 1973.

———. *California: A History.* New York: Modern Library, 2005.

Stokes, Mason. *Color of Sex: Whiteness, Heterosexuality, and the Fictions of White Supremacy.* Durham: Duke University Press, 2001.

Streeby, Shelley. *American Sensations: Class, Empire, and the Production of Popular Culture.* Berkeley: University of California Press, 2002.

———. *Radical Sensations: World Movements, Violence, and Visual Culture.* Durham: Duke University Press, 2013.

Sturken, Marita. *Tangled Memories: The Vietnam War, the AIDS Epidemic, and the Politics of Remembering.* Berkeley: University of California Press, 1997.

Tantaros, Andrea. *Varney and Company.* Fox Business News, recorded December 22, 2015.

Thompson, Jerry D. *Cortina: Defending the Mexican Name in Texas.* College Station: Texas A&M University Press, 2007.

———. *Juan Cortina and the Texas-Mexico Frontier, 1859–1877.* El Paso: Texas Western Press, 1994.

Thompson, Mark. *American Character: The Curious Life of Charles Fletcher Lummis and the Rediscovery of the Southwest.* New York: Arcade Publishing, 2001.

Tocqueville, Alexis de. *Democracy in America, and Two Essays on America.* Translated by Gerald A Bevan. New York: Penguin Books, 2003.

Trujillo, Carla, ed. *Living Chicana Theory.* Berkeley: Third Woman Press, 1998.

Tuck, Ruth. *Not with the Fist: Mexican Americans in a Southwest City.* New York: Harcourt Brace, 1946.

Turner, Jack. *Awakening to Race: individualism and Social Consciousness in America.* Chicago: University of Chicago Press, 2012.

Turner, John Kenneth. *Barbarous Mexico.* Chicago: Charles H. Kerr and Company, 1910.

Valdez, Luis. "Bandido." In *Zoot Suit and Other Plays.* Houston: Arte Público Press, 1992.

Vallejos, Tomás. "Jose Antonio Villarreal." In *Dictionary of Literary Biography*, Chicano Writers: First Series, vol. 82 (1989): 282–88.

Venegas, Daniel. *The Adventures of Don Chipote, or, When Parrots Breast Feed.* Translated by Ethriam Cash Brammer. Houston: Arte Público Press, 2000.

Villaseñor, Victor. *Macho!* Houston: Arte Público Press, 1991.

Wallace, Maurice O. *Constructing the Black Masculine: Identity and Ideality in African American Men's Literature and Culture, 1775–1995.* Durham: Duke University Press, 2002.

Wandersee, Winifred D. "The Economics of Middle-Income Family Life: Working Women during the Great Depression." In *Decades of Discontent: The Women's Movement, 1920–1940*, edited by Lois Scharf and Joan M. Jensen. Westport: Greenwood Press, 1983.

Warner, Michael. *Letters of the Republic: Publication and the Public Sphere in Eighteenth-Century America.* Cambridge: Harvard University Press, 1990.

Wasserman, Mark. *Everyday Life and Politics in Nineteenth Century Mexico: Men, Women, and War.* Albuquerque: University of Mexico Press, 2000.

Weber, David. *Foreigners in Their Native Land.* Albuquerque: University of New Mexico Press, 1977.

Weber, John. *From South Texas to the Nation: The Exploitation of Mexican Labor in the Twentieth Century.* Chapel Hill: University of North Carolina Press, 2015.

Wiegman, Robyn. *American Anatomies: Theorizing Race and Gender.* Durham: Duke University Press, 1995.

Windell, Maria. "Sanctify our Suffering World with Tears." *Nineteenth-Century Literature* 63, no. 2 (September 2008): 170–96.

Young, Elliott. *Catarino Garza's Revolution on the Texas-Mexican Border.* Durham: Duke University Press, 2004.

Young, Julia. *Mexican Exodus: Emigrants, Exiles, and Refugees of the Cristero War.* New York: Oxford University Press, 2015.

Zamora, Emilio. *Claiming Rights and Righting Wrongs in Texas: Mexican Workers and Job Politics during World War II.* College Station: Texas A&M University Press, 2009.

———. *World of the Mexican Worker in Texas.* College Station: Texas A&M University Press, 1993.

INDEX

Page numbers in *italics* indicate illustrations.

ABOUT THE AUTHOR

Alberto Varon is Assistant Professor of English and Latino Studies at Indiana University Bloomington.